SIDNEY CRAIGE PERHAM, NINTH GENERATION, BY THE OLD HEARTH-STONE. See page 276.

Footprints of the Patriots

BESIDE OLD HEARTH-STONES

Abram English Brown

Author of *Beneath Old Rooftrees, Glimpses of
Old New England Life, History of Bedford*, etc.

*The stranger at my fireside cannot see the forms I see,
Nor hear the sounds I hear;
He but perceives what is; while unto me
All that has been is visible and clear.*

—Longfellow's *Haunted Houses*

HERITAGE BOOKS
2022

HERITAGE BOOKS

AN IMPRINT OF HERITAGE BOOKS, INC.

Books, CDs, and more—Worldwide

For our listing of thousands of titles see our website
at
www.HeritageBooks.com

A Facsimile Reprint
Published 2022 by
HERITAGE BOOKS, INC.
Publishing Division
5810 Ruatan Street
Berwyn Heights, Md. 20740

Originally published:

Boston
Lee and Shepard Publishers
10 Milk Street
1897

Typography by C. J. Peters & Son, Boston
Presswork by Rockwell & Churchill

International Standard Book Number
Paperbound: 978-1-55613-332-9

TO THE HONOR

PREFATORY NOTE.

In this volume, as in the first of the series, I have endeavored to bring to light some of the obscure movements of the early patriots.

The search for these has called me to the outer circle of the battlefield of the opening Revolution, where footprints of the minute-men have escaped the eye of the tourist.

I desire to acknowledge the continued courtesy of the members of the families now occupying the old farms from which their ancestors went out determined to have liberty or death.

In offering this volume to the public, it is with a sincere desire that all descendants of the early patriots, whether located on the old homesteads or in homes far distant from New England, may have a just appreciation of the cost of the glorious heritage of freedom to which they are born.

It is my purpose to continue this search, and I shall be glad to receive any suggestions whereby better results may be obtained for the promotion of good citizenship.

ABRAM ENGLISH BROWN.

CONTENTS

LIST OF ILLUSTRATIONS

BESIDE OLD HEARTH-STONES

CHAPTER I

> So through the night rode Paul Revere,
> And so through the night went his cry of alarm
> To every Middlesex village and farm, —
> A cry of defiance and not of fear,
> A voice in the darkness, a knock at the door,
> And a word that shall echo forevermore.
>
> LONGFELLOW.

LEXINGTON ALARM IN NORTHERN MIDDLESEX. — GROTON PLANTATION. — GROTON PATRIOTS ON APRIL 19, 1775. — IN CAMP AT CAMBRIDGE. — THE DEATH-ROLL AT BUNKER HILL. — THE PRESCOTT FAMILY. — CHAMPNEY HOUSE. — GRAVE OF CAPTAIN ABRAM CHILD

No time was lost in extending the " Lexington Alarm," and so thorough had been the planning that but little or no time was wasted in the most distant towns before the patriots started for the relief of the distressed. Northern Middlesex had given no uncertain sound during all the time when the troubles were culminating. The older citizens were familiar with the war cry, many of them having repeatedly rushed to arms in the early

wars; and the fireside tales were those of personal
sufferings in the Indian troubles and French wars.
In many a home was reference made to the family
record in the well-worn Bible, and the pine torch
lighted in order that the youngest listener might
be duly impressed by reading for himself such
entries as "Killed at Crown Point; Died at Champlain; Killed by Indians at Fort George." Ticonderoga and Crown Point were household words,
kept vividly in mind by the old musket that had
done service in that well-known region. No fairy
tales found listeners in these homes; for the siege
of Louisburg and the destruction of the peaceful
Acadian villages, scenes in which these people
had a part, furnished ample subject for twilight
pastime.

There was a tract of land, more than thirty
miles inland, granted to Dean Winthrop and
others, and incorporated as early as 1655 by the
name of Groton. It was named for the home of
the Winthrops, in Groton, England. Seven years
passed before the record appears of the erection
of that all-important building, a meeting-house,
and of the election of those well-known New
England functionaries, selectmen. These settlers,
like other pioneers whom we delight to honor,
exemplified true Christian heroism. With their
minister, Rev. Samuel Willard, they faced the
hardships of frontier life with a resignation hard
to be understood in these days of luxury and

comfort. "They lived on the rough edge of civilization; and nothing stood between them and an unbroken wilderness." Christian civilization was apparent, when King Philip's war broke out, and sorrow settled upon the place. The greater part of the houses were destroyed, including the meeting-house; some of the people were killed, and others carried into captivity. Although forced to abandon the undertaking for a while, those people heroically took up the burden again, and went on successfully. While it was the descendants and successors of the pioneers who indelibly stamped their names on the records of this settlement during the later Indian troubles and with the French, they manifested no half-hearted spirit in the repeated emergencies.

Territorially Groton admitted of many divisions; and the natural increase of population, together with the influx from the lower towns, led to the formation of several new districts or townships before the beginning of hostilities with the mother country. Distance only prevented these patriots from having a share in the well-known scenes of April 19; but no better record was made at camp in Cambridge, and in battle at Bunker Hill, than is found to the honor of these people of northern Middlesex.

GROTON.

In my search for hidden footprints in the town of Groton, I was conducted to the home of Mrs.

Abigail Moors, who in her ninetieth year was mistress of her own home.   Referring to her father, Imlah Parker, a soldier of the Revolution, this interesting woman emphatically said, "I have always thought he was the nicest man that ever lived."   With memory undimmed, she, the last of a family of nine children, lives in the full enjoyment of filial affection, bearing testimony to the fact that the true parent is the real patriot.

It has been shown in "Beneath Old Roof Trees" that the people of Groton received no encouragement from their pastor towards resistance to British aggression ; in fact, if they had followed their minister, they would all have been classed with the Tories.   But from the spring of 1765, when the odious Stamp Act was passed, they had been outspoken in the interests of the Colonies, regardless of their spiritual leader.   Two companies of minute-men were enlisted in the town agreeably to the recommendation of the First Provincial Congress, in its resolve of October 26, 1774, at Concord.   The alarm of April 19 was quickly met by the response of these companies, under Captains Henry Farwell and Asa Lawrence.

The alarm of the previous day, already explained in this series, had started Captain Nathan [1] Corey and other Groton men to Concord in advance of the companies, and hence given Groton some representatives at Old North Bridge.   Two companies

[1] Not Aaron.

of militia followed the minute-men on the 19th, and all gathered at Cambridge before that April day had closed. There is sufficient reason for believing that General Artemas Ward found the Groton men to be faithful soldiers. He had a special interest in the old families of that town. His wife, Sarah Trowbridge, to whom he was married in 1750, was daughter of Rev. Caleb and Hannah (Walter) Trowbridge of Groton. When the immortal scroll of June 17 was made up, it appeared that Groton had suffered great loss. Among the dead was Sergeant Benjamin Prescott, a nephew of Colonel William Prescott.

The following names appear on the bronze tablets at Charlestown : —

PRESCOTT'S REGIMENT.

Parker's company. — Peter Fisk, David Kemp.

Lawrence's company. — James Dodge, Stephen Foster, Abraham Blood, Benjamin Wood,[1] Simon Hobart, Robert Parker.

Farwell's company. — Jonathan Jenkins.

Moors's company. — Sergeant Benjamin Prescott.

Corey's company. — Chambers Corey.

Although the Colonel Prescott homestead was lost to Groton through the dismembership of the town, the name has been closely identified with it. Various members of the family are notable in its annals.

[1] See Pepperell Death-roll. Chapter IV. of this volume.

The first to appear in the town was Jonas, son of John the immigrant, who came to this country about 1640, and settled at Lancaster, where often, in a coat of mailed armor, he appeared to the troublesome Indians, impressing them as of supernatural origin. Jonas, at Groton, was a captain of the yeomanry militia at the time when the savages were committing their depredations. Benjamin, a son of Jonas, was born in 1696, and was a man of military and civil distinction. He obtained lands on the border-line of the town. A monument standing at an angle of the road nearing the centre of Groton tells the following: "Colonel William Prescott Commander of the American forces at the Battle of Bunker Hill, was born on the 20th of February, 1726, in a house which stood near this spot." Brothers of Colonel William were Dr. Oliver and Judge James Prescott, each of whom honored the town of his nativity. One of the selectmen in 1775 was Oliver Prescott; Honorable James Prescott was. a member of the first, second, and third Provincial Congress, and of the Board of War in 1776. Oliver Prescott was a member of the Council in 1777. The family was also represented in other important positions during the war; and Honorable James Prescott was the representative from the town in the first General Court of the Commonwealth of Massachusetts, which assembled on Wednesday, October 25, 1780. It thus appears

STONE MARKING BIRTHPLACE OF COLONEL WILLIAM PRESCOTT, GROTON

that the heroism of John the immigrant was perpetuated in his descendants, who proved themselves to be true patriots and good citizens in the
time of great trial.

Some interesting facts are here added in regard
to the personality of Colonel William Prescott,

CHAMPNEY HOUSE, GROTON

given by his grandniece, Mrs. Sarah (Chaplin)
Rockwood, to Dr. Samuel A. Green. Her father
was Rev. Daniel Chaplin, D.D., of Groton; and
her mother was Susanna, eldest daughter of Judge
James Prescott, brother of the colonel. She was
ten years of age when the hero of Bunker Hill
died.

" She describes him as a tall, well-proportioned man, with blue eyes and a large head. He usually wore a skull-cap ; and he parted his hair in the middle, wearing it long behind, braided loosely, and tied in a *club* with a black ribbon, as was common in those days. He had a pleasant countenance, and was remarkably social and full of fun and anecdotes. He was dignified in his manner, and had the bearing of a soldier."[1]

Authorities agree on the value of early impressions ; and we can but credit this description of the personal appearance of Colonel Prescott, for it was indelibly stamped upon the youthful Sarah Chaplin when sitting upon the knee of the old soldier. She attained the remarkable age of one hundred and four years.

The Champney house is one of the few dwellings remaining to remind us of the patriots of Groton who left their homes in exchange for the life of the camp and field of battle.

---

[1] This fact in regard to the dress of the hair was not brought to the notice of the sculptor, William W. Story, the modeller of the Prescott statue at Bunker Hill.

In the old burying-ground of Groton is a stone on which is the following record of a patriot who was born at Waltham : —

" Man lives his little hour and Falls too oft unheeded down."

SACRED TO THE MEMORY OF

CAPT. ABRAM CHILD.

WALTHAM 1741–1834. 93 YEARS.

He entered the army in the French War at the age of 17 years. Was
with Gen. Amherst at the capture of Ticonderoga and Crown
Point in 1759. He was a Lieut. among the
minute men and aided in the Concord fight and the Battle
of Bunker Hill in 1775. Joining Washington he was one of the Immortal Band which crossed the Delaware Dec. 25, 1776, and turned
the tide of war in the victories of Trenton and Princeton. De-
tached to the North he fought in the two battles of Stillwater, and witnessed the surrender of Burgoyne in 1777.
Rejoining Washington he bore equally the frosts
of Valley Forge and the Heats of Monmouth.
in 1778. Detailed with Gen. Wayne, he crowned his
military career by heading the Infantry as oldest Capt. in the
gallant capture of Stoney Point in 1779 where he received the only wound
that marked his eventful services.

———

The blood of our fathers, let it not have been shed in vain.

WEBSTER.

CHAPTER II

"Tell ye your children of it, and let your children tell their children, and their children another generation." — JOEL i. 3.

ORIGIN OF SHIRLEY AND PEPPERELL. — PEPPER-
ELL'S RELIEF FOR BOSTON IN 1760. — COLONEL
WILLIAM PRESCOTT. — REVEREND JOSEPH EMER-
SON. — TOWN AND CHURCH RECORDS. — PATRI-
OTIC ACTS IN PEPPERELL

AMONG the towns once included, either whole
or in part, in Groton Plantation, are Pepperell and
Shirley. Besides being offshoots from the mother
township, they had other early and later interests
in common which make it almost impossible to
separate them entirely. It was a custom of the
early days of the Colony for a town to become
such by degrees. In many cases the remote settlers set up the plea of the great distance to be
travelled to get to the meeting-house, and a pre-
cinct would be established in which better ecclesiastical advantages were enjoyed; the next step
was, in some instances, the formation of a district,
which gave added privileges ; and then followed
the right of sending a representative to the General Court, when the fully equipped town appeared

upon the records.[1] Pepperell passed through each of these preliminary stages, but Shirley was at first recognized as a district and then as a town. As early as 1742 " Groton West Parish " appeared in the records; but it was not until eleven years later that it was dignified by a name entirely distinct from that of Groton, and still later before it was classed as a town. It is difficult to tell when the political connection with the mother town was severed; for in the exigency of the opening Revolution, Pepperell, as other districts, had its own representative. William Prescott was the district's representative in the General Court convened at Salem on Friday the seventh day of October, 1774, by order of Governor Thomas Gage, and which resulted in the First Provincial Congress, that met at Concord on the eleventh. When duties in the field required the presence of William Prescott, he was succeeded by Edmund Bancroft, who served in the second and third Provincial Congress.

In 1753 Shirley was incorporated as a district, without having taken the course of first building a meeting-house and settling a minister.

In following the plan of a biographer, I have at first given the antecedents of these towns of enviable record in north-west Middlesex, and next turn

---

[1] During the reign of George the Second, there were objections on the part of the royal authorities to forming new towns in the New England Colonies, whereby more representatives appeared in the local government, hence districts were more commonly formed.

to the origin of the names assigned them.   The
notable officials William Shirley and William Pepperrell are closely allied in our Provincial history ;
and as portions of Groton Plantation became districts during the popularity of these men, it was
natural that their names should be perpetuated in
this manner.

William Shirley was governor of the Province
from August, 1741, to September, 1749.   He was
appointed by the king under the second charter.   It was during this period that the south-
westerly part of Groton became a district, and
later a fully equipped town ; hence, it was given
the name of Shirley in honor of the governor.

William Pepperrell of Kittery, Maine, was colonel of a regiment of militia, and a merchant of
great success and popularity.   Being well and favorably known in Massachusetts and New Hampshire, he was selected by Governor Shirley as
commander of the expedition fitted out in 1745
to capture the fortress of the French at Louisburg, Cape Breton.   The marvellous success of
the expedition turned public attention to the merchant commander, and no honor was too great to
be conferred upon him ; hence the northern part
of Groton, first called " Groton West Parish,"
when becoming a town, was named Pepperrell, in
honor of the hero of Louisburg.

The facts that men from these towns were included in the six thousand who made up the army

in command of Colonel Pepperrell, and that the
minister of the latter town was a chaplain in the
expedition, must have strengthened the desire to
name the town Pepperrell.[1] It may seem extremely
far-fetched to cite the part of these towns in the
capture of the " Gibraltar of America" as a reason for the remarkable record of the later patriots
of the locality ; but the thirty years which intervened between the experiences at Louisburg and
Lexington could not have effaced the record, and
with such a spiritual leader as had the town of
Pepperell in the Rev. Joseph Emerson the fire
of patriotism could not go out.   In his sermon to
his parishioners in the spring of 1758, just before
starting under command of Captain Thomas Lawrence for the French war, this patriot preacher
said from his pulpit, " Let it never be said of a
Pepperell soldier that he was afraid to face his
enemies, or that he ever turned his back on
them, and cowardly deserted the cause of his
country."

The name of Emerson is of itself enough to
give the town of Pepperell an honored place in
the annals of the Colonies ; but when combined
with that of Prescott there is a union of strength
which must have exerted an influence upon all
subsequent generations of the early heroes.   It
is claimed that William Prescott was one of the

[1] The Pepperrell family repeated the " r." The same form
was used in the name of the town for many years.

town's representatives at Louisburg, and it is certain that he was lieutenant in the Provincial troops sent out to remove the French neutrals from Nova Scotia in 1755.

While we may deplore this measure of war, we cannot deny the patriotism which impelled those who responded to the call. While our emotions are stirred by the slightest reference to those Acadian villagers "on the shores of the Basin of Minas," who, "at peace with God and the world," were swept from their homes, we cannot refrain from according honor to our townsmen who were led in the expedition, and also rejoice that in some measure our ancestors atoned for the wrong by sharing their meagre comforts with the Evangelines who were left at their doors.

The early settlers of Pepperell were familiar with the hardships of frontier life. Rev. Joseph Emerson, who became their minister in 1746, was accustomed to seeing little companies of his parishioners start off to face the Indians and their French allies; fifteen of his people are recorded as having perished in that service between the years 1748 and 1756. Under the judicious leadership of their minister their hearts were softened by sorrow and sacrifice, and they were ready to share their hard earnings with others in distress; a notable instance being shown at the time of Boston's great fire of March 20, 1760, when it was estimated that the loss was one hundred thousand

pounds sterling. Rev. Mr. Emerson made the following record in the church book : —

" The governor Pownall sent Briefs thro' the Province for
a general contribution, accordingly we had one here and collected £64 12*s*. o*d*. Old Tenor, and when paid the following
Receit was given.

BOSTON, 16*th April*, 1760.

Received of ye Church in Pepperell, whereof the Rev. Mr.
Joseph Emerson is Pastor, the sum of sixty four pounds,
twelve shillings old tenor for ye sufferers in the late fire.

JOHN PHILLIPS."

With the many publications which treat of the
Revolutionary period at our command, there is no
way in which the patriot of to-day may become so
fully impressed by the moral heroism with which
each town met its share of suffering and made
its sacrifice, as by carefully studying the worn yellow leaves of the records of the town meetings.
There each successive step appears in all its significance, recorded in the cramped handwriting of
the clerk, in many cases spelled without rule, but
unmistakable in meaning. The student of these
files cannot fail to read much between the lines,
and detect in each blot and period a spirit of determination that knew no compromise.

The town of Pepperell has an old church record
in addition to that of the town clerk, which gives
added testimony to its patriotism. Each resolution adopted by this town, if not in the language
of the Committee of Correspondence of Boston,

bears the impress of the mind of the patriot preacher, whom they gladly followed, and whose work for his people and his country was sealed by his death in October, 1775.

In viewing early pastoral acts from the present standpoint, when the preaching of politics from the pulpit is at the risk of an immediate change in spiritual leaders, it is difficult to understand much that took place in Pepperell and other towns during the contention between Parliament and the Provinces. But when fully realizing the exact position of the parson of that time, which has been set forth in chapter vii. of "Beneath Old Roof Trees," one may more easily comprehend the situation. Rev. Mr. Emerson, the zealous apostle of liberty in this town, found a faithful co-worker in William Prescott, one of his parishioners, who, besides having inherited peculiar talents for leadership, had the advantage of the experience of mature life. They both had been schooled in military service, and had eyes and ears to detect the first indications of the trouble with the mother country. But while this preacher was bold in his denunciations of the infringements on their rights, he was equally positive in declaring from his pulpit, "We have a king who is well worthy of our affection and obedience." They saw in the Stamp Act an occasion for positive declaration. They had suffered personally in the king's service against the French, and had seen the stalwart

young men of the town go out from their midst
to return no more. They had also shared in the
unusual drain upon the town's treasury, and they
most naturally deprecated any act whereby the
Colonies were to be burdened with greater taxes
to meet the king's indebtedness. Theirs was the
voice of the town when, in October, 1765, they instructed their representative in the General Court,
closing thus : —

"As the trade of this province is greatly obstructed, and
the people labor under an almost insupportable debt, we
expect you will use your utmost endeavors, in the General
Assembly, that the monies of the province drawn from the
individuals, may not be applied to any other uses, under any
pretence whatever, than what is evidently intended in the act
for supplying the province treasury."

The repeal of the Stamp Act was an occasion
for one of Rev. Mr. Emerson's patriotic sermons,
which was printed; and copies of it are now treasured in the homes of the descendants of those
who most heartily indorsed its sentiments.[1] Mr.
Emerson called the repeal one of the great deliv-
erances in English history. He urged his people
to cultivate in their minds and in the minds of
their children an affection for their mother country. He said, "Let us have reverence for and be
duly subject to lawful authority. Government is
drawn from God, though the practical form of it
is left to the prudence and discretion of men."

[1] Printed and sold by Edes and Gill in Queen Street, MDCCLXVI.

Pastor and people were not slow in learning that it was policy rather than justice that actuated the British ministry in repealing the Stamp Act ; and early in the year 1773 they chose a committee of nine "to consider what is proper for this district to do, at this alarming time, respecting the encroachments that have been made upon our civil privilege." The result of the town's committee, communicated to the town of Boston through its Committee of Correspondence, was most encouraging, coming as it did from the remote border of the Province. They at first acknowledged the receipt of the letter and pamphlet sent to them in common with other towns, by the authorities at Boston, in which particular and minute accounts were given of the encroachments made upon their charter privileges. The Boston patriots were fully assured of the alarm of their sympathizers at a distance. They say : —

"We of this place are unanimous ; no less than one hundred have signed a request to the selectmen to call a meeting, though we count but one hundred and sixty families ; and when met the fullest meeting that was ever known on any occasion, and not a dissenting vote or voice. We feel for ourselves, we feel for our posterity, we feel for our brethren through the continent. We tremble at the thought of slavery, either civil or ecclesiastical, and are fully sensible of the near connection there is between civil and religious liberty. If we lose the former the latter will not remain ; our resentment (not to say our indignation) rises against them, let them be in whatsoever relation they may, who would dare invade our natural or constitutional rights."

The voters gave their representative positive advice, and at the same time voted to add two casks of powder with lead " answerable to their stock of ammunition."

In showing the successive steps in the town of Pepperell which led up to the 19th of April, 1775, there is left no room for doubt that the acts of the Boston leaders were as leaven to all the communities affected by the king's arbitrary measures. So thoroughly aroused were the people at this northern border of the Province that more than a year before the Declaration of Independence was formulated, they concluded a series of resolutions thus : —

" We therefore instruct you, sir, that you, in our name and behalf, signify to the Great and General Court, of which you are a member, that our opinion is, that independence is the only alternative for the safety of this oppressed land, and that if the honorable Congress should think it best for the safety of the United Colonies to declare them independent of Great Britain, we acquiesce heart and hand, and are determined, at the risk of life and treasure, to support the measure."

Wm Prescott

The appeal of the Boston Committee of Correspondence met with a prompt response from the patriots of Pepperell. Their letter, signed by William Prescott, was the third in order of date. It accompanied forty bushels of grain and promises of further assistance with provisions and with men, and invoked them " to stand firm in the common cause."

Something was yet needed to prove to all generations that these people were not as " sounding brass or a tinkling cymbal." The Lexington alarm reached these remote homes, and the proof was readily furnished. The patriots of that day are largely represented by name and blood in the residents of to-day, but their homes have almost all disappeared, or been greatly changed; yet there is one to which I most gladly invite my readers.

MONUMENT ON SITE OF THE MEETING–HOUSE IN
THE MOTHER TOWN

CHAPTER III

We have no title-deeds to house or lands;
Owners and occupants of earlier dates,
From graves forgotten stretch their dusty hands,
And hold in mortmain still their old estates.
                                        EMERSON.

THE PRESCOTT FAMILY. — PRESCOTT HOMESTEAD.
— ECHOES FROM ITS WOOD–CAPPED HILLS. —
SOCIETY OF THE CINCINNATI. — CONNECTION
WITH GOVERNOR ROGER WOLCOTT. — ALLIANCE
WITH THE LINZEE FAMILY. — CHARACTERISTICS
OF COLONEL WILLIAM PRESCOTT

THE Prescott family home is on the northern
border of the town of Pepperell, and on the rising
ground that soon merges into the hills of the
Granite State. Its present territory of two hundred acres was included in the grant of 1655 to
Mr. Dean Winthrop and others. Benjamin Prescott was the first of the family to secure a title to
this remote section. He was doubtless impelled
by that spirit of adventure which actuated many
of the early settlers of New England to push out
where land was abundant, having been impressed
that such property was the basis of wealth and
influence in the mother country. Benjamin Pres-

cott began early to exert an influence in the West
Parish ; and his son William, who had nearly attained his majority when the Pepperell home was
established, found there ample opportunity for the
development of his powers.   No better combina-
tion of blood, brain, and muscle could be found
than that which made up the young man William
Prescott, who, well matched with Abigail Hale, his
wife of Puritan stock, developed this home on
the frontier, and continued the family possession.
This young farmer was a power in the struggling
town, whose records show that he was among the
first to protest against injustice.

   We can imagine the influence of his words upon
the distressed people at the blockaded port of
Boston, voicing as they did the sentiment of the
northern border of the Province at the time when
the mandamus councillors took their oath of office.

   " Be not dismayed nor disheartened in this day of great
trials.   We heartily sympathize with you, and are always
ready to do all in our power for your support, comfort, and
relief; knowing that Providence has placed you where you
must stand the first shock.   We consider that we are all
emerged in one bottom, and must sink or swim together.
We think if we submit to those regulations, all is gone.   Our
forefathers passed the vast Atlantic, spent their blood and
treasure, that they might enjoy their liberties, both civil and
religious, and transmit them to their posterity.   Their children have waded through seas of difficulty, to leave us free
and happy in the enjoyment of English privileges.   Now, if
we should give them up, can our children rise up and call us

blessed? Is not a glorious death in defence of our liberties better than a short, infamous life, and our memory to be had in detestation to the latest posterity? Let us all be of one heart, and stand fast in the liberty wherewith Christ has made us free; and may he of his infinite mercy grant us deliverance out of all our troubles."

In driving over the delightful hills of the town from the village of Pepperell to the Prescott home, one can but see in fancy the dignified figure of the patriot preacher, as upon his horse he galloped over this route to the same homestead to take counsel with his gallant young parishioner and avowed patriot. Young Prescott was appointed captain of the militia company soon after his return from the expedition to Nova Scotia, and was promoted in 1774 to the position of colonel of the regiment of minute-men from Pepperell and adjoining towns.

Although remote from any centre of habitation, a powerful influence was exerted from this home during the months of anxiety which preceded open hostilities. Colonel Prescott was nearly fifty years of age, and besides enjoying the esteem and confidence of his townsmen, was well and favorably known in all that locality; Province line was no barrier to his popularity in both civic and military circles. The semiweekly drillings of the Pepperell minute-men under Colonel Prescott, and the bold statements from the pulpit by Rev. Joseph Emerson, kept the peo-

ple in constant expectation; so that when the
news of April 19 was received they were not
long in making final preparations. A mounted
messenger reached the town in the middle of
the forenoon, declaring that the Regulars had
come out from Boston, and killed eight men at
Lexington, and were fighting at Concord. The
despatch with which Colonel Prescott buckled
on his sword, and bade wife and only son William, then thirteen years of age, a tender farewell as he galloped off the hill, may be known
without resorting to imagination; for his habits
of early years and later experience are in proof
of this. His order was for the Pepperell company and that at Hollis to march at once to
Groton, and there join the company of the latter
town, while he proceeded directly to Groton. The
effect of the more immediate contact with Colonel
Prescott is seen in the report that the company
from his town reached Groton before the men
there were ready to march. The selectmen were
then together distributing arms and ammunition
to their soldiers. Dr. Oliver Prescott, chairman,
brother of the Colonel, upon hearing the music
and seeing the Pepperell company marching to
the Common in full ranks, said, "This is a dis-
grace to us!" But if the reader has studied with
care the first volume of this series, "Beneath Old
Roof Trees," he remembers that a portion of the
Groton company marched during the hours of

the previous night, and consequently represented the town in the fight at Old North Bridge.

Since it is the Prescott homestead that we are now considering, we will leave the minute-men, and return to the historic place. Weary with the tumult of war, Colonel William Prescott, in the spirit of a Cincinnatus,[1] returned to his home, and resumed the peaceful employment of cultivating his paternal acres. War did not deter the only son of the colonel from his school course. In the autumn of 1776 he left the old hearth-stone to attend school at Byfield, where he fitted for Harvard College, from which he graduated, and become the eminent jurist, Judge William Prescott. While his life was largely spent elsewhere, he never lost his interest in the old home. Of the next generation to cherish the ancestral homestead came William H. Prescott, the historian. Often weary of city life, he packed his books in huge trunks, and took passage in the old stage-coach for this family home among the hills, where he found tonic in the pure atmosphere, and inspiration from the invisible presence of his grandsire, the hero of Bunker Hill. The fifth generation in possession of the well-known estate was Mr.

[1] "The officers of the American Army having been taken from the Citizens of America possess high veneration for the character of that illustrious Roman, Lucius Quintius Cincinnatus, and being resolved to follow his example, by returning to their citizenship, they think they may with propriety denominate themselves the Society of the Cincinnati."

William G. Prescott, the only son of the eminent
scholar and historian. It was his greeting that
assured me of a cordial welcome to the home, as
he gave me to drink from the well where the sixth
generation quaffed from the brimming bucket,
while a representative of the seventh generation
prattled in innocency at our feet.[1]

I would fain share with my reader the courtesy
shown me by Mr. William G. Prescott ; but since
that is beyond my power, I now invite him to the
enjoyment of a June day at the old homestead.

One of the many precious heirlooms with which
this house abounds is the commission to Colonel
Prescott in the army of " The United Colonies,"
signed by John Hancock, making him " colonel of
the 7th regiment of foot." It hangs in the room
made sacred by the life of the one to whom it was
given. Another reminder of the colonel is a frag-
ment of the flowing gown, or banyan, which made
Colonel Prescott conspicuous in the redoubt at
Bunker Hill on the 17th of June. He threw aside
his military wrap in the heat of the engagement,
and appeared in this peculiar garment, which,
slashed by many a sword thrust, was long treasured in the home after the colonel had passed
away. The majestic figure of Colonel Prescott in
this peculiar dress attracted the eye of General
Gage, as by the aid of his glass he reviewed the

[1] Child of Hon. Roger Wolcott, now Governor of Massachusetts, and Edith Prescott, daughter of William G. Prescott.

scenes of that June day. Intent on duty, Colonel
Prescott was unmindful of danger, scarcely heed-
ing the shots as they came screaming over his
head from the sloops of war which lay off in the
stream. The eye that directed the shots from one
vessel of the fleet was, strangely enough, destined
to be changed from that of an enemy of the Provincials to that of a stanch friend ; and among
the attractions of the home, reminding one that
truth is stranger than fiction, are two cannon-balls,
supposed to have been fired from the sloop Falcon
to the redoubt on Bunker Hill. These are rusty
with the age of one hundred and twenty-one years,
but are kept near the picture of the man, Captain
Linzee, who it is supposed directed their course.

Captain John Linzee of the royal navy, in the
service of the king, was bent on the destruction
of the American army at Bunker Hill, and later
harassing the people of the shore towns. But he
afterwards became a friend of the Republic, and
in the days of peace his granddaughter was united
in marriage with a grandson of Colonel William
Prescott (William H., the historian). The romance of history is brought out most vividly by
these rusty missiles of war, and by the strong features of the man who steered their course. What
wonder Thackeray should make note of this in the
opening of the " Virginians."

" On the library wall of one of the most famous writers of
America there hang two crossed swords which his relatives

wore in the great war for independence. The one sword was gallantly drawn in the service of the king, the other was the weapon of a brave and honored republican soldier. The possessor of the harmless trophy has earned for himself a name alike honored in his ancestors' country and in his own, where genius like his has always a peaceful welcome."

THE SWORD
OF
COLONEL WILLIAM PRESCOTT
WORN BY HIM
WHILE IN COMMAND OF THE
PROVINCIAL FORCES
AT THE
BATTLE OF BUNKER HILL
17 JUNE, 1775,
AND
BEQUEATHED TO THE
MASS: HIST: SOCIETY
BY HIS GRANDSON
WILLIAM H. PRESCOTT.

THE SWORD
OF
CAPTAIN JOHN LINZEE, R.N.,
WHO COMMANDED THE
BRITISH SLOOP OF WAR FALCON WHILE
ACTING AGAINST THE AMERICANS
DURING THE BATTLE OF BUNKER HILL.
PRESENTED TO THE
MASS: HIST: SOCIETY
14 APRIL, 1859,
BY HIS GRANDCHILDREN,
THOMAS C. A. LINZEE
AND
MRS. WM. H. PRESCOTT.

These crossed swords are treasured in the rooms of the Massachusetts Historical Society at Boston, and remind one of the fulfilment of the prophecy, "And he shall judge among the nations, and shall rebuke many people: and they shall beat their swords into ploughshares, and their spears into pruninghooks: nation shall not lift up sword against nation, neither shall they learn war any more" (Isaiah ii. 4).

Another treasured relic of war is the hilt of the sword used by the first Napoleon. The buffet near by in the corner is loaded with the china of the united English and American families. The most precious are pieces used by Colonel William Prescott in his ancient home. A large share of richly carved furniture is in use to-day, as it was when brought across the water for Judge William Prescott, when setting up housekeeping with his beautiful bride, Catherine G. Hickling. On the right of the front hall of the original house is the spacious library of to-day, full of the reminders of the historian, whose sweet and thoughtful features are represented in a lifelike bust in marble. Hundreds of volumes suggest his struggle over his invaluable histories. After winding up the staircase with its ancient wainscoting of oak, one enters the room where the historian did much of his indefatigable labor. The peculiar arrangement for light reminds the visitor of the story of the crust of bread thrown by a careless student, which caused the historian to lose the sight of one eye forever.

In all the vivid reminders of the successive generations of the family, there is nothing to be seen that more forcibly recalls the hero of Bunker Hill than the brass door-knocker, so often manipulated by the old soldiers when calling upon the colonel, their leader, and the rude chair, with its wooden seat and arms, in which Colonel Prescott was in the habit of sitting when he entertained his friends by the crackling fire.

So free-handed was the colonel that he never refused anything asked by a soldier who fought under his command. Hence the colonel left his estate in debt, which his son, the judge, cleared, and transmitted, in all its rural beauty, to later generations.

> " Pleas'd with his guests, the good man learn'd to glow,
>   And quite forgot their vices in their woe;
>   Careless their merits or their faults to scan,
>   His pity gave ere charity began.
>   Thus to relieve the wretched was his pride,
>   And even his failings lean'd to virtue's side."

TABLET SEEN IN THE MOTHER TOWN

CHAPTER IV

Say then, O poet! when sages
Shall anew the tale relate,
Not for a thousand ages
Was a little battle so great;
Yea, write, besides, on your pages,
With an adamantine pen,
Not for a million ages
May such battle be fought again.

THOMAS W. PARSONS,
Dedication of Tablets at Charlestown.

REV. CHARLES BABBIDGE GIVES THE GENERAL RE-
PORT OF THE BATTLE OF BUNKER HILL AS
HE HEARD IT FROM THE OLD SOLDIERS. — THE
PREACHER IN CAMP. — PEPPERELL'S DEAD AT
BUNKER HILL. — COLONEL PRESCOTT'S GRAVE.
— GRAVES OF OTHER HEROES. — LIEUTENANT
JOSEPH SPAULDING. — THE SWORD OF BUNKER
.HILL

I KNOW of no other town in New England having so large part in the opening Revolution whose
story comes to us to-day in as direct manner as
does that of Pepperell. Of the more than fourscore soldiers of the town who left their homes
on April 19 and fought at Bunker Hill, a full
score were living when Rev. Charles Babbidge,

who is now pastor emeritus of the first parish
church, began his work in that town. It was my
good fortune to receive from this venerable clergyman the reports of the personal experience of
the Pepperell soldiers as he gathered them from

REV. CHARLES BABBIDGE

the lips of the veterans when, in his early ministry, he talked with them by the wayside, or gave
them the consolations of the gospel in their
homes. Rev. Charles Babbidge, now a nonagenarian, began his ministry in Pepperell in 1833.
He is one who has never statedly ministered to

any other people than those of his first choice. For more than sixty-three years he has been recognized as the pastor of the first parish, although of late not in active service.

In addition to all the ecclesiastical functions of a faithful pastor, Rev. Mr. Babbidge has never allowed the fire of patriotism to go out on the altar so early kindled in that town by his predecessor, Rev. Joseph Emerson, and kept burning through all the years of the town's history. How far this may be attributable to the location, and to the score of heroes of Bunker Hill to whom he ministered until they joined their comrades, we may not be able to determine. When from the standpoint of a nonagenarian this pastor reviewed his early years at Pepperell, he expressed himself in the semi-scriptural language, " Did not my heart burn within me as I walked and talked with them by the way, and as they opened to me the secrets of their lives?" But his patriotism was not sentiment alone ; for at the commencement of the Civil War he was chaplain of the Sixth Regiment, and the first minister in the country to enlist. He thus followed in the footsteps of the town's first minister, who is said to have offered up the first prayer in camp at Cambridge. Having served through the three months' campaign of "the Old Sixth," Rev. Mr. Babbidge was commissioned chaplain of the Twenty-sixth Massachusetts Regiment, in which he served three years, when he

returned to his people.[1] With this introduction to
a modern patriot of Pepperell, my reader must be
prepared to catch an impulse for good citizenship
from the story as he received it from survivors of
the Revolution : —

"Having been in camp since we arrived there on the 19th
of April, we had become restless and anxious for some more
active service, and our order to march over to Charlestown
on the night of June 16 was gladly received. We were always ready to follow our neighbor, Colonel Prescott. It was
our regiment, with detachments from others, that marched
from Cambridge Common to Charlestown, and took possession of the heights. Our colonel was at the head. He was
dressed in a simple, loose blue coat and three-cornered hat.
Two sergeants carried dark lanterns ahead of him ; the intrenching-tools were in carts in the rear. We had our arms ;
and most of us had one day's rations in our knapsacks, although some did not obey the order and were not so well
provided, not realizing what was in store for them. There
were one or two halts for consultation of the officers ; but we
reached the hill about midnight, and began work in earnest.
It went very well until the June sun of the 17th licked up the
dew, and we began to be weary. We had no sleep, and but
little refreshment; yet we could not give up so long as our
colonel was with us, and cheering us on as he walked lei-
surely around on the top of the redoubt, giving directions,
and uttering words of approval, and cracking an occasional

[1] "There is one consideration that may afford you consolation:
you will never again receive a letter from one, who, like myself,
played in his childhood in and out of the redoubt on Bunker Hill
while it still remained precisely as it was when Prescott left it, and
when Warren moistened it with his blood." — Letter from Dr.
Babbidge written for, and read on, the centennial of Colonel William Prescott's death.

joke. He knew that he was detected by the British, but seemed perfectly unconcerned. When it was nearly noon on the 17th we were pretty tired and sleepy, and our officers urged the colonel to send over to General Ward at Cambridge for fresh troops; but the colonel would not hear to it, and said ' The men who have raised these works will best defend them; they have had the merit of the labor, and should have the honor of victory if attacked.'

" General Warren came up with his musket in hand a short time before the fight began. Our colonel had heard that he had been commissioned major-general the day before, and hence offered him the command, to which he replied, ' No; I have not received my commission. I have come as a volunteer, and am happy to learn service from a soldier of your experience.'

" We watched the landing of the enemy, and also the cannon-balls as they came over our heads. We could see the roofs of the houses over in Boston covered with people, watching to see what would be the result of the king's army as they landed and marched up the hill. Up the hill they came, firing as they advanced. But we kept silent behind our embankment, for we knew we had no ammunition to waste. ' Aim low, boys,' whispered Colonel Prescott; ' fire at their waistbands, and wait till you see the whites of their eyes. Waste no powder.' When the redcoats were almost up the hill, their plumes nearly level with its crest, bang! bang! went our fifteen hundred muskets at once, and down went scores of the brave Britishers, cut down as the scythe cuts the waving grass.

" We did the best we could; but when our ammunition was gone, there was no other way for us but to retreat while the smoke from the burning town enveloped us. The hardest part of it all was to leave so many of our neighbors dead and wounded in the redoubt. But after all that we had suffered since leaving Cambridge, we would gladly have gone back that night with more men and supplies, and retaken the heights, or perished there with our townsmen who were dead, and others who, missing, we supposed were dead.

"The grief in these Pepperell homes when the news of the battle reached here, we may well imagine. Our people were not altogether unprepared for the sad tidings; they had distinctly heard the roar of the cannon. Our faithful pastor made his record; and there on the church book the boys' names appear in his handwriting, the same as though they had died here peacefully at home."

The anxiety of Rev. Mr. Emerson for his people in camp was so great that he repeatedly made journeys to Cambridge that he might minister to the survivors. On one occasion while there he took a severe cold, which terminated his useful life. Another hand completed the record; but it is apparent that pastor and eight of his people laid down their lives early in the war for freedom. The names of the Pepperell men who fell on the 17th of June, as they appear on the bronze tablets at Charlestown, are as follows: —

PRESCOTT'S REGIMENT.

Nutting's company. — Nathaniel Parker,[1] William Warren, Edmund Peers,[2] Wainwright Fisk, Ebenezer Laughton, Jeremiah Shattuck.

Asa Lawrence company. — Lieut. Joseph Spaulding, (unassigned) Amasa Fisk.[3]

---

[1] Nathaniel Parker was junior. His father, Nathaniel senior, aged sixty-eight years, died on the same day of fever at his home in Pepperell.

[2] Edmund Peers should be Pierce.

[3] Amasa Fisk must have died later from wounds or disease in a

Deaths.

1775

271. Jan. 4. Wife of Joseph Spaulding Æ. 35 nervous fever
72.   9 Daughter of John Green still born.
73.   15. Wife of John Green Æ. 45. in child bed.
74.   19. Jonas Wright aged 35 Years 5 Month. consumpt
75 March 4. Samuel Shattuck aged almost 79 Years. Fever
76.   6. Son of Widow Anna Wright aged 5 Months. 15 D. Consump
77.   15. Son of David Wright aged 7 Months. 20 D. Fever.
78 May 14. Isaac Williams aged 75 Years some months Consumption
79 June 5. Aaron Hosley aged 33 Years. 1 M. 2. D. Fever
80.   17. Nathl Parker about 60 Years of age Fever
81.   17. Joseph Spaulding Æ. 37 killed in ye Battle at Charlstown
82.   17. Nathl Parker jun. Æ.   killed   at Charlstown
83.   17. Willm Warren Æ. 28. killed   at Charlstown
84.   17. Ebenr Laughton Æ. 27 killed   at Charlstown
85.   17. Wainwright Fisk Æ. 24. killed   at Charlstown
86.   17. Jerah Shattuck 3. Æ.   killed   at Charlstown
87.   17. Edmund Pierce Æ. 44 killed   at Charlstown
88.   17. Benjn Wood Æ. 20 killed   at Charlstown
89.   20. Nathl Bowers Æ. 60. Fever.   Fever Oct. 4
90 July 26. A son of Darius Hudson aged almost 1 Year 18 M.
91 Aug. 27. A Daughter of Tho. Lawrence aged near 8 Y. 9. M. Dysentery
92 Sep. 4. A Son of Benjn Wright aged 9 Years. 6 M. 25. D. Dysentery
93.   9. The Wife of James Nutting aged about 77 Years
94.   12. The Wife of Benjn Jewet aged almost 49 Years. Dysentery
95.   20. Isaac Pierce in the 31 Year of his age. nervous fever
96 Oct. 28 Daughter of Nehemiah Shattuck still born
97 Oct 29 Revd Mr Emerson aged 51 yes. 1 M. 24 D. nervous fever

FAC-SIMILE OF PAGE, PEPPERELL CHURCH RECORDS

NOTE. — The church record of deaths of Pepperell men at Bunker Hill seems to be unquestionable as authority, although tardy in its appearance. It must have been made soon after the 17th of June, as it is in the handwriting of Rev. Joseph Emerson, whose own death occurred in about four months after the loss of his parishioners. Its acceptance is an admission of inaccuracy on the memorial tablets at Charlestown. Benjamin Wood, credited to Groton, belonged to Pepperell.

The name of the patriot preacher of Pepperell, who died from disease contracted in the service, is seen on the rude slab erected by the town, on which is read :—

Weep not for me, but weep for yourselves and for your children

ERECTED BY THE TOWN OF PEPPERELL

TO THE MEMORY OF

THE REV. JOSEPH EMERSON

FIRST PASTOR OF THE CHURCH HERE,

who deceased Oct. 29th 1775 in the 52d year of his age, and the 29th of his ministry.

Steadfast in the Faith once delivered to the Saints. Fixed and laborious in the cause of Christ & precious souls. Exemplary in visiting & sympathizing with his flock — Diligent in improving his Talents — A kind Husband and a tender Parent — a faithful Reprover — a constant Friend — & a true Patriot.

Having ceased from his labors his works follow him.

Colonel Prescott remained in service until the end of the year 1776; and in the autumn of the following year he went as a volunteer with some of his former officers and townsmen to aid in the capture of General Burgoyne, which was his last

prison, and, if belonging to Pepperell, was not recorded by his pastor, who may have died before him.

military service. After the enjoyment of peace
and his country's independence at the old homestead, he died in 1795, at the age of sixty-nine
years. In the old burying-ground at Pepperell,
where rests the patriot preacher, and within the
shadow of the old church, stands a plain tomb,
built of four upright granite slabs, forming a
square enclosure about three feet high, upon the

GRAVE OF REV. JOSEPH EMERSON, PEPPERELL

top of which rest two horizontal tablets of slate-
stone, bearing the following inscriptions : —

THIS STONE IS ERECTED

IN MEMORY OF

COL^L. WILLIAM PRESCOTT

OF PEPPERELL,

Who died on the 13th day of October, Anno Domini 1795,
in the seventieth year of his age.

IN-MEMORY OF

MRS. ABIGAIL PRESCOTT,

WIDOW OF THE LATE

COL. WILLIAM PRESCOTT,

Who died Oct. 19, A.D. 1821, Æ. 89.

The grave of Colonel Prescott is surrounded by those of his neighbors and friends. The flags floating from the bronze markers of the S. A. R. remind the visitor that, as in life, so in death the gallant colonel is in the midst of his soldiers.

CAPT. EDMUND BANCROFT,

DIED OCT. 23, 1805, Æ. 79.

In common with his neighbors, love of country was his ruling passion. He was ever ready to offer up his own life, and the lives of his sons, a sacrifice on the altar of liberty during the darkest period of the Revolution.

ERECTED IN MEMORY OF

GEN. HENRY WOODS,

Who died March 5th, 1804,

Aged 70 years.

He served his country in her contest for the obtainment of freedom and independence, and has since sustained with honor several important offices, both civil and military. He was no less endeared to his family and connections by his disposition to disseminate knowledge, promote the social virtues, than to the community by his public spirit and charity.

THIS MONUMENT IS ERECTED IN MEMORY OF

MR. BENJAMIN CHAMBERLIN,

Who departed this life in the Continental army at Valley Forge,

In the year 1778, in ye 17th year of his age.

He was the son of Mr. Phineas Chamberlin, and Mrs. Lydia, his wife.

CAPTAIN JOHN NUTTING,

DROWNED MAY 25, 1816, AGED 85.

(He passed through the Battle of Bunker Hill in command of a company.)

THIS MONUMENT IS ERECTED TO YE MEMORY OF

MESSRS. DANIEL AND JOEL HOBART,

SONS OF MR. NEFB. HOBART AND MRS. RACHEL, HIS WIFE.

Daniel fell in the Battle of White Plains Oct. 28, 1776, aged 28 yrs.
Joel was drowned at ye Eastward Oct. 9, 1785, aged 20 yrs.
Erected by the brethren.

WILLIAM KENDALL,

Died 1819, aged 69.

THOMAS LAWRENCE,

Died 1833, æ. 77.

CAPT. NATHANIEL SARTELL,

Died Sept. 1847, æ. 87.

MAJOR THOMAS LAWRENCE,

Died July 27, 1822, æ. 65.

IN MEMORY OF

LIEUT. JOS: SPAULDING,

Who was slain in the memorable Battle on Bunker Hill,
On the 17th of June, 1775, in ye 37th year of his age.

On the same stone is read : —

HERE LIES THE BODY OF

MRS. PHEBE SPAULDING,

WIFE OF LIEUT. JOS. SPAULDING,

Who departed this life January 4th, 1775, in ye 38th year of her age.

NOTE. — On the top, in the face of this moss-covered stone, is
rudely carved the representation of a sword.   To the present generation this has lost its significance, but meant much to the family
who erected this memorial, as is seen in the following family narrative.

"Fight on, brave boys, they fall like pigeons!" were the last words of Joseph Spaulding, First Lieutenant of Captain Asa Lawrence's company in the Battle of Bunker Hill.   When this brave son of Pepperell yielded up his life, the Provincials expected to win the day.   They had full confidence in their leader, Colonel William Prescott, and believed that with him they were sure to come off victorious ; in fact, they were ready to die for him if need be.   Tradition says that Lieutenant Spaulding, early in the battle of the 17th of June, voluntarily took a position of danger in place of Colonel Prescott.   In order to fully estimate the patriotism of the yeomen soldiers of the opening Revolution, one needs to know something of the sacrifice made in order to leave their homes to enter the service of their country.   With the opening of the year 1775, Lieutenant Joseph Spaulding had seen the grave close over the lifeless form of his beloved wife, leaving him with the care of a young son and daughter.   It was when his hands and heart were full that the Lexington alarm was sounded through the town, and Lieutenant Spaulding was quick to respond.   If he had retired from service after the experiences of April 19, no one would have thought of censuring him ; but the brave young man only returned to make provision for his children, and then rejoined his comrades in camp at Cambridge, where he was found when orders came to march over to Charlestown with intrenching-tools, etc., on the night of the 16th of June. Through the busy hours of that night, and on the following morning, his thoughts must have been divided between the motherless children at home in Pepperell, and the movements of the British army in and around Boston. But regardless of the natural yearnings for the welfare of his children, Lieutenant Joseph Spaulding manfully faced the enemy; and when he fell, it was with a word of encouragement upon his lips. "They fall like pigeons!" No words could have been more natural, or suggestive of the spring and fall game of those towns, and of the manner of capturing the great flocks of wild pigeons that made their semi-annual visits to the towns in Middlesex County. These were the last words uttered by Lieutenant Spaulding. They were meaningless when first reported to the orphans at Pepperell; but as they advanced in years their full significance became apparent, and they have been transmitted from generation to generation with that spirit of patriotism which prompted their utterance in the hour of death in the redoubt on Bunker Hill. In addition to the message, there was brought to the home the sword taken from the dead soldier. This has been equally precious, and is now treasured as the Sword of Bunker Hill by a great-grandson, Edgar Oliver Spaulding, at Plymouth, N.H.

Says the owner: "I am a son of Oliver Spaulding and Sarah Ann Hawkins of Rumney, N.H.

My father was a son of Oliver Spaulding and Sarah Greenough, and grandson of Lieutenant Joseph Spaulding."

Says the proud owner of the sword, " My grandfather left Pepperell about the year 1787. Being

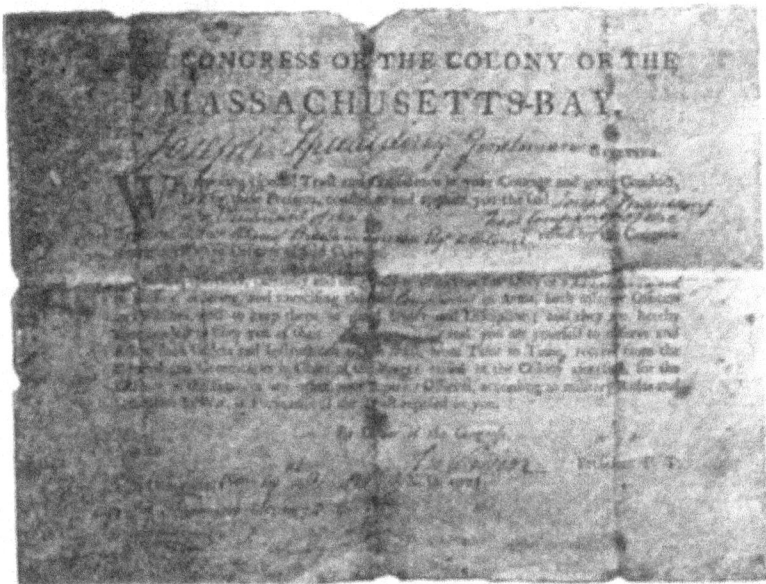

LIEUTENANT JOSEPH SPAULDING'S COMMISSION

an orphan and so early removed from the town where his parents were best known, he did not have the record of family joys and sorrows, and could tell but little save the simple story, ' My mother died a few months before my father was killed at Bunker Hill, after which my sister and myself lived for a time at grandsir's.' " This story by the great-grandson of the hero of Bunker Hill is strengthened by the silent testimony of the stone at the grave of the wife of Lieutenant Joseph Spaulding. This rude memorial was erected by a provision made for that purpose in the last will of William Spaulding of Pepperell, father of the hero. The will, admitted to probate Sept. 29, 1770, directs that gravestones shall be put up to the memory of his deceased wife, and to that of his son Joseph and wife. In addition to this, there appears in the old church record of deaths, in the handwriting of the patriot preacher, Rev. Joseph Emerson, that which time has not effaced.

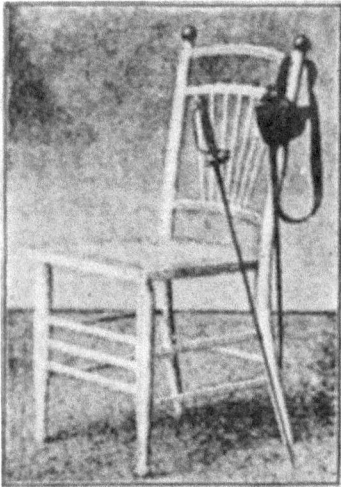

THE SWORD OF BUNKER HILL

The first entry of the year 1775 is the death of the wife of Joseph Spaulding, Æ38, — nervous fever. The eleventh entry is Joseph Spaulding, Æ37, — killed in ye battle at Charlestown. Being the oldest of the eight Pepperell men who perished at Bunker Hill, Lieutenant Spaulding's name is placed at the head of the list of patriot dead.

The Spaulding sword, like many of the weapons carried by the minute-men on the 19th of April and 17th of June, dated back to the Colonial wars. It was owned by Major Rogers, a British officer in the French war. The owner accidentally dropped it into a lake, from whence it was recovered by Lieutenant Spaulding, who voluntarily dived for it, and was successful in bringing it from the sandy bottom. But upon offering it to its owner, he was rewarded for his daring feat by the gift of the weapon. The young man carried it home to Pepperell as a trophy of the French war, naturally took it with him when next called to service, and used it as faithfully against the king as it had ever been used in the service of his Majesty in the hand of Major Rogers.

"The God of Freedom blessed the Sword of Bunker Hill."

WALLACE

CHAPTER V

They helped to light the torch of liberty's fires. A man who makes a sacrifice for his fatherland, be he never so lowly, his name should be forever written in the history of the nation. — HON. JOHN R. MURPHY, *June* 17, 1889.

REV. CHARLES BABBIDGE'S EXPERIENCE WITH OLD SOLDIERS OF THE REVOLUTION. — THOMAS PAINE'S "COMMON SENSE." — NO GOVERNMENT HOMES FOR VETERANS OF THE WAR. — MILITARY SERVICE OF HARVARD COLLEGE. — STORY OF EDMUND BANCROFT. — BURGOYNE'S OFFICERS AND THEIR DOGS. — STORY OF EDMUND BLOOD

BESIDES the general narrative, the young pastor gathered much in the way of incidents from the ôlder members of his parish, who, as they neared the threshold of eternity, seemed to live over again the experiences of their early years, particularly those of the war. Says Mr. Babbidge, "I sat by the bedside of an old soldier, one of my parishioners, about to depart this life. His thoughts, dwelling upon the future, led him to desire to discuss the works of Thomas Paine. There had been placed in his hand, while in camp, a pamphlet entitled "Common-Sense," written in a popular style by Paine. In this he advocated the cause of the American Colonies against the mother country. The success and influence of the publication were extraordinary ; and it won the author the friendship of Washington, Franklin, and other distinguished leaders, as well as the confidence of the soldiers fighting for their independence. This Pepperell soldier had treasured the pamphlet, and naturally been led to study other works by the same author, and been greatly impressed by his infidel opinions, which seemed to be clouding the light of revelation as he was nearing his end. I was impressed by this experience with the fact that these old veterans had not only scars of body, but of mind, as the result of their early service in the war."

Our country was in no condition to make the liberal provisions for the soldiers after the Revolution that it did after the Civil War, and not a few of them ended their lives in the almshouse. " This was the case in Pepperell," said the clergyman ; "and I frequently visited old soldiers at that institution when in the discharge of my parochial duties, and there caught anew from the veterans the impulse of patriotism. They were old and worn-out men ; and no one could look upon them, and think what they had sacrificed and endured, and not be drawn to them very strongly. There was Moses Blood, 'an Israelite without guile,' and Jedediah Jewett, ' Uncle Jeddie,' as he was famil-

iarly known, and Mr. Wright, all tenderly cared
for in that most excellent home.   Each had his
peculiarities, and was allowed to indulge them.
Their sayings are frequently quoted in the town
to this day.   The wit of one of them, Thomas
Seward, seemed to sharpen with advancing age.
Rev. Mr. Bullard, my predecessor, called at the
almshouse, and there met the veteran.   Desiring
to know how many inmates there were, he said to
Mr. Seward, ' How many here are supported by
the town ? '   The reply was, ' Two, sir ; myself
and you, and being the older I put myself first.'
This, to the minister, whose support was provided
in town-meeting, in much the same manner as
was that of the poor, was so well put that the
pastor did not fail to report it."

While the town of Pepperell has never been neg-
lectful of the anniversary of April 19, and with
the other towns in that locality duly appreciates
it, their especial day of annual observance has
been that of the 17th of June.   As long as any
of the old heroes lived, they were the central
figure in the local celebration.   A military spirit
always prevailed in the town ; guns were fired in
all parts on the 17th, a dinner was served, the
Prescott Guards were on duty, and an oration was
always delivered.

" The military discipline throughout the State,"
said Mr. Babbidge, " if properly conducted, tends
to cultivate obedience and good manners, and thus

is conducive to proper life. This was true in a
large degree throughout the Commonwealth as
long as the organization was kept up. When I
was in Harvard College we had one of the finest
companies in the State, consisting of the students.
The State provided our arms, and we drilled for
exhibition four times each year. Robert C. Winthrop was our captain. While sitting here by my
hearth-stone and looking backward, I can but at-
tribute much of the success of the Northern army
in the Civil War to the familiarity with arms which
dates back to those days."

Among the Pepperell men who served at Bunker
Hill was Sergeant Edmund Bancroft, who is represented there to-day in blood and name by his
grandson, Edmund Bancroft. There is no more
convincing evidence of the character and ability
of the yeoman soldiery of 1775 than is found in
this town, where one of their men, a sergeant,
who fought at Bunker Hill, served the town later
in the second and third Provincial Congresses.
The home of the soldier and representative to
Provincial Congress has disappeared ; but on the
same acres is the home of his grandson, Edmund
of to-day. This man repeats the familiar narrative as he received it, a fireside tale, confirming
that of many others ; but he naturally introduces
that later experience of the war in which the
town had a most interesting share, the surrender
of Burgoyne. Colonel Prescott, with other men of

the town, were in that service when the Northern army surrendered.[1]

After the surrendered army arrived at Cambridge, several of Burgoyne's officers were sent out to Pepperell on parole. Two of them were boarded in the Bancroft family, and others were quartered in the neighborhood. This provision was doubtless made through the influence of Mr. Bancroft. Says the present Edmund, "My father, who was Edmund second, was a boy in the family, and much in company with these prisoners. His recollection of the guests, as they went about wearing their side-arms, was very vivid; and he frequently furnished the evening's entertainment for us children, as we sat about the open fire, by telling the stories of those disappointed men who had been obliged to surrender. They provided their own support and had attendants, as was frequently the case with the British and German officers when in this country. These had dogs with them, called by the names of Barstow and Bisbee. Our boy nature was greatly aroused by the incidents in which these dogs played a part." It is claimed that these officers were permitted to meet at a certain place once a week for friendly conference, a monument having been erected to commemorate the tradition. The story by Mr. Bancroft, of quartering the officers in the remote towns, is strengthened by the history of the times; and Longfellow

[1] For narrative see subsequent chapter.

gives us a glimpse of their dogs in "The Open Window," —

" The large Newfoundland house-dog was standing by the door."

Among the many family mementoes of the Bancroft home proudly shown by the Edmund of to-day is the powder-horn carried by his grandfather in the fight. It is elaborately carved, and bears the initials " E. B.," with dates, etc. As evidence of an inheritance of the family military spirit on the part of the one who now bears the name, appears the record of service of Edmund the third as major of a regiment of militia in which were the Lowell City Guards, when Benjamin F. Butler was a lieutenant, and learned military tactics of this officer.

Neither the deaths at Bunker Hill, nor the loss of their patriotic minister in the cause of freedom, deterred the men of the town from responding to the successive calls for service and money. At first it was necessary that a man should be of full height, of age, and of good health, to "pass muster;" but there came a time when it was not so easy to keep the depleted ranks of the Continental army full, and men were accepted although not recorded as "liable to do military duty." Boys were admitted who had prematurely reached the stature of manhood, although they had not attained the age of sixteen years. Edmund Blood of Pepperell was found in the service when yet in his

teens. He was but eleven years of age when the
Lexington alarm called the people of Pepperell to
action ; but fired with the spirit so generally per-
vading the town, he anxiously waited the time
when he, too, could enter the service, and seized
the first opportunity, which was the call of June,
1780. He is recorded as of light complexion, and
"5 ft., 7 in." in stature. His service was at
North River, New York. Having served out his
time, he returned to his home in penury, — the
condition to which a large share of the soldiers
were reduced. In many instances they were discharged hundreds of miles from their homes, with
no provision for the journey. They counted themselves fortunate if they were not forced to make
the journey on foot, with not even as much as a
remnant of a shoe or stocking, thus destitute and
weary coming back to the old home to share the
burden of debt occasioned by the war. A most
convincing proof of this general condition of discharged soldiers is found in the family home of
Edmund Blood at Pepperell. A son of the young
soldier, bearing his father's name and culivating
his paternal acres, has a discharge paper, — his
father's passport from Fishkill, N.Y., to Pepperell, Mass.

Mr. Blood of to-day is but sixty years of age, yet
is one of the few living children of a soldier of the
Revolution who has had the tale of personal experience from his father's lips.

" I marched July 4, 1780, arrived at Springfield July 8, and went on to New York. I was in the Eighth Division, under Ebenezer Kent, and chiefly occupied in doing guard duty. I frequently saw Washington, and early learned to admire his manly form, open, frank countenance, and uniform courtesy to all, regardless of rank. When we were discharged, Dec. 5, 1780, each received a written certificate bearing the signature of the Colonel. This was proof that we were not deserters, and also a recommendation to the charity of the farmers, whose aid we sorely needed. We had no money of any sort, and when we were finally paid off, it was in the worthless currency, which had nothing but bulk to commend it."

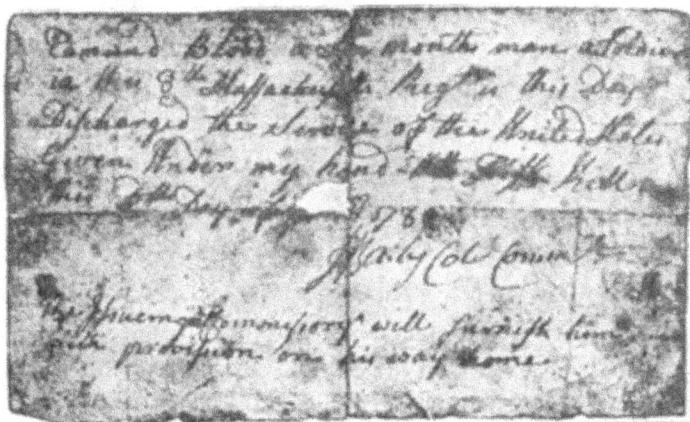

DISCHARGE OF EDMUND BLOOD

This slip of paper, carried by Edmund Blood in his waistcoat pocket from Fishkill to Pepperell, has been kept in the home where the returned soldier put it, and is *prima facie* evidence of what many have accepted as doubtful tradition.

It would seem as though this experience were

enough to satisfy the young man's love of adventure, but Edmund Blood soon appears with twenty
of his townsmen in the privateer service.[1]   A
statement of his final settlement with Captain
Manley, showing his share in prizes captured, is

THE BLOOD HOMESTEAD

one of the family treasures at the Blood homestead, from which comes the Pepperell spring
water, now being shipped to the same State in
which the young soldier did service for his country.

[1] See Story of Privateering in this series.

CHAPTER VI

When we assumed the soldier, we did not lay aside the citizen.
GEORGE WASHINGTON.

PEPPERELL CONTINUED. — WILLIAMS'S PLACE. —
PARKER HOMESTEAD. — THE PLOUGH IN THE FUR-
ROW. — SHATTUCK FAMILY. — BLOOD FAMILY. —
WARNER HOME. — JEWETT'S BRIDGE. — "PAUGUS
JOHN "

FURTHER research in the town of Pepperell
brought me to the Williams home, where I was
met by a busy farmer, Mr. Luther H. Williams,
who carries on the farm which his father and
grandfather conducted before him.

"My grandfather, Isaac Parker," said the owner,
"was one of Colonel Prescott's regiment. He
was in Captain John Nutting's company, responded
to the Lexington alarm, and was in the battle of
June 17th. My grandparents frequently rehearsed
the experiences of that time, in which this town
had a creditable part. Grandmother, who lived
to be ninety years of age, forgetting for the time
the age of her grandchildren, would say to me, a
restless boy to be amused, ' Do you remember the
battles of Concord and Bunker Hill? I do; I re-

member how the guns roared, for I heard them on the day of the battle at Charlestown, when so many of our folks were killed.' "

My next halt was at the Parker home, where five generations of the name have made a record. The last are the children of Charles S. Parker, who now conducts the farm. The line running backward

OLD PARKER PLOUGH

from the present owner is Allen S. Parker, his father, Thomas, his grandfather, and Nathaniel Parker, whose name is found among those who did valiant service on Bunker Hill. Says Mr. Parker, " My great-grandfather was ploughing in the field when the April alarm was sounded; and he lost no time in preparation, but left his team, took his gun, and started. We have kept the old plough here on the farm as a reminder of that day, and also to show by way of contrast the progress that

has been made in farm implements since the Parkers first began to cultivate these acres." The
plough that belonged to the soldier ancestor was
brought from its hiding-place; and a picture was
taken of it, together with the chain in use at the
same time.

A superficial student of the history of Pepperell
cannot fail to be impressed with the consanguinity
of its people from the earliest settlement to the
present time. Shattuck and Blood have been pre-
dominant names. They owned large tracts of land
on both sides of the Nashua River, suffered greatly
from the depredations of the Indians, and were
well trained in warfare long before the Revolution.
" Few persons nowadays can have an accurate
conception of the toil, suffering, and dangers endured by the early settlers of our frontier New
England towns. The workmen as they went forth
to their labors were not sure of returning again in
safety to their homes, or, if they did, that they
should find their loved ones alive. The tomahawk, scalping-knife, and other deadly weapons,
were in the hands of foes whose approach was
often stealthy and when least expected."

Two of the grandsons of the first William Shattuck settled in that part of Groton which became
Pepperell. They were allied with the Bloods
through marriage; and so common were the two
names, that it was said a stranger in the place was
perfectly safe in addressing a citizen as Mr. Shat-

tuck, and, if failing of recognition, turning to the name of Blood. " Rev. Mr. Emerson is said to have remarked, that 'he sometimes regretted that he did not marry a Shattuck, for he should then have been related to the whole town.'" The widow of the regretful minister's son Joseph, how-

COLONEL SHATTUCK'S HOME, PEPPERELL

ever, made amends for the mistake by marrying Calvin Shattuck in 1811.[1]

The town furnishes no more favorable vantage-ground for tracing the footprints of the patriots

[1] The Bloods were of that family early found in Concord, Mass., to which reference has been made in " Beneath Old Roof Trees."

in these families than the home of Colonel Samuel
Pepperell Shattuck ; the beautiful house of the
present day identifies that of John Shattuck, which
was one of the garrison houses maintained as late
as 1750. The owner was called "Canada John,"
because occupying the outpost between civilization in the Colony and Canada ; and doubtless the
name distinguished the garrison-keeper from other
John Shattucks. A large elm-tree now on the
place is said to have sprung up through the stone
chimney of the old garrison when gone to decay.
Colonel Shattuck, the present occupant of this
old estate, represents the younger branch of the
original settler's family ; while Mrs. Shattuck, who
was a Shattuck before marriage, represents the
older branch. In company with Colonel and Mrs.
Shattuck, both worthy descendants of a self-sacri-
ficing ancestry who have left footprints on the
sands of time, I gathered facts of peculiar interest. In driving through the centre of the town,
Mrs. Shattuck proudly remarked that "here is
where our grandmothers met and publicly burned
their tea, thus following the example of the patriots of Charlestown, Providence, R.I., and other
towns, when the king was trying to force them to
submission."

The relations between the Pepperell minister
and his people at the opening of the Revolution
are brought vividly to mind when calling at the
old Shattuck home, and listening to the family

story from Augustus L. Shattuck: "My grandfather, Jonathan Shattuck, was a millwright. In
company with his neighbors he started from home
in response to the Lexington alarm, but was told
by his far-seeing minister that his place was at
home, because much of the supplies for the army
depended upon the millers; hence grandfather returned, hung up his gun, and went to work in the
mill." It will be remembered that during the
early months of the war the patriot army was supplied by contributions from the families. There
consequently was but little uniformity in the rations. One good woman of Pepperell, familiar with
the Bible account of David taking ten cheeses into
the camp of the Israelites,[1] insisted upon sending
a cheese of her make to her son in camp at Cambridge, by a neighbor, who was returning from the
town after a furlough.

In our drive about the town we came to the
crossroads where it is alleged a Pepperell woman
met her husband on that April morning, and delivered to him his coat, with admonitions to make
haste, for the Regulars are out. Passing a fertile
field, I was told that "Jeremiah Shattuck was
working here when he heard the alarm gun; and
he instantly left all, jumped the fence, joined the
company, went to Cambridge, and gave up his life
at Bunker Hill with other Pepperell men."

There are but few houses in the town that have

---

[1] 1 Sam. xvii. 18.

not undergone radical changes since the Revolution, but there is one at the corner of Pepperell and Townsend which remains much the same as when the roaring of the cannon on Bunker Hill was heard at its door. Joseph Warner was the first of the family on the place; he took up his abode there in 1777, when his son Richard was eight years of age. Both completed their lives at this farm, and were followed by the present occupant, who is Walter Warner; he is eighty-six years old, and conducts the business of the farm after the plan followed by his father. Mr. Warner of to-day recalls with interest the story told him by his father, who, as a boy in the centre of Pepperell, watched the gathering of the minute-men and their hasty departure in martial manner on April 19, 1775. The impression made on the youthful mind by the report that many of the townsmen had been killed at Bunker Hill, and more were wounded, was one that remained as long as life lasted; and the oft-repeated story has found lodgment in the memory of Walter Warner. His natural aversion to anything modern inclines him to derive the most complete satisfaction from the recollections of his youth.

Our further drive about the town brought us to Jewett's Bridge, which spans the Nashua River. Colonel Shattuck reminded us of the bravery of his patriotic grand-aunt, Mrs. David Wright, who with an associate, Mrs. Job Shattuck, posted themselves here, and arrested Captain Leonard Whiting, a noted Tory, the bearer of treasonable despatches from Canada to Boston (*see* "Woman in the Revolution"). Passing down the river road, which winds gracefully through the town, following the course of the Nashua, we came to the

COLONEL SAMUEL P. SHATTUCK

place where an earlier patriot made a record that will endure as long as the history of the New England Colonies is read. It was at this place that John Chamberlain killed young Paugus, and saved his own life. While this story is of days that preceded the Revolution, the descendants of the hero were active in the war for independence, and are represented to-day in the town, one of my venerable guides, Mrs. Shattuck, being a grand-niece of John Chamberlain.

STORY OF PAUGUS JOHN.

Condensed from published reports.

John Chamberlain was one of Captain Lovewell's company in the famous fight with the In-

dians in 1725 near Fryeburg, Me. In the general
engagement John's gun became foul, and he went
to the edge of the pond to wash it out. While
there he discovered Paugus, the chief, engaged in
the same act. Chamberlain had personal acquaint-
ance with Paugus, and they at once resolved to see
who should be the
survivor of the hour.
" Now, Paugus," said
Chamberlain, " I ' ll
have you ; " and with
the spirit of an old
h u n t e r sprang to
l o a d i n g his rifle.
" Na — na, me have
you," said Paugus ;
and he handled his
gun with a dexterity
that made the bold
heart of Chamber-
lain beat quick, and
he almost raised his

MRS. SAMUEL P. SHATTUCK

eye to take his last look upon the sun. They
rammed their cartridges, and each at the same
instant cast his ramrod upon the sand. " I'll
have you, Paugus," repeated Chamberlain, as in
his desperation he almost resolved to rush upon
the savage with the breech of his rifle, lest he
should receive his bullets before he could load.
Paugus trembled as he applied his powder-horn to

the priming. Chamberlain heard the grains of his powder rattle lightly upon the leaves beneath his feet ; he struck his gun-breech violently upon the ground, the rifle "primed herself," he aimed, and his bullets whistled through the heart of Paugus. As the chief fell, the bullet from the mouth of his ascending rifle touched the hair upon the crown of Chamberlain, and passed off without avenging the death of its dreadful master.

The children and successors of Paugus, long after this event, determined to avenge the death of the chief. They entertained the opinion that whoever should kill Chamberlain would be considered the greatest chief of the nation ; and they made several attempts to do it, the last one having taken place at the Nashua River in Pepperell, where Chamberlain had a mill.

In the year——, towards the close of one of those fair days in autumn which make up the "Indian summer," a number of the villagers of Groton had gathered in their one-story tavern to talk over their little politics, as was their custom, when they were surprised and startled by the entrance of a young Indian among them. An Indian at that time was a rarity in the town. He was tall, over six feet, and finely formed, after the fashion of the forest. He had a belt of wampum around his waist, and from it hung his tomahawk. A long gun was in his hand ; and he stood in moccasins, with the grace and dignity of the son of a chief.

He placed his gun behind the door, and silently
took his seat by himself. A little before sunset
the farmers left the inn, and returned to their
homes. An old hunter remained with the landlord and the young savage. The hunter eyed the
Indian with keen attention; his suspicions were
aroused at the sight of this warrior, armed, so remote from the residence of the nearest tribe, and
in a time of peace. He was acquainted with the
Indians in the old wars ; and his suspicions were
heightened and confirmed when he heard the
young chief ask the landlord, in a low and indiffer-
ent tone, if " one Chamberlain dwelt in the village." The landlord pointed out to him the mill
where the old man labored, and the cottage where
he dwelt. The Indian took his gun, and went
out. " Some of the blood of old Paugus," said
the hunter, " and, I'll venture my life, come to
avenge the death of that chief upon Chamberlain.
I'll give the old man warning." He stepped out,
and made haste to the mill where the old man
was still at his toils, and made known his suspicions. Chamberlain's cheek turned ashy pale ; and
he sternly replied, " Tell young Paugus I have the
gun that slew his father, and he had far better return to his forest than molest me in my old age."
As he spoke he pointed out the long gun as it
hung upon prongs of the moose-horn, driven into
the sawmill plate ; and near it was suspended the
bullet-pouch and powder-horn of the same cam-

paign.   After giving his warning the hunter retired.   Chamberlain took down his gun, tried his
flint, charged it, took the pouch and horn and flung
them upon his side, hung up near the saw-gate
the old garment he had worn at work through the
day, hoisted the gate of the mill and set the wheel
in motion, looked keenly around him in every direction, and retired to an eminence a few rods distant, crowned with a clump of thick bushes, and
crouched down to await the approach of his mysterious enemy.   He was not, however, mysterious
to Chamberlain.   The old man remembered every
trait in the Indian character, and calculated with
great accuracy as to the time and manner of Paugus's advance.   Just as it was growing too dusky
to distinguish a human form, except towards the
west, the old man descried him creeping cautiously
from a bunch of bushes, eight or ten rods above
the mill, by the torrent, with his cocked rifle before him, and his hand upon the lock.   The young
savage heard the noise of the saw-frame, and could
discern it in rapid motion, and shrunk back into
the thicket.   He came out again, a little distance
from where he entered, and, with the wary motions
of the ambush, reconnoitred the mill, Chamberlain marking him all the while.   Young Paugus
came out of the bushes the third time, and in a
new quarter, and was stealthily advancing when
something seemed to catch his eye in the form of
his father's slayer.   He stopped short, brought his

rifle to his eye, and with quick aim fired. The report rang sharp and low upon the still air, as if the gun itself were muffled, or afraid to speak above its breath. Young Paugus crept out upon a mill-log that extended over the rapid, and stretched himself up to his full height, as if to ascertain, without advancing, the success of his shot. The old man could spare him no longer. He saw the well-remembered form of the old chief, as the young savage stood against the western sky, which was still red with the rays of the sunken sun. He levelled the fatal gun; it blazed; young 'Paugus leaped into the air as the ball whistled through his heart, and his lifeless body fell far down into the rapid that foamed below him, while his vengeful spirit fled and mingled with that sterner one which parted long before at Lovewell's Pond. The next morning a bullet-hole through the centre of the old garment he had hung at the saw-frame admonished him that the aim, as well as the vengeance, of old Paugus had descended to his son.

Standing near the spot where John Chamberlain killed young Paugus, the water of the same stream still coursing by, I could but hear in their gentle ripple, —

"For men may come, and men may go,
But I go on forever."

The story of the narrow escape of John Chamberlain from the avenging hand of young Paugus led to the display of some rude articles of domestic

use, treasured by my guides in the home as mementoes of the time when their ancestor plied the
craft of a miller in this town. Together with the
small articles was brought forward the long chest,
or magazine, kept previous to and during the Revolution in the upper loft of the meeting-house ; and
in it were stored the town's supply of powder, balls,
flints, etc. From it, doubtless, were filled the pow-

PEPPERELL MAGAZINE

der-horns of the eighty-four men who went from
the town with Colonel Prescott on April 19, 1775.
Surely the ancient magazine has become the property of the right man ; for Colonel Samuel P. Shattuck is of himself the embodiment of military zeal,
having served in the State militia from the rank of
private to that of colonel in the Sixth Regiment.

The names of the pioneers of the town were
prominent during the Revolution and in later wars.

There were nine Shattucks in Colonel Prescott's
regiment from Pepperell, while Bloods and Cham-
berlains were numerous. These and the other
patriots of that town are still met in the form of
their descendants on the same estates from which
they made a hasty departure on April 19, 1775. On
the lid of the magazine is read the following : —

" Joseph Warner
Returned his powder
& Balls.　　　Deken Blod⁵ sun recd　8 — 0 — 2
　　　　　　Joseph Warner sun　"　　0 — 2 — 7 "

EDMUND H. N. BLOOD, PEPPERELL

CHAPTER VII

FIRST SETTLERS OF SHIRLEY. — LONGLEY AND
HAZEN. — LONGLEY HOMESTEAD. — STORY OF
"WILL THE MILLER." — JOSHUA LONGLEY AND
BRIDGET MELVIN. — HON. GEORGE S. BOUTWELL
AS A SCHOOLMASTER. — HOLDEN FAMILY

We call them savage, O, be just!
Their outraged feelings scan;
A voice comes forth, — 'tis from the dust, —
The savage was a man!
Think ye he loved not? Who stood by,
And in his toils took part?
Woman was there to bless his eye, —
The savage had a heart!
Think ye he prayed not? When on high
He heard the thunders roll,
What bade him look beyond the sky?
The savage had a soul!

My researches in this part of Old Groton were
under the direction of Mr. John E. L. Hazen, a
lineal descendant of the heroes of the early wars
and also of the Revolution. Two families prominent in the beginning of the record of Shirley
were Longley and Hazen. They have continued
in prominence and influence during the almost
century and a half of the town's corporate existence.

The romance of history appears in all its fasci-
nation in the story of early members of the Longley family. We are fortunate in having the record
from direct descendants, who cultivate the acres
reclaimed by their ancestors when the musket was
the yeoman's constant companion. William Longley, son of Richard of Lynn, located in Groton as

HAZEN HOME, SHIRLEY

early as 1659. His wife Joanna was sister to
Deputy Governor Thomas Goff, and with her husband shared the hardships of frontier life. The
first William lived until King Philip had made his
last desperate effort to exterminate the white settlers. William Longley, the second clerk of the
town, suffered more severely at the hands of the
Indians. It was in 1694 that several of the fam-

ily fell victims to the savage hand of the lurking foe.

"The Indians, having lurked about the premises undiscovered the day previous to the slaughter watching a favorable opportunity to effect their purpose, early in the morning of the fatal day turned the cattle out of the barnyard into a corn-field, and lay in ambush. This trick had the desired effect to draw out some of the family, probably Mr. Longley and his sons, unarmed, to drive the cattle from the corn. The Indians then rose upon them, and killed or captured the whole family. It is said, however, that Jemima, a daughter of Mr. Longley whom they had tomahawked and scalped, was found alive, sitting upon a rock, and that she survived many years, married, and had children." Three who escaped the tomahawk were carried away into captivity. Betty died there of starvation. Lydia was sold to the French in Canada, and never returned to her people. It remained for John to perpetuate the name in this line of the family. He was about twelve years of age when his family was massacred, and himself carried into captivity by the savages.

An interesting incident of the life of this boy is told by his descendants. Says Melvin W. Longley, "My grandsire, John Longley, after going some distance from the old home with his captors, when they came to a halt told the Indians that his father's sheep were shut up in the barn, and

would starve unless they would permit him to go
back and release them, and that having done this
he would at once return to them. They allowed
the boy to go, and he kept his promise. My
ancestor pursued a wild life with his captors five
years, when he was ransomed by the government.
The romance of his captive state was not altogether averse to him, and it required some time to
accustom himself to life in Groton after his return
to his native town. He became a useful citizen,
being clerk of the town for six years, and was
thrice elected as representative to the General
Court. He was a deacon of the church twenty-
eight years."

John Longley married Sarah Prescott, an aunt
of Col. William Prescott, and subsequently married
Deborah Houghton.

It is apparent that the stronger characteristics
of this family were perpetuated through successive generations. Mr. Longley's three eldest sons
manifested the greatest bravery and perseverance
in overcoming all obstacles and establishing homes
on a section of the original grant. William, the
eldest of the three Shirley emigrants, settled in
the south part of the town, and together with
Samuel Hazen, the founder of the other pioneer
family, set up the first grist-mill in the place. In
my tour about Shirley I was early directed to the
site of the mill, which is still of interest to the
descendants of the first proprietors. The waters

of the Catacunemaug still ripple through the meadows as when the early millers utilized the pure stream; and some of the primeval oaks shed their autumnal foliage upon the smooth, glassy surface as when William Longley turned out his grist a century and a half ago.

SHIRLEY OAK

The influence of the hearth-stone narratives of the redeemed captive and father upon the Longley-Prescott children, and upon all who heard the familiar tales, may best be judged by tracing the acts of the patriots of that town.

The Indian depredations had ceased before the incorporation of

Shirley; yet the French war, which terminated in the surrender of the Canadas to the English government, was still being waged, and the town's first human sacrifice in that struggle was Joseph Longley, who was wounded at Fort William Henry, and died at Greenbush, N. Y., in 1758. He was first selectman and town clerk. That spirit which prompted them to fight for the king impelled them to take up arms against him when such a course was needed to sustain the rights and liberties of the Colonies. The Stamp Act brought them to action. They held a town meeting October 18, 1765, and unanimously instructed their representative, who was Abel Lawrence, Esq.: —

" Is it a matter of wonder that every thinking person in the Colonies of North America is greatly alarmed by the late act of Parliament, called the Stamp Act, as it affects the state and liberty of every loyal subject of said Colonies? . . . We look upon said act as a burden, grievous, distressing and insupportable; not only likely to enslave the present but future generations. The great and heavy load lying upon us, occasioned by the late war, with its increasing interest, and all other incidental charges at home for the support of the government, &c., have sunk us so low already that we are wholly unable to bear the duties imposed upon us by the stamp act, which, if it takes place, must and will immediately prove our certain ruin. . . . We are far from saying or acting anything whereby we might be charged with disloyalty, as subjects to the best of kings, or that we have not a proper sense of the British Court, but we do think that our charter privileges, and natural rights, as the free-born sons of Britain, are infringed upon by said stamp act. Our advice, instruction and direction, therefore, to you is, that upon all proper occasions you use and exercise your utmost endeavors, and strongest efforts, in a modest, becoming and respectful manner, to prevent said act from taking place in the government; and that you with a watchful eye, upon every occasion, diligently guard and protect the liberties of your country, to the utmost of your power, against all encroachments and innovations. . . .

By order of the Committee,
JOHN LONGLEY."

On January 11, 1773, the people indorsed the act of the Committee of Correspondence in Boston, saying, —

"We are fully persuaded, if the Judges of the Superior Court of this Province have their salaries from the king, . . . that our liberties are greatly infringed thereby, and that we shall have no better chance for justice, no better security of life and property, than the people have in the most despotic government under heaven." They further say "that our grateful acknowledgments are due to the inhabitants of the town of Boston, for their vigilance upon this and many other occasions of like nature.

JOHN LONGLEY, *Dis. Clerk.*"

The passage of the act on *tea* by the British Parliament brought out the people of Shirley in a series of resolutions, which bear the impress of decided patriots. They stand out upon the town book in bold hand. Art. I. is: —

"*Voted*, that we will neither buy, nor sell, nor drink (nor suffer it to be drunk in any of our families) any tea that is subject to an American duty."

The name of Obadiah Sawtell, another patriot, appears as district clerk at the conclusion of this series of resolutions.

Thus far sympathy and acquiescence with the Boston patriots had only been shown by words, but the Port Bill brought out something more real. They held a town meeting on January 18, 1775, and chose a committee to receive donations for the poor of Boston and Charlestown. They continued in sympathy with each progressive act of the people of the lower towns, and were ready to respond to the alarm of April 19, 1775. Every man old enough to bear arms, with the exception of seven, responded to the messenger, and made haste towards the scene of danger. Eighty names appear upon the roll of the Lexington alarm in command of Captain Henry Haskell, and thirty-five appear as serving for eight months during the siege under the command of Captain Robert Longley of Bolton. They were in the regiments of Colonels Whitcomb and Prescott.

Some of the personal experiences of the soldiers of this town are told by their descendants on the old farms.

Melvin W. Longley, already quoted, was met at his cheerful farmhouse, where were also two sisters of the same generation. Soon after the Revolution this house "was built by my great-grandfather, Joshua Longley, on a part of the original grant. My children represent the fifth generation who have gathered about the old hearth-stone, and the sixth who have trodden these acres, while three earlier generations have lived in this territory when it was included in original Groton." The first of these was William, the proprietor of the mill.

THE STORY OF WILL THE MILLER.

William Longley the father, and William the son, were both millers. In order to distinguish the craftsmen, the good farmers of the locality, who brought their grist to be ground at the mill on the Catacunemaug, called the elder "Old Will the Miller." No disrespect was implied; for the rugged yeomen looked upon Old Will as their great benefactor. He had been the first to set up that indispensable institution, a mill, thus relieving them of much of the burden of life.

The Longley and Hazen mill was rude indeed, but in keeping with the dwellings of the farmers, made as they were from rough-hewn logs, and affording but little beyond the bare necessities. The farmers, young and old, delighted in listening to Old Will's recitals of his father's experience during the five years of his life in captivity. Waiting for grist was no hardship for them if Old Will, dressed in powdered apparel, was tending the stones. The elder William was a sufferer from rheumatism, and not in a mood for story-telling

at all times; but when he was at his best in describing the life among the Indians, the farmer's
boy was reluctant to leave. In fact, the fathers
were known to tarry long after Old Will had taken
his toll, and emptied a fresh sack into the hopper.

These stories of savage warfare served a two-
fold purpose. They amused the miller's patrons,
and prevented their being impatient while waiting their turn, and also kindled a fire of patriotism in the minds of the farmers, which served them
well when the time came for opposing the king.

The news of the Stamp Act aroused the miller
to a high state of indignation, and he declared
his readiness to fight against all such oppression.
The Port Bill reanimated his spirit of patriotism,
and he dipped deep into his toll-bin for the aid of
the poor of the distressed port.

He had reached almost the allotted age of man
when the Lexington alarm was sounded through
the town. The exemption from service granted to
millers was no excuse for him. The ardor of youth
possessed his spirit when his sons, neighbors, and
friends were hastening to and fro in preparation
for the march. But his bowed and crippled form
made it impossible for him to join the company;
yet he insisted, saying, "True, I cannot handle a
musket, yet I will fight the redcoats with my two
canes;" at the same time brandishing those for-
midable weapons as though his words were not to
be disregarded. He reluctantly remained at home

with the few who were compelled to stay because
of age or infirmity. But no citizen of the town
evinced more genuine patriotism, watched the
progress of the war with more interest, or manifested more joy when the yoke of oppression was
thrown off, than did Old Will the miller.

"Joshua, son of 'Will the miller,' 'my great-
grandfather, was among the eighty men who
marched from this town on April 19, 1775," said
the present occupant of the estate. "He remained
in the camp until the 30th of the month, and later
entered the service for eight months. He was in
the battle of Bunker Hill, escaping with but little
injury." At this point of the narrative a cannon-
ball was brought forward which a family tradition
says was fired from the British side, and when
well-nigh spent carried away a portion of the skirt
of Joshua Longley's coat.

"My great-grandfather's trip to Concord on that
eventful morning was not the first that he had
made to that town. He had been over that familiar route to Concord in quest of the young
lady who became his bride in March, 1770." She
was Bridget Melvin, daughter of Eleazer and Mary
(Farrar) Melvin, and had connection with noted
families already described in "Beneath Old Roof
Trees."

NOTE. — Eleazer Melvin and his brother David served in that
fight at Pigwacket in 1725, and were both in the expedition to
Louisburg, and in later campaigns of the Colonial wars.

A Melvin powder-horn, now in the possession of John E. L. Hazen, one of the Longley family connections, is a memorial of the Concord patriots as well as those of Shirley.

Joshua Longley carried on the farm, besides acting as a miller and builder, until his death in 1814. A stone in the old burying-ground tells the following : —

> JOSHUA LONGLEY,
> BORN AT GROTON, MASS., JULY 23, 1751,
> DIED AT SHIRLEY, NOV. 7, 1814.
>
> BRIDGET MELVIN, HIS WIFE,
> BORN AT CONCORD, MASS., DEC. 9, 1751,
> DIED AT SHIRLEY, FEB. 27, 1817.

The next generation on this farm was Stephen, who was followed by his son, Stephen Melvin, who is succeeded by Melvin W. Longley ; and so it appears that the grandsire's union with the Concord family is pleasantly remembered by perpetuating the name of the bride of Joshua, while the beneficent life of the patriot has not lost its effect upon succeeding generations.

In the southerly part of Shirley, not far from the original Longley-Hazen mill site, and on a portion of the territory first settled by Samuel Hazen, I met a great-great-grandson of the pioneer of Shirley, Mr. Thomas L. Hazen. He said, " My great-grandfather, Samuel Hazen, Jr., was at work on these acres when the alarm of the 19th of April reached him. He immediately left his plough, ran to the house, took his gun and powder-horn,[1] and said to his wife (Elizabeth Little), 'Betty, you take care of the children and the cattle! I must go!' The family then consisted of five children, the eldest not ten years, and the youngest less than two months. He, with the others from this town, reached Acton about eleven o'clock, where they heard of the fight at Concord and of the retreat; but they concluded to march on, and pursued the enemy to Cambridge. Samuel Hazen remained there thirteen days, and later joined the army, and was made captain of the Shirley company.

On a stone at his grave is read : —

CAPT. SAMUEL HAZEN,
DIED MAY 6, 1815,
AGED 74 YEARS, 11 MONTHS.

One of the old dwellings now standing in Shirley is that known as the Joseph Hazen House. It is a well-kept reminder of the days when the children and grandchildren of Samuel the patriot were taught beneath its roof the lessons of patriotism. Near by was the old Pound Hill schoolhouse, where many a rustic youth was taught the rudiments of education under the supervision of Mr. Joseph Hazen, "the committee-man." Said Mr. Herman S. Hazen, "My father enjoyed a peculiar satisfaction in having employed for a win-

---

[1] Powder-horn now in possession of Thomas L. Hazen.

ter term a young man from Lunenburg, who has
since acted well the part of a patriot." George
S. Boutwell taught Pound Hill school from December, 1834, to February, 1835. He passed his

SHIRLEY SCHOOLHOUSE. *"A ragged beggar sunning"*

seventeenth birthday while teaching in Shirley.
He received sixteen dollars a month and board.
But four[1] of the pupils are now living who recall

[1] The four pupils are Mr. and Mrs. Sullivan Davis of Pepperell,
Mrs. Henry Edgarton of Shirley, and Charles Anderson of Minne-
apolis, Minn.

the erect figure and genial countenance of the young man who went in and out before the youth upwards of sixty years ago.   The schoolhouse still remains "a ragged beggar sunning."

The master's desk is gone; but there may be seen —

> "The warping floor, the battered seats,
>   The jack-knife's carved initial."

A BATTERED SEAT FROM SHIRLEY SCHOOLHOUSE

> "The charcoal frescoes on its wall,
>   Its door's worn sill betraying
> The feet that creeping slow to school
>   Went storming out to playing!"

Among the minute-men of Shirley was James Dickerson, who heard the April alarm while in the field engaged in planting corn. He left his hoe, took his musket and powder-horn, and joined the company. His wife Priscilla[1] took up the hoe, finished the planting, and carried on the labors of the farm until her husband's return.

In passing through the southerly part of the town, I met Mr. Elihu Longley, who at fourscore

OLD HOME, SHIRLEY

years dwells on a portion of the original grant. At the well, dipping " the moss-covered bucket," I met Mr. Edward A. Jenkins, who is the fifth generation on his farm. When gathering his children

[1] This Priscilla, born in Shirley, March 6, 1749, and wife of James Dickerson, was a daughter of Francis and Susanna Harris. Harris was one of the foremost men of the town. Eleven times selectman, also town clerk and treasurer. He was the delegate of the town in the first and second sessions of the Provincial Congress.

and grandchildren about him, he boasts of seven generations who have drunk from the same well. Mr. Jenkins recalls the face of his great-grandfather, Moses Jennerson, who was among the patriots of 1775.

At the northerly part of the town I passed the farm where lived two patriots, Timothy Bolton and his brother William. The latter was a drummer in the Shirley company when it left the town on April 19, 1775.

Near the Bolton home was the old tavern kept by Obadiah Sawtell. Here were lively times when the Shirley company gathered to discuss the questions of those trying days. But "Flip and Toddy" never gave out as long as the company remained. Obadiah Sawtell, Jr., was one of the alarm band, and also in later service, to the credit of the town. This noted landlord was the town's first representative to the General Court under the Constitution, and a member of the convention that adopted the Constitution of the United States.

In passing I made note of the home of John Dwight, who was wounded at the battle of White Plains.

In the easterly part of the town lived Jonas Longley, the third son of John, the redeemed captive. Although sixty-four years old at the opening of the Revolution, this old hero and his son Jonas shouldered their fowling-pieces, and marched to Cambridge on April 19, 1775. It is of interest to note that the present town clerk of Shirley is Jonas Longley, a great-grandson and namesake of the old veteran.

In passing I was shown the homes of the Page family, from which went Jonas and Simon to the war ; of Samuel Walker, who lived almost a century, and told his story of the Revolution to four generations ; also that of Deacon Joseph Brown, who was in the ranks.

At the southerly part of the town is the old brick house from which John Edgerton went to the service of his country, in company with Ivory Wilds, who later renounced the world, and became a member of the Society of Shakers.

Among the treasured relics of the days of peculiar trial is a package of the Continental currency, shown by members of the Parker family, who are thus reminded of the service of their patriot ancestor, Captain James Parker.

Continuing the journey, I came to the old family seat of the Holdens, who have been numerous through the entire history of the town. Seven of the name were in the Shirley company on April 19, 1775, five of whom enlisted for eight months, and were in service on the 17th of June. There was another of the family, John Holden, who made record during the war, although too young to be registered with the soldiers at the beginning.

CHAPTER VIII

SHIRLEY CONTINUED. — JOHN HOLDEN THE BOY
FIFER. — OLIVER HOLDEN THE COMPOSER OF
"CORONATION." — THE MEETING-HOUSE A MAG-
AZINE. — GIFT OF MADAM LYDIA HANCOCK. —
BOUNTY COAT

AMONG the sixteen children of Amos Holden
was John, born on May 21, 1765. His name stands
as the sixth in the register of the family Bible. Although but a babe in swaddling clothes when the
Stamp Act aroused the Colonists to a realizing
sense of the cloud of war gathering about them,
the boy John Holden was fully aware of the duty
of a patriot when the Lexington alarm summoned
the men of Shirley to arms. Like David of old, the
boy John Holden had been trained to tend sheep
on his father's farm, and while in that quiet and
retired service there had developed within him a
talent for music. The fife was the popular musical instrument in this boy John's day, as was the
harp in the days of David, the son of Jesse.
When John Holden learned to play the fife no one
knew, in fact he could scarcely tell himself, unless
it was on training-days, when he followed the militia company about the town as they kept step to

the music of the fife and drum in the hands of his well-known neighbors.

Amos Holden found it difficult, with his large family, "to make the ends meet;" but the longing for a fife which had grown to be little less than a passion in the boy John must be gratified, and the indulgent father procured one, and brought it home for a birthday present to the lad. The boy could hardly believe his own eyes, but lost no time in perfecting himself in its use. It was at the time when the whole country was in a state of ferment and dread. War seemed inevitable, and the oppressive rule of the English was the theme of conversation everywhere.

Young John heard much of it, and longed to be a man that he might join the Shirley company of minute-men now holding semiweekly drills. One day he received a compliment which gave rise to aspirations not dreamed of by his parents.

A Boston gentleman paid a visit to the Holdens at the old farmhouse, when the chief topic of conversation was the prospect of war with the mother country. While the guest was present, Amos Holden asked his son to play a tune on his fife. The boy struck up with a stirring march, which elicited the exclamation of surprise, " The boy has the soul of music in him ; he will be ready to meet King George's army."

John sat still for a while in a meditative manner ; but before retiring for the night went shyly up to his father, and said, " If the British do come, shall I go to the war with my fife?" — "Why, yes," replied the father laughingly; "they could not get along without you."

These words, spoken by the father without a second thought, as are too many from parental lips, sank deep into the heart of the boy John. He revolved them over and over in his mind, as he applied himself to the use of his fife. When he was far away in the fields tending his father's flocks and herds, the stirring notes of the fife could be heard by the neighboring farmers, who predicted that the time was not far away when John Holden would be the fifer of the Shirley company.

At length, on a delightful April morning of 1775, an alarm was sounded over the hills of Shirley, "The Regulars are coming." It was not long before the men were on the march towards Concord. Amos Holden was among them. The boy John, with fife in hand, begged to go too, but was dissuaded from what he had believed to be his father's promise with the excuse, "You are too young; wait a while, and if they don't get enough of it to-day, when we meet them, you may have a chance later." The time soon came when youth was no barrier, if the requisite stature had been attained; and three of the sons of Amos Holden entered the army. John was one of them. Instead of a musket, this boy soldier carried his fife, and

did a patriot's duty on the march, in the camp, and
on the field. At times, when everything seemed
dark and doubtful about the company, the notes
of John Holden's fife could be heard above the din
of battle, and many a weary and homesick soldier
took on new courage, and went forth to victory.
For twenty long months the boy fifer was away
in the service; at first with Colonel Prescott, and
later with Washington at New York, under the
immediate command of General Knox. This lad,
with a beardless face, dressed in a soldier's suit
gay with brass buttons, was a favorite with the
regiment. Said one of the officers, " This boy is
a captain-general of us all. I have never known
him to whimper or say 'I can't,' although he is
the youngest of us."

At the conclusion of his service in the war,
John Holden returned to Shirley, and in 1791
married Sally Sanderson of Lunenburg, and removed to Franklin, Vermont, where he was living
in 1833, when he received a pension from the
United States Government, which was continued
to him until his death in 1847. He was classed
as a private and musician, in the pension department. In the archives of the State of Massachusetts, he is recorded as fifer.

OLIVER HOLDEN AND "CORONATION."

Another of the Holden family of Shirley, born
four months after John, was Oliver, son of Nehe-

miah.   He was cousin to John the fifer, and like him endowed with rare musical talent.   These boys were happy in each other's society in their humble homes, romping over the hills of Shirley, and trudging off to the little schoolhouse under the hill.   But soon after the Revolution, Nehemiah Holden and his family removed to Charlestown, where there was a demand for mechanics in the work of rebuilding the town destroyed by the minions of George III.   Oliver labored as a housewright with his father for a while, and then, following his natural inclination, gave his attention to mercantile life.   This afforded him a better opportunity for indulging his musical talent. While conducting trade, he composed tunes, taught singing-school, and published several volumes of choice hymns and tunes.   Among his occasional odes was one for the reception tendered General George Washington when upon his third and last visit to Boston, in October, 1789.   Oliver Holden trained a choir of young men for the occasion ; and when Washington passed under the triumphal arch at the Old State House, the choir sang to this ode the words, "George Washington, the hero, is come."

But that which has immortalized this son and patriot of Shirley is the tune "Coronation."   This was composed in 1793, soon became a favorite in the churches, and now, after more than a century, retains a prominent place in church psalm-

ody.   During the Civil War it became a battle
hymn, and many a weary soldier on the march
has quickened his pace by the inspiration of grand
old "Coronation."

The words have been traced to Rev. Edward
Perronet, son of Vincent Perronet, vicar of Shore-
ham, England. They were first sung to the tune
of "Miles Lane;" but the production of Oliver
Holden was better adapted to them, as millions
cheerfully testify to-day.

On Old Burial Hill, Charlestown, where are yet
to be seen scars made[1] by the bullets of Gage's
army, is the burial-place of this noted man.   On a

---

[1] From a table monument near the John Harvard obelisk : —

HERE LIES INTERRED THE BODY OF
RICHARD RUSSELL, ESQ.,
WHO SERVED HIS COUNTRY AS TREASURER
MORE THAN A TREBLE PRENTISHIP &
AS A MAGISTRATE SIXTEEN YEARS,
WHO DEPARTED THIS LIFE
THE 14TH OF MAY 1676.
BEING THE SIXTY-FIFTH YEAR OF HIS AGE.

A Saint, a Husband, a faithful Brother
A friend far excelled by any other
A saint that walked high in either way
Of Godliness and Honesty all say.
A husband rare to both his darling wives
A father politic, faithful and kind.

.   .   .   .

" N. B.   The ravages of time, and an accident during the siege of Bos-
ton in 1775, having destroyed the monument erected at the decease of
Mr. Russell, this being a true copy of the original was replaced by his
Relatives, A.D. 1787, in testimony of their regard to his memory."

bronze tablet placed in the brick wall of the family
tomb may be read : —

HERE SLEEPS THE SWEET SINGER
OLIVER HOLDEN,
COMPOSER OF THE TVNE " CORONATION."
BORN IN SHIRLEY, SEPT. 18, 1765,
DIED IN CHARLESTOWN, SEPT. 4, 1844.

To his dear memory, this tablet is placed by his Granddaughter.[1]

All hail the power of Jesus' name,
Let angels prostrate fall.
Bring forth the royal diadem,
And crown him Lord of all.

It was when the storm-clouds of the Revolution
were gathering that the people of Shirley went
to work to build a meeting-house in place of the
rude structure that had served them for a score of
years as the only place for public convocation,
religious, municipal, and military.   On Thanksgiving Day of 1773 the voice of prayer was first
heard in that house.   It was the only occasion of
the kind when " God save the King " from the
pastor's lips met with an " Amen " from the people.   Before the next autumnal festival the port
of Boston had been blockaded, and Shirley farmers
had shared their crops with their distressed brethren in Boston.   It was a custom of these towns
to use the upper gallery of the meeting-house as a
magazine for military stores.   The building usually stood on or near the training field, was away

[1] Mrs. Fanny A. Tyler.

LONGLEY BALL,
PICKED UP
AT
BUNKER HILL

SHIRLEY RELICS
OF THE
REVOLUTION

from other houses, and was entirely free from any means of heating, consequently was regarded as the safest place for powder. A portion of the upper gallery in the Shirley meeting-house was early set apart for this purpose. While the minister was urging resistance to British oppression, there was in the loft above the high pulpit the material to give emphasis to his instruction. In the hasty distribution of the cartridges to the minute-men, some dropped and rolled out of sight, and after a full century were found, and brought forth to the light, and are now treasured by my guide as reminders of those days of peculiar trial.

The patriotic people of Shirley have for generations derived a peculiar satisfaction from the gift of the pulpit Bible by Madam Lydia Hancock of Boston. This benevolent woman was the widow of the merchant, Thomas Hancock, and with his nephew John was enjoying the luxuries of the famous Hancock estate in Boston at the time of this gift. The occasion was the opening of the new meeting-house ; and Madam Lydia testified by this gift to the town her regard for her niece and namesake, Lydia Bowes of Bedford, who had but recently become the wife of the minister of Shirley, Rev. Pheneas Whitney. It will occur to the reader that a sister of Mrs. Whitney, Lucy Bowes, was the wife of Rev. Jonas Clark of Lexington, and that they were daughters of Rev. Nicholas Bowes of Bedford, and Lucy, daughter of Rev. John Hancock of Lexington. Hence they were cousins of John Hancock, the famous patriot. This family connection must have stimulated the patriotism in the town of Shirley.

THE BOUNTY COAT.

During the summer of 1775, when the Provincial troops were in an unsettled condition, and the siege was progressing, the Provincial Congress made a demand for thirteen thousand coats for the use of the patriot army, to be ready before the cold weather. There were no shrewd millers to take the contract, and turn the public emergency to their personal advantage ; but at each hearthstone there were set up a mill and a tailor's shop.

The committee of supplies was directed to apportion the coats on the towns by a schedule, made in accordance with the last Provincial tax. This burden largely fell to the women, and following what they had sacrificed, was trying indeed; but with their characteristic zeal, they went to work to get the coats ready before the first day of October. The selectmen of each town were required to cause a certificate to be sewed to the inside of each coat, telling from what town it came, by whom the coat was made, and, if the cloth was manufactured in this country, by whom it was manufactured. Here was an opportunity for proving personal ability, and the spirit of competition was rife throughout the Province.

Rolls of wool laid aside for family use were brought out, carded, spun, and woven under the same roof; and while the great wheel was humming in one room, there was the continual preparation of food for the absent soldier boys. The coats were to be of "good, plain cloth, preference to be given to that of home manufacture."

LONGLEY WELL.

Having signed the protest against the use of foreign manufactures, there was the greater struggle with each town to meet its demands from its own looms. The coats were to be "made in the common plain way, without lapels, short, and with small folds, and faced with the same kind of cloth of which they were made." They were to be "buttoned with pewter buttons, those of each regiment respectively to have buttons with the

same number stamped upon the face of them."
This course was to put into use a uniform, in
place of the variety of garments in which the
hastily improvised army were clothed.

The committee of supplies in each town let out
the contract to the different families, and in many
a town's record book may be read the account of
paying the different parties interested. The fact
that these supplies were possibly for some of their
own people may have urged the manufacturers
to greater faithfulness, but we have no reason to
think that any one would have slighted any part
of this duty. The different towns reported what
might be expected of them, and some of their reports may be seen to-day. Among them is that
of the town of Shirley, which reads : —

To the Gen^tmen, Committee of suplies appoynted by Congress, &c. To see to the Providing Clothing for the army.

Gen^tmen, — These are to Inform you that the Dis^t of Shirley have agreed to provide the Parte of Coats, Shirts, Stock-
ins, and Britches to them Assigned, and thirty Pare of Shoes
for the Benefitt of the Continentle army, &c.

By order of the Selectmen.

OBADIAH SAWTELL. *Dis^t. Clerk.*

SHIRLEY, *August ye* 10*th, A.D.* 1775.

Each man volunteering to serve for a term of
eight months was promised a coat, and it was regarded as quite a possession ; so much so that
representatives of those who were killed at Bunker Hill, or who died before receiving the coat,

were granted a certain sum of money in lieu of the coat, etc.

The names of those enlisted for eight months, with the promise of the coat, are found on what is known as the "Coat Roll;" while those who turned out on April 19 are recorded on what is known as "The Lexington Alarm List."

CHAPTER IX

STORY OF THE TOWN OF HOLLIS, N.H. — MOVE-
MENTS OF HOLLIS PATRIOTS. — AT OLD HOME—
STEADS. — EVIL WORK OF A TORY WOMAN. —
HOLLIS GUN—MAKERS

" The kindly spot, the friendly town, where every one is known,
And not a face in all the place but partly seems my own."

HOLLIS, after making a record for about seven
years as the west parish of Dunstable, became a
fully equipped town. It was chartered in April,
1746, when Benning Wentworth was the governor
of New Hampshire.

In tracing the footprints of the patriots of Hollis, I was early impressed with the fact that I was
considering the acts of descendants of the settlers
of towns near Boston, and that the people of
Hollis were bound by ties of blood and kinship
with those of Concord, Littleton, Bedford, Marlborough, Billerica, Reading, Salem, Woburn, and
other towns of lower Middlesex and Essex Counties from which they or their parents had migrated.

Having so many common interests of long standing, it was natural enough for their military af-

fairs to be somewhat united. This was particularly the case with the towns which formed the
northern boundary of Middlesex County and their
neighbors in the adjoining towns on the southern
border of New Hampshire. The popularity of
Colonel William Prescott was recognized in the

JOHN COLBURN

towns of both colonies; family ties also inclined
the soldiers of Hollis, N.H., to cast in their lot
with the trusted Colonel's regiment.

It mattered little whether in this or that town,
in one Province or the other, the same motives actuated the one people; and I invite my readers to
turn with me to the hearth-stones of Hollis, where

still glows the fire of patriotism kindled by the pioneers of that locality. Age entitles Mr. John Colburn to the first hearing.

Although in his ninety-seventh year, Mr. Colburn has other qualifications for speaking of the patriots of Hollis. He was born there, and his parents were also natives of the town. Said the veteran, when met in his home, seated by his wife, who was also a nonagenarian, "We have both spent the greater part of our long lives near the place of our birth, and these beautiful hills and valleys are a delight to us." On his maternal side this veteran is descended from Eleazer Flagg, one of the earliest permanent settlers of that territory. Anticipating my call on his ninety-seventh birthday, Mr. Colburn prepared a carefully written statement for me. Rising from his chair, and buttoning his Prince Albert coat about his stately figure, he passed into an adjoining room, and returned with his notes, saying, —

"I have always avoided the pronoun 'I,' never seeking nor desiring publicity; but since you desire it, I presume I cannot more profitably spend these hours than in aiding you in tracing out the footprints of the patriots, and in doing it I must sometimes speak of myself.

"I suppose to you who are young the story of the opening Revolution seems like ancient history; but to me Concord, Lexington, and Bunker Hill are as much a reality as are Gettysburg or Bull

Run and other battlefields of the Civil War, in which my son participated, and has often described.

"While driving the oxen to plough the fields yonder, father used to tell me of his and his neighbors' experience in camp and battle; and especially on or near the 19th of April, would rehearse the whole story, becoming so interested at times that he would stop the team in order to better illustrate positions. He and mother would devote whole winter evenings to talks about those days. It was a delight to us children — for I was one of thirteen for whom my parents toiled and sacrificed. Mother, who was a Hardy (Lemuel's daughter), could help along the stories; for her folks were in it as well as the Colburns. With a good blazing fire on the hearth, and a plenty of four-foot wood at hand to replenish it, a dish of good apples, some butternuts, and a mug of cider, what cared we for the driving snow? We drew up to the fire in a group, some on the settle and some in the chimney-corner. To be sure, there would occasionally come a contrary blast down the chimney, and fill our eyes with smoke and ashes; but it was soon over, and we children were calling for more story. To make it more vivid, father would pause at times, and say, 'Now imagine that north-east blast against the window to be a volley of bullets from the redcoats;' at which we would hide the closer behind the high back of

the settle, or snuggle more securely in the arms
that were ever ready for some of us. My father
was too young to have any part in the town meetings just before the war; but he knew what was
going on, and was anxious to be in the company
when they were drilling for an emergency.

" On November 7th the people took action at
the polls, and chose three of their leading men
to represent them in the County Congress on the
following day at Amherst. They made record as
follows : 'We, the inhabitants of the town of
Hollis, having taken into our most serious consideration the precarious and most alarming affairs of
our land at the present day, do firmly enter into
the following resolutions : —

" ' That we will at all times endeavor to maintain
our liberty and privileges, both civil and sacred,
even at the risque of our lives and fortunes, and
will not only disapprove, but wholly despise all
such persons as we have just and solid reason to
think even wish us in any measure to be deprived
of them.' Deacon Stephen Jewett, Ensign Stephen
Ames, and Lieutenant Reuben Dow, equipped with
such authority, were sent to Amherst.

" In the very last of December they chose a delegate to meet in a Province convention to consider
a Continental Congress. It was John Hale, Esq.,
who had this honor.

" They also voted 'that we do cordially accede
to the just statement of the rights and grievances

of the British Colonies, and the measures adopted
and recommended by the Continental Congress
for the restoration and establishment of the former,
and for the redress of the latter.' Three deacons
with others were constituted a committee to ob-
serve the conduct of all persons touching the association agreement.

The town of Hollis has in its archives three original rolls of military companies. Two of them
were made out in January, 1775, and the third on
June 7. The rolls were named respectively, " A
List of the Company of Militia in Holles under
the command of Capt. Joshua Wright," " Alarm
List," and " The List of the present Militia Company of Holles, Exclusive of the Minute-men and
all that have gone into the army, June ye 7th,
1775." These companies appear to have contained all the able-bodied men of the town. They
held frequent meetings, and in every way kept
pace with their neighbors across the line in
Massachusetts. On April 3 they chose Deacon
Stephen Jewett and Deacon Enoch Noyes as delegates to the County Congress, and "to see what
method should be taken to raise money for the
Continental Congress at Philadelphia." " Thus
far it had been only drilling and voting ; but soon
there came something more exciting," said Mr.
Colburn's father, "and Governor Wentworth, down
at Portsmouth, found that we were in earnest. The
alarm did not reach us on April 19th until it was

too late to be of any service on that day, but
our ninety-two minute-men made a record later
that compares favorably with the Massachusetts
towns."

Mr. John Colburn's repetition of his father's
fireside story was concluded by his description of
Bunker Hill, where in his youth he visited the
earthworks thrown up on that June night of 1775.
Said he, "They had not begun to talk of a monument, and everything was in a very rough condition. I walked over that redoubt, and identified
the locations just as my father had described them
to me, where he, with so many Hollis men, faced
the enemy in the heat of the battle, where a number of them gave up their lives."

Seated by the side of Mr. Colburn during his
birthday recital was his faithful wife, who was
ninety-one years of age, and a life-long resident
of the town. She was Naomi Boynton, granddaughter of Deacon John Boynton and Ruth
Jewett. This interesting woman was not only an
intelligent listener, but a most helpful prompter,
and in her turn modestly said, "It was my grandfather, Deacon John Boynton, who first received
the April morning message, and spread it through
the town." These words of Mrs. Colburn, modestly dropped, resulted in my retracing the steps
of the messenger of 1775, in company with Mr.
Cyrus F. Burge, and in gathering the facts as we
made our way. Beginning at Runnell's bridge,

we first came to the land where were recalled the homes of Ebenezer and Thomas Jaquith, who responded to the urgent call of General Sullivan on November 30, 1775. It was through the special efforts of Colonel Samuel Hobart, paymaster of the New Hampshire troops, that the large number rallied in Hillsborough County, and responded at Cambridge. Colonel Hobart had been in the king's legislature, was also recorder and treasurer of his county at this time, and was a manufacturer of gunpowder in the Province of New Hampshire.

We next came to the home of William J. Rockwood, grandson of Dr. Ebenezer Rockwood, who served in Thatcher's regiment. The one thing in his possession to-day reminding of his grandsire's patriotic service is his commission as surgeon from the Massachusetts Bay Colony. In passing remarked my guide, "Near these trees lived Isaac Stearns, who served the town in the French war, and was one of the minute-men of Hollis to respond to Deacon Boynton's alarm. He also served in the Continental Army, and after the war migrated to Plymouth, N.H."

Forty rods away lived Ebenezer Cummings, son of Deacon William. He went into the war, and died of the smallpox in 1778.

This dreaded scourge brought sorrow to the town through the instrumentality of a woman who was a Tory of the most bitter nature. It is alleged that she spread infected clothing through the families, and thus caused the death of ten of the innocent citizens. Among the victims were Daniel Mooar and daughter, Edward Johnson and infant son.

Halting at the home of Andrew Jewett, we were saluted by a grandson of Ebenezer Jewett, who was in service at Bunker Hill. Said Andrew, " My grandfather's gun gave out before the powder failed, and he did the best he could by hurling stones at the British soldiers. He frequently entertained the young people in times of peace by describing his rough and tumble experience at Bunker Hill. Grandfather brought home from the war a negro man, Pompey, who lived in the family many years on this farm, which was in part my grandfather's.'

In passing through a part of the town, we noted the hill on which the alarm-gun was fired in order to arouse other families, who lived farther away. Three important minute-men, Lieutenant John Goss, Captain Reuben Dow,[1] and Deacon Boynton, lived near the State line in this locality. We drew rein at the Boynton home, and there heard from the lips of the present occupant facts of interest.

[1] Captain Dow was with his sons, ploughing in the field, when the alarm reached them. The father, with two sons, Evan and Stephen, made haste to the Centre, or place of rendezvous, while Daniel, but six years of age, was left to care for the oxen, with the aid of his mother and sisters.

In the hasty preparations for marching, the families contributed such food as they had. The salt-pork barrel, partially full, was brought out of the cellar; and the strips of pork were divided between the minute-men who assembled here at the home of their captain. This Dow farm is one of the many of Hollis that has been retained in the family of the patriot who went from the same door on that eventful morning. The line of descent has been: Reuben, Stephen, Jeremiah Dow; the latter's daughter, who married John C. Bell; succeeded by Charles Dow Bell, whose son, Charles J. Bell, is now the thrifty farmer, and is surrounded by an interesting family. Thus seven generations have enjoyed these scenes; the last not failing to be duly impressed with the part taken by the first, Captain Reuben Dow, in the struggle for liberty.

Standing on the well-worn door-stone, I saw in the distance the Colburn home, where I took my first lesson in New Hampshire patriotism. Nearer by we halted at the well from which the Goss family drew their supply. To the west from Captain Dow's home lived Amos Eastman, and we made haste to that old family site. Here Amos Eastman was well established when he went as the captain of a company under General John Stark into the French war. He and his son Amos manufactured guns at this place for the patriots; and a gun of their make was used as the alarm-gun at Hollis Common later in the war, an alarm being three guns fired in rapid succession.

Indisputable evidence of this branch of industry is found in State papers:

WEDNESDAY, *January* 24th, 1776.

Voted, that the balance of the account of Amos Eastman for guns, amounting to thirty-two pounds, sixteen shillings, be allowed and paid out of the Treasury, and that the President of the Council give orders on the Treasury for payment thereof.   Sent up by Mr. Clough. — *N. H. State Papers*, vol. viii., p. 56.

NOTE. — In the year 1752 Amos Eastman, Senior, then living at Penacook, being on a hunting expedition in the northerly part of New Hampshire with General John Stark and others, was, with Stark, taken prisoner by the Indians, and both of them taken to an Indian village in Canada.   On their arrival at the village, both the captives were compelled to run the gantlet between two files of savages, each armed with a switch or club with which to strike them as they passed between the lines.   Stark, as is said, escaped with but slight injury; but Eastman was cruelly beaten, and was afterwards sold to a French master, kindly treated by him, and soon after redeemed, and went home.

The Eastman family possession has been in the male line from Amos to son Amos, then Alpheus to son Oliver Perry Eastman, who now tills the paternal acres. He is aided by another generation, who cherishes the family record at this old hearth-stone.

Continuing on our route towards the centre of

Hollis, we came to the Worcester home. No school-child who has turned from his task to Worcester's Dictionary for help can fail of having an interest in the estate, from which went out generations of noble men and women to bless the world, prominent among whom was the lexicographer.

CHAPTER X

HOLLIS CONTINUED. — THE WORCESTER HOME. —
THE LEXINGTON ALARM AT THE WORCESTER
DOOR. — TOWN MEETING CALLED. — DEATH-ROLL
AT BUNKER HILL. — EQUIPMENTS LOST IN THE
BATTLE OF JUNE 17, 1775. — CALL FROM GEN-
ERAL SULLIVAN. — BOY SOLDIERS. — THE WOR-
CESTER FAMILY IN THE WORLD. — THANKSGIVING
DAY AT THE OLD HOME

THE Worcester home is a little south of the
centre of Hollis, and has been in the family possession since the year 1750.

The pioneer of the family in this country was
Rev. William Worcester, who came from Salisbury, England, and became the minister at Merrimack, later called Colchester, and permanently
named Salisbury. Although in a rude log meeting-house, the settlers were in favor of order, and
voted, " Every freeman when speaking in meeting
shall take off his hat, and rise when speaking,
and put it on when done." The pioneer died at
Salisbury in 1662. We next find the family at
Sandwich, Mass., where Rev. Francis Worcester,
great-grandson of the Rev. William, was born.

He married Abigail Carleton, and there kept the family record good until 1750, when he moved with his large family to Hollis, and so became the founder of the noted family in that town.

The house to which Rev. Francis Worcester took his family was small, but through various additions has become a very large dwelling, yet none too large for some of the generations which have flourished there. Attracted by the family record elsewhere to this old and well-kept house, I received a cordial welcome from the present occupant, Miss Lucy E. Worcester, who is of the fifth generation at that home, and of the eighth in this country.

Said Miss Worcester, " It was Captain Noah, my great-grandfather, who was the man of affairs here when the war broke out. He was then forty years of age, was ensign of a company of militia, town clerk, committee of observation, and in other positions of trust. Having been active in all the town's meetings during the agitation, Noah Worcester was not altogether surprised when the outbreak came. It was about noon on the 19th of April when Deacon John Boynton, one of the committee of observation, and who lived in the south part of the town, came riding through the streets of Hollis at the top of his horse's speed, calling to every one as he passed, 'The Regulars are coming, and are killing our men.' He drew rein at the door of Captain Worcester, who was chairman of the Committee of Safety. Captain Noah, my great-grandfather, had just finished dinner, and was standing before his looking-glass, with face well lathered, in the act of shaving. Without stopping to finish his toilet, but with one side of his face still whitened for the razor, he hurried to the stable, mounted his horse, and in that plight assisted in spreading the alarm. Other messengers were despatched to different parts of the town ; and in the afternoon of that day ninety-two men met on Hollis Common with muskets and powder-horns, each man furnished with one pound of powder and twenty bullets."

The Hollis company made choice that afternoon of Reuben Dow as captain, John Goss, first lieutenant, and John Cumings, second lieutenant. They marched off toward Concord, and went into camp at Cambridge. A part of them volunteered for eight months. The minute-men of Hollis who continued in service after the Lexington alarm went into other companies, and were mustered into the Massachusetts regiment commanded by Colonel Prescott, whose family seat, as we have seen, was very near Hollis, and who was connected with families of that town, his wife being Abigail Hale of Hollis, a sister of Colonel John Hale.

"Another patriot who turned out from this home on the 19th was my great-uncle, Noah Worcester, Jr., who was but sixteen years of age. He went as fifer.   Captain Noah, who had his title as a member of the State Militia, was town clerk at this time, and we are indebted to his faithfulness for many facts.

We find that the first town meeting after the experience of April 19 was on the 23d inst.   Colonel John Wentworth sent out a letter to each town on the day after the Lexington alarm.   That sent to Hollis is recorded in Noah Worcester's handwriting, and is as follows :—

Gentlemen, — This moment melancholy intelligence has been received of hostilities being commenced between the troops under the command of General Gage, and our brethren of the Massachusetts Bay.   The importance of our exerting ourselves at this critical moment has caused the provincial committee to meet at Exeter, and you are requested instantly to choose and hasten forward a delegate or delegates to join the Committee, and aid them in consulting measures necessary for our safety.   J. WENTWORTH.
                                  In behalf of the Committee of Safety.

PROVINCE OF NEW HAMPSHIRE ⎱
  HILLSBOROUGH COUNTY, SS.   ⎰

SPECIAL TOWN MEETING.
April 23, 1775.

Pursuant to the above notice and request, the inhabitants of the town of Hollis being met unanimously voted, that Samuel Hobart, Esq., be and hereby is appointed to represent the town at Exeter, with other delegates, that are or shall be appointed by the several towns of this Province, for the purpose above mentioned.

NOAH WORCESTER, *Town Clerk.*

To any one who studies the records of Hollis, kept by the patriot clerk Noah Worcester, it must be apparent that everything was done with system, and that their response on the 19th was serious and deliberate. The special town meeting of the twenty-eighth shows us that while in governmental affairs they were obliged to work with the Province of New Hampshire, their affiliations were with the patriots of Massachusetts. Noah Worcester records : —

SPECIAL MEETING.
April 28, 1775.

Colonel John Hale, Moderator.

At a meeting of the town of Holles called on a sudden emergency in the day of our public distress.

1st. *Voted*, that we will pay two commissioned officers, four non-commissioned officers, and thirty-four rank and file, making in the whole forty good and able men, to join the army in Cambridge, paying said officers and men, the same wages the Massachusetts men receive, and will also victual the same till such time as the resolution of the General Court or the Congress of the Province of New Hampshire shall be known respecting the raising of a standing army the ensuing summer.

They also made arrangements at this meeting for providing for poor families of those patriots who were in camp at Cambridge, and that the grain raised for the poor of Boston be divided between the army and the needy families of the soldiers.

These records show that " Province of New

Hampshire " was used in all warrants for town meetings until after the battle of Bunker Hill, from that time till July 4, 1776, the word "Colony" was used, and after the Declaration of Independence the word "State" took the place. Men absent in the army were allowed to have a written vote in town affairs, which was counted the same as if the men were present in person.

"The most trying experience of the men of our town did not come until the 17th of June, when we had our share in good measure. Most of our men were with Colonel Prescott, but a few were with Colonel Reed; and all were present at the battle of Bunker Hill, which sent sorrow to the homes of Hollis as to no other town in the Province. The loss of Hollis in killed was fully equal to two-fifths of the killed and missing in the two New Hampshire regiments, and greater than that of any other town of New Hampshire.

The list recorded on the memorial tablets[1] at Charlestown is as follows : —

PRESCOTT'S REGIMENT.

Dow's company. — Sergt. Nathan Blood, Phineas Nevers,[2] Thomas Wheat, Jr., Peter Poor, Isaac Hobart, Jacob Boynton.

Moors's company. — Ebenezer Youngman.

These names are among the list on Soldiers Monument at Hollis.

[1] Thomas Colburn, credited to Dunstable, is claimed by Hollis.
[2] The family spelling is Nevens.

BUNKER HILL MONUMENT

The wounded were Captain Reuben Dow, Ephraim Blood, Francis Blood, Francis Powers, Thomas Pratt, William Wood. Caleb Eastman was killed at Cambridge two days after the battle by the bursting of his gun. James Fisk and Jeremiah Shattuck died of sickness at the Cambridge camp before the battle.

The Hollis patriots furnished all their own equipments, and also their clothes, as did the soldiers generally during the first year of the war. Many articles were lost on the 17th of June, and subsequently each person filed a list with their estimated value. It is headed as follows : —

CAMBRIDGE, *Dec.* 22, 1775.

This may certify that we, the subscribers, in Capt. Reuben Dow's company, in Col. William Prescott's regiment, in the Continental army, that we lost the following articles, in the late engagement on Bunker Hill on the 17th of June last.

The one meeting with' the greatest loss was Nahum Powers : —

" 1 knaps'k 1*s.* 4*d.*, 1 tump'e 1*s.* 2*d.*, hat 3*s.*, jacket 8*s.*, bayonet 6*s.*"

Noah Worcester, Jr., was one of the losers : —

" Knapsack 1*s.* 8*d.*, 1 tumline[1] 1*s.* 2*d.*"

[1] " A tump-line was a strap to be placed across the forehead, to assist a man in carrying a pack on his back." — *Worcester's Quarto Dictionary.*

The inventory of lost articles perpetuates the names of twenty-eight men of Hollis who were in the battle of Bunker Hill, besides the commissioned officers. Another paper, in the handwriting of Captain Dow, shows the loss of equipments of the six men of Hollis belonging to his company killed in the battle.

CAMBRIDGE, *Dec.* 22, 1775.

NATHAN BLOOD,   ISAAC HOBART,   JACOB BOYNTON,
THOMAS WHEAT,   PETER POOR,   PHINEAS NEVINS.

The men whose names are above written belonged to Capt. Dow's company and Col. William Prescott's regiment, and were all killed at Bunker Hill on the 17th of June last, and were furnished each of them with a good gun, judged to be worth Eight Dollars a piece — also were furnished with other materials, viz., Cartridge Boxes, Knapsacks, and Tumplines, and were well clothed for soldiers. Also had each of them a good blanket. Nathan Blood had a good Hanger.

Eight Hollis soldiers, who were in Colonel Reed's regiment and in service on that day, lost various articles. Phineas Hardy lost; "1 blanket, coat, shirt, breeches." As Hardy's loss must have been his extra clothing, it appears that the good people of Hollis saw that their soldier boys in camp at Cambridge were well clothed.

Our men fought in their shirt-sleeves; the heat of the day caused them to throw aside their coats as when in the hayfield. This accounts for the loss of so many coats and other garments.

The Hollis patriots who served to the credit of Massachusetts had a share in the bounty of a military coat. A receipt signed by forty-seven men is their acknowledgment of the bounty. The heirs or widows of the deceased soldiers received an equivalent for the coats. In some cases it devolved upon the selectmen to decide who was the person legally entitled to the pay, as the following voucher shows : —

WE HEREBY CERTIFY that the widow Experience Shattuck is the proper person to receive the clothing belonging to Jeremiah Shattuck who belonged to Capt. Reuben Dow's company in Col. Wm. Prescott's regiment and is dead.

NOAH WORCESTER, }
JACOB JEWETT, } *Selectmen.*
OLIVER LAWRENCE, }

The selectmen also certify that Captain Dow is the person to receive the clothing due to Peter Poor, a transient person, who belonged to the Hollis company, and was killed at Bunker Hill.

It was when Hollis's cup of sorrow was brimful that an urgent call was made for more men. It came from General Sullivan, then in command of the Continental troops at Winter Hill, to the New Hampshire Committee of Safety, and reads as follows : —

WINTER HILL, *Nov.* 30, 1775.

Sirs, — Gen. Washington has sent to New Hampshire for thirty-one companies to take possession of and defend our lines in room of the Connecticut forces who most scanda-

lously refuse to tarry till the 1st of January.   I must therefore entreat your utmost exertions to forward the raising
those companies, lest the enemy should take advantage of
their absence and force our lines.   As the Connecticut forces
will at all events leave us at or before the 10th of next month,
pray call upon every true friend of his country to assist with
heart and hand in sending forward these companies as soon
as possible.

Sirs, I am in extreme haste,

Your Obt. Serv't.,

JOHN SULLIVAN.

To the COMMITTEE OF SAFETY *at Exeter*.

The demand was met, and two thousand New
Hampshire patriots were soon in service, remaining till the following March, when the British
evacuated Boston.   Miss Worcester continued her
story : —

" Two-thirds of the Twenty-sixth Company volunteered from Hollis ; and my great-grandfather,
Noah Worcester, was captain, going from this
house, leaving the cares of a large family to be
shared between his wife and aged father.   The
young men were so fired with patriotism that they
were anxious to enter the service before they were
liable to do military duty, and so great was the
need that many of them were accepted before they
were sixteen years of age.   My grandfather, Jesse
Worcester, was scarcely fifteen when he entered
the service ; as he was too short, he put pebbles in
his shoes for fear he would not pass muster."

This boy soldier was one of twenty-five who

went on a six-months' campaign to the northward. Daniel Emerson, Jr., was captain of the company.

In different campaigns to the end of the war these patriots from Hollis were found doing faithful service. It is worth our while to pause at the Worcester hearth-stone, and consider the character of the patriots of 1775 as manifest in after life.

WORCESTER HOMESTEAD, HOLLIS, N. H.

Four of the sons of Captain Noah Worcester became prominent clergymen, and filled honored positions; but they never forgot this old home, and loved to return to it, and here, laying aside all restraint, live over again those days when they went out from this home to do service for their country. Thanksgiving Day was their annual jubilee. The day when these dignified ministers, fully six feet tall, roamed over the farm, and gath-

JESSE WORCESTER

ered around the festive board, where lay prostrate the best turkey of the flock, surrounded by pies and puddings, and every thing that culinary art could devise. After dinner they would walk the rooms, and join in singing "Coronation."

Prominent upon the walls of the best room of this Worcester mansion are the portraits of Jesse and Sarah (Parker) Worcester. This boy soldier, Jesse, after the Revolution, obtained an education, and taught school; but failing health sent him back to the home farm, where he lived for many years. In conclusion my hostess informed me, —

"Turned aside from a professional life, my grandfather was not discouraged, but with his amiable companion, my grandmother, made a commendable record. Fifteen children were born to them. Seven of their nine sons obtained a liberal education. Two of them

SARAH WORCESTER

followed the legal profession (one becoming a member of Congress from Ohio during the Civil War), one was a teacher, and the others were ministers, with the exception of Joseph E., who was the author of several histories, geographies, etc., but best of all, the dictionary which bears his name." The daughters all honored homes of their own.

HOLLIS TRAINING FIELD

CHAPTER XI

HOLLIS CONTINUED. — TENNEY HOMESTEAD. — DEA-
CON ENOCH JEWETT COLBURN. — WASHINGTON'S
SOLDIERS MAKE MAPLE-SUGAR FOR THE ARMY.
— WHOLE FAMILIES IN THE WAR. — THE NEVINS
BOWLDER. — SCHOOLTEACHERS' PAY IN THE REV-
OLUTION. — THE OLD BURYING-GROUND

OUR next halt was at the Tenney homestead,
where the sixth generation of the family and name
were met in peaceful contentment. The first was
William Tenney, who settled here in 1747 with
his wife, Anna Jewett, from Rowley. The Lexington alarm called from this home the son William, who had not yet attained his majority. He
went out as a minute-man, performed the part of
a patriot at Cambridge, and later responded to
the urgent call for troops to take the place of the
Connecticut forces during the first winter of
the war. Notwithstanding the repeated calls for
personal service in the army, William Tenney,
who was known as captain, married Phœbe Jewett
in 1776, and they together conducted the business
of the farm. Of their ten children, the youngest,
Hon. Ralph Emerson Tenney, born in 1790, set-

tled at the homestead. This son was named for Ralph Emerson, who, according to a gravestone record, was instantly killed by the accidental discharge of a cannon, while exercising the matross on the day before the advent of the Tenney son. Thus the parent showed his regard for a neighbor, fellow-soldier in the war for liberty, and a son of

TENNEY HOMESTEAD, HOLLIS, N.H.

the honored minister of the town, Rev. Daniel Emerson. Of the next generation at the Tenney farm came William N. Tenney, followed by his son Ralph E. Tenney, who, with his children, enjoys the shade of the same spreading trees that have protected their ancestors from the scorching rays of the sun, when walking through the familiar path leading from the highway to the old home.

Passing through the village in a northerly course to the southerly end of Long Pond, we made note of the former homestead of Phineas Hardy, from which three sons went into the army. Our next halt was at the home of Deacon Enoch Jewett Colburn, whose story was so full of interest that we could but tarry and hear it through. This genuine New England farmer and church officer accepts no tradition that is not well founded, but having good evidence of the origin of the family in Hollis, tells the following : —

" Our family has no traceable connection with the other Jewetts of Hollis. Enoch, my grand-father, did not serve this town in the war, but it was the Revolution that led him to come here. He was with Washington's army during that dread-ful winter at Valley Forge, and shared in the hard-ships of the soldiers."

" On retiring from White Marsh to Valley Forge, the tents of the American Army were exchanged for log huts, which constituted acceptable habitations to his nearly naked and barefoot troops, who had tracked their way from White Marsh, by the blood, which, running from the bare and mangled feet of the soldiers, stained the rough and frozen road throughout its whole extent. They were in a destitute and deplorable situation ; and, to add to their miseries, fam-ine began to make its appearance. The British in Philadel-phia gave good gold for what the farmers brought to town, while Washington could only pay them in Continental scrip, which, already depreciated, became less in value."

" As the spring of 1778 opened," said Mr. Colburn, " Washington sent out squads of men to gather provisions. My grandfather was one of a squad sent into northern New England to tap the maple-trees, and make a quantity of maple-sugar. They chanced to come to this town, where they built a cabin and began the business. Grandfather, then young and venturesome, liked the place, and after the war closed came back, married, and settled down in the extreme north part of this town. These trees and stone walls are continual reminders of him whose name I bear, and whom I delight to honor."

Our route now takes us within the limits of the original town of Monson, whose story is told under the title of " A Lost Town." Its heroes are necessarily classed with the soldiers of Hollis and Amherst. Notable among these was the Youngman family on Pine Hill, who gave themselves up to the interests of the country. There were five of them, whose time spent in the service aggregated twenty years. Ebenezer Youngman of Captain Moors's company was killed at the battle of Bunker Hill. The other brothers were in the Continental regiments. Thomas was among the victorious at Trenton and Princeton in New Jersey, and Nicholas was in the northern campaign. Other Old Monson men were Joseph French, and Ebenezer, Christopher, and Stephen, sons of Lieutenant Benjamin Farley of Bedford,

Mass., the first innkeeper in West Dunstable
(Hollis).

Ensign Samuel Leeman, who turned out at the
Lexington alarm, was in the battle of Bunker
Hill, in the Continental army, and killed near
Saratoga, October 10, 1777.

Thomas Emerson and Thaddeus Wheeler were
of the number who had seen the old town of
Monson abandoned. There were also the Farleys,
who had come from Billerica in Massachusetts.
Caleb, on Pine Hill, the pioneer and head of the
family, had served in the French war of 1755, to
the credit of his native town. He served in a succession of campaigns in the Revolution, but passed
safely through it all, and attained the ripe old age
of one hundred and two years and five months.
There was Captain William Kendrick, who discharged the alarm-gun that aroused the Monson
people on April 19. He was of the Hollis Committee of Safety in 1776-7, and in Captain Emerson's mounted company at Rhode Island. The
Nevens family acted well their part. They had
come from Newton and Bedford in Massachusetts,
and had strong attachments for the people of that
Province. Five of the sons of William left an
indelible record in the war. They were William,
Joseph, Benjamin, John, and Phineas.

"Early in the afternoon of the 19th of April,
three of these brothers were at work with their
crowbars in digging stone for a farm wall at a

short distance from their home. At the coming
in sight of the messenger, they had partially
raised from its place a large flat stone embedded
in a farm roadway. Seeing the messenger spur-
ring towards them at full speed, one of the
brothers put a small bowlder under the large stone
to keep it in the position to which it had been
raised, and all stopped and listened to the message
of the horseman. Upon hearing it, leaving the
stone as it was in the roadway, with the little
bowlder under it, they hastened to the house, and
all three of them, with their guns and equipments,
hurried to the Hollis Common to join their company. One of these brothers, Phineas, was killed
at Bunker Hill; another, William, the spring following lost his life in the service in New York."
John enlisted for the Canada expedition, and was
never heard of by his people. As a family memorial of this incident, the large stone, supported by
the small one, was permitted to remain as the
men left it when they answered the call of their
country; and now (1897) it has been transferred
to the Common, or " Old Training Field," and so
located as to indicate the line of march of the
ninety-two minute-men who left that town for
Lexington, April 19, 1775. On this bowlder has
been placed a bronze tablet on which the names
of the patriots are read, together with the following : " The Nevens Brothers were at work on this
stone, on their farm, April 19, 1775, and left it in

this position at the Minute Men's alarm, to join
their comrades on this Common." While the old
town of Monson has been lost, and the Nevens
home gone to decay, the rough stone upon which
the brothers were peacefully laboring when the
war-cry reached them has been set up as their
pillar of memorial and of their comrades.

As neighbors to the Nevens family were the
Baileys. They had a sawmill, and were there at
work when they received the Lexington alarm.
Daniel, the father, with sons Daniel, Joel, and
Andrew, without stopping to shut down the gate,
made a hasty response.

There were the Wallingsfords, who had gone
from Bradford, Mass., to Old Monson. Lieutenant David, leaving his hoe in the cornfield,
appeared with his gun at the Common, and was
of the company who so nobly represented Hollis.
He entered the Continental army, and was credited with opening the fire at Bennington.

The loss of Old Monson occasioned the removal
of many of her families, and consequently these
homes went to decay; but in our route we have
seen the family sites, and, attracted by the few
struggling trees, with the tenacious lilacs, have
traced the neglected hearth-stones of the patriots
of Old Monson.

Although beyond the limits of Middlesex County
and of Massachusetts, the town of Hollis has been
the first town to set up a monument on which can

be read the names of all who responded to the alarm of April 19, 1775. They are : —

REUBEN DOW, *Captain.*

JOHN GOSS, *1st Lieutenant.*

JOHN CUMINGS, *2d Lieutenant.*

Nathan Blood.
Joshua Boynton.
William Nevens.
Minott Farmer.
Sampson Powers.
James McIntosh.
James McConnor.
Ephraim Blood.
David Farnsworth.
Noah Worcester.
Uriah Wright.
Thomas Pratt.
Elias Boynton.
Francis Blood.
Ezekiel Proctor.
Jacob Spaulding.
Ebenezer Ball.
Thomas Colburn.
Samuel Hill.
Benjamin Cumings.
Samuel Jewett.
Israel Kenney.
David Ames.
William Wood.
John Campbell.
Libbens Wheeler.
Abel Brown.
Nahum Powers.
Isaac Stearns.
Samuel Hosley.

Daniel Taylor.
Thomas Kemp.
Amos Taylor.
Jacob Read.
Thomas Wheat.
Ebenezer Farley.
Ebenezer Youngman.
James Fisk.
Josiah Fisk.
Jonathan Eastman.
Amos Eastmam.
Aaron Hardy.
Benjamin Boynton.
Ephraim Pierce.
Jonas Blood.
James Colburn.
William French.
Ebenezer Wheeler.
Benjamin Wright, Jr.
Joseph Bailey.
Benjamin Wright.
Nathaniel Wheat.
Benjamin Nevens.
Joseph Nevens.
Nathaniel Ball.
Benjamin Sanders.
Ebenezer Gilson.
Thaddeus Wheeler.
Thomas Patch.
Samuel Johnson.

Benjamin Abbott.
William Tenney.
Samuel Conery.
Benjamin Farley.
Jonathan Russ.
John Philbrick.
Ebenezer Jaquith.
Manuel Grace.
Robert Seaver.
Nathan Phelps.
Daniel Blood, Jr.
Edward Johnson.
Jacob Danforth.
Bray Wilkins.
Israel Wilkins.
Job Bailey.
Samuel Leeman.
Joseph Minot.
James Dickey.
Jonathan Ames.
Randal McDaniels.
David Wallingsford.
Richard Bailey.
Nathan Colburn.
Abner Keyes.
Joel Bailey.
John Atwell.
Jesse Wyman.
Ephraim Howe.

The Hayden home is one of the few that sheltered the patriots of 1775 and of 1861. The ancient house stands with as much apparent firmness
as when Samuel Hayden came from Marlborough,
Massachusetts, and located here in 1761. He was
attracted, doubtless, by the mill privileges which
the swift stream afforded, and which has furnished business for the several generations who
have made a most commendable record at this
place. Josiah, a nephew of the pioneer, was the
second of the family, and was followed by his
son Samuel, the drummer of the Old Monson company. He is succeeded by two sons, who cherish
the home, till the soil, and tend the mill after the
most approved plan. A family reminder of not
only the Revolution, but of the French war, is a
powder-horn, on which are carved figures representing a line of Indians with their war implements, and the words : —

SAMUEL HAYDEN, HIS POWDER-HORN.

If I do lose, and you do find,
Give it to me, for it is mine.

This horn and the family musket were taken
down from their places above the open fire, and
carried by Samuel Hayden into the Revolution.
The maternal head of the Hayden family was Hannah Bailey, daughter of Samuel who was killed at
Bunker Hill. Hannah was a schoolteacher in An-

dover when the troubles with the mother country
broke out. At the close of a short term of her
school, there was a great scarcity of money, and
the school committee allowed the teacher to take
her choice between the bills of credit of the
time or rolls of wool, in payment for her services.
She took the latter, and spun them into yarn, and
made cloth, which later became useful to her in
completing her wedding outfit. In proof of this,
her grandsons at the old home brought forward
a liberal sample of the fabric.

Our journey through Old Monson was made
doubly interesting by an additional guide, — Mr.
Charles S. Spaulding, son of Asaph S. Spaulding
and Hannah Colburn. In common with other residents of Hollis, our guide has a connection with
Middlesex families. He says, "There were inducements held out for immigration, a special effort
being made by means of handbills circulated
through Middlesex and Essex Counties.

Having completed the circuit, I halted at the
home of my efficient guide, Mr. Cyrus F. Burge,
on the farm where his father has spent his days,
and where his great-grandfather settled in 1762,
and from which Ephraim Burge went into the
war, doing service in the northern campaign when
Burgoyne surrendered.

The old burying-place of Hollis is a typical
churchyard as far as there can be one in a comparatively new country. Having completed my

search for the footprints of the patriots around the old hearth-stones, and remembering that —

"The paths of glory lead but to the grave,"

I turned in to the narrow acre with its grass-grown paths, and sought for a few hints of the chapter of patriotism chiselled on the moss-grown, tottering slabs which stand like weary sentinels.

First I read : —

ERECTED TO THE MEMORY OF
DEA. JOHN BOYNTON,
WHO DEPARTED THIS LIFE OCTOBER YE 29TH, 1787,
IN YE 68TH YEAR OF HIS AGE.

It was so soon after the war that the people had not begun to fully realize the import of the message so promptly spread through the town by this faithful deacon.

I next read the name of —

LIEUT. AMOS EASTMAN,
WHO DEPARTED THIS LIFE
MARCH 6, 1808, IN THE 89TH YEAR OF HIS AGE.

Even at this date no note is made of the part taken by this village hero. The common grave at Bunker Hill where were buried so many of the pride of Hollis is recalled by the brief note on a stone, on which is read, " Lucy Baldwin, daughter of Thomas Wheat, who was killed at the Battle of Bunker Hill."

The grave of Captain Reuben Dow recalled that scene on the Common opposite, when he at the head of the Hollis minute-men marched off to Cambridge. He lived till 1811, having completed more than fourscore years. An erect stone tells that Doctor John Hale was born October 24th, 1731, and died October 22d, 1791. He was colonel of a regiment, and resigned to enter the service as surgeon, serving through the war. Near by we read that Dr. William Hale was born, July 27th, 1762, and died October 10, 1854. He entered the service as aid to his father at the age of fifteen years, and served through the war.

Among these stones, " with uncouth rhymes and shapeless sculpture deck'd," are reminders of the Emerson family, of which New England is justly proud. As I shall refer to the Emerson clergymen of this locality in another connection, I will only call the attention of my readers to the record of some of the sons of Rev. Daniel Emerson of Hollis who lie buried with those whom they served.

IN MEMORY OF

DANIEL EMERSON, ESQ.,

HAVING FAITHFULLY AND INDUSTRIOUSLY SERVED HIS GENERATION,

AS AN OFFICER OF THE CHURCH,

AS A DEFENDER OF FREEDOM,

AS A MAGISTRATE AND LEGISLATOR,

AS A FRIEND OF THE POOR,

AND AS A ZEALOUS PROMOTER OF THE REDEEMER'S KINGDOM,

HE RESTED FROM HIS LABORS

OCTOBER 4, 1820, ÆT. 74.

On a stone at the grave of another son of the Hollis minister is read : —

ERECTED TO THE MEMORY OF
LIEUT. RALPH EMERSON
WHO WAS INSTANTLY KILLED BY THE ACCIDENTAL
DISCHARGE OF A CANNON WHILE EXERCISING
THE MATROSS
OCTOBER 4, 1790,
IN THE 30TH YEAR OF HIS AGE.

We drop apace.
By nature some decay,
And some the gusts of fortune sweep away.

NEVENS'S BOULDER

CHAPTER XII

JOHN COLBURN TELLS HIS FATHER'S STORY OF
THE NORTHERN CAMPAIGNS. — BURGOYNE'S AL-
LIANCE WITH INDIANS. — KING GEORGE III. HIRES
THE GERMANS TO FIGHT THE PROVINCIALS

> When on that field his band the Hessians fought,
> Briefly he spoke before the fight began :
> "Soldiers, those German gentlemen were bought
> For four pounds eight and seven pence per man,
> By England's King; a bargain, it is thought.
> Are we worth more? let's prove it while we can;
> For we must beat them, boys, ere set of sun,
> Or my wife sleeps a widow." — It was done.
>
> HALLECK.

IT was my good fortune to meet Mr. John Colburn [1] on the celebration of his ninety-sixth birthday at his home in Hollis, N.H. He was strong
in mind and body, and spent the hours of this anniversary in recalling the scenes of the past. It
was like breaking the seals of closed volumes to
many in attendance.

"I was one of thirteen children born to my
parents, James and Susannah (Hardy) Colburn.
We had a hard struggle in our youth, for my
father was not a strong man. He lost his health

---

[1] See story of Hollis.

in the northern campaigns of '76 and '77. My
earliest recollections are of his accounts of service
in the war. He used to tell us, ' I was only in
my teens when I entered the Provincial service.
I passed through the battle of Bunker Hill safely,
while my neighbors and townsmen fell around
me. But I endured great hardship in the campaign at the north when following up Burgoyne
and his army. Bridges were scarce at that time,
and we were compelled to ford the rivers. In
wading across the Mohawk I took a severe cold,
from which I never fully recovered; but we pushed
on, filled with contempt for Burgoyne, who had
written a long proclamation to the Americans
soon after his arrival in the country. He promised great things to them if they would lay down
their arms and surrender peaceably to the British,
but threatened terrible things if they continued to
oppose the king. Among other evils, he said he
would let the Indians loose among them if they
refused to surrender.

NOTE. — The manner in which the Indians were inducted into
the service of killing the patriots of America is seen by the following: " We went to-day to headquarters in Montreal, to be present
at a meeting between General Carleton and all the nations of wild
men, since, in order to make it as impressive as possible, all the
chief officers of the army were expressly invited to attend. The
chiefs of the so-called Iroquois nation, namely, many of the Onan
tais, Anajutais, Nonlaquahuques, and Kanastaladi, met at six o'clock
in the evening, in the old church of the Jesuits, which had been
expressly prepared for the occasion. The high choir was covered

with carpets, upon which were placed a row of stools.   In the centre was a large armchair for Governor-General Carleton, who during the whole of the meeting kept his hat upon his head.   Behind him was a table, near which sat the adjutant generals, Captains Foy and Carleton, who served as secretaries.   There were also benches, upon which sat three hundred wild men, with their pipes lighted.   Every nation had its chief and interpreter, the latter acting as spokesman and translating into French all that was said to General Carleton.   In order, however, that there might be no mistakes or misunderstandings, General Carleton had also his interpreter.   Thus each nation spoke for itself.   The substance of what they said was that they had heard the rebels [Americans] had risen against the English nation; that they praised the valor of General Carleton as shown in frustrating the designs of the enemy; that they, therefore, loved and esteemed him, and that they had come to offer their services against the rebels. . . .   All these nations were engaged for one year, and had their posts assigned them.   Before leaving they all passed by General Carleton, shaking hands with him and the rest of the officers.   The evening and night were spent by them in feasting and dancing, which had already lasted seven days.   They had brought with them a few scalps of rebels whom they had killed, and with which they honored Generals Carleton, Burgoyne, and Phillips.''   Other Indian nations were also brought into this abominable service.   They offered '' their grandfather, the King of England, and their father, General Carleton '' their services against the Bostonians.   One of the leaders of the company wore at this time the coat of General Braddock, whom he had killed in the fatal expedition of 1755. That proud general's vest was also worn by a nine-year-old son of the Indian chief.   The appropriation of a dead British general's clothes could not have been a very agreeable sight for the present actors in the great drama.

'' 'This announcement filled the Americans with indignation, especially the army engaged in the north.   Every day there was a new story told of

Indian barbarity. Even the British could not safely trust their savage allies. A Tory officer sent a party of Indians to escort a young lady named Jane McCrea, to whom he was engaged in marriage, within the British lines. When on the way, the Indian escorts fell into a quarrel over the reward they were to receive, and in the difficulty, killed the girl, and bore her scalp away, leaving her mangled body in the road.

" ' This brutality committed near her neighbors and friends filled the whole country with horror and indignation, and even General Burgoyne saw that he had made a mistake in placing confidence in such allies.

" ' I was with General John Stark, in whom we had the greatest confidence. Seth Warner and the " Green Mountain Boys " were with us in the latter part of the campaign. About the middle of September, 1777, the two armies of the north were near each other, waiting for action. Burgoyne was on the heights of Saratoga. Gates, the American general who had succeeded Schuyler, was on some heights back of the old tavern known as " Bemis Inn." On the 19th of September we met, near the village of Stillwater, in bloody battle, which lasted several hours without any apparent result to either side. On the 7th of October we had it again, in about the same place. We fought until dark. General Frazer, Burgoyne's favorite general, was shot through the body, and soon died. Soon after this battle, when there was yet doubt as to what the final results were to be, we saw the enemy in their intrench-ments, and kept up our cannonade, not knowing that they were carrying out the dying request of General Frazer, and burying him in the trench on the height where he had received his mortal wound. While we were waiting in uncertainty, the generals of the two armies were carrying on a correspondence in regard to terms of Burgoyne's surrender. It was at length agreed that his army should lay down their arms, and march to Boston as prisoners of war, and be sent to Europe, under a promise to take up arms no more in the war. I had no love for any of those who were fighting against us, but especially despised the Hessians, whom we thought were willingly hired to come to this country to subdue us. By a special act of generosity on the part of General Gates, none of us were allowed to see the enemy when they marched out to the fields of Saratoga and there stacked their guns; but when the march off to-wards Boston was begun, it became necessary to have a guard, and I was of that number. Up to this time I had entertained nothing but contempt for the women, wives of the German soldiers, who followed the army; but when I saw the family of the Brunswick general, I came to the conclusion that they were people of distinction, and were actuated by other than sinister motives. My sympathies went out for them in the long journey across the country, as we guarded the captured thousands to Cambridge, Mass., where they were lodged in the abandoned barracks of the army which kept the British shut up in Boston.'"

To the above story of James Colburn, a soldier of the Revolution, as told to me in substance by his son John when lacking but four years of a century of life, I am indebted for the suggestion of the following story of the German soldiers who fought for George III. in the Revolution : —

NOTE. — Much has justly been said in condemnation of the English Government for employing Germans in the war for the subjugation of her revolted American Colonies, and generations of the descendants of those who fought the hirelings have naturally imbibed feelings of contempt for the German army. But it should be remembered that at that time the German soldier belonged, body and soul, to him to whom he had sold himself. He had no country. He was severed from every tie; in fact, he was, in every sense of the word, the property of his military lord, who could do with him as he saw fit. They did not prove to be as helpful as it was expected, but were found totally unfit for the business in which they were engaged. They could not march through the woods and encounter the difficulties incident to war in our then almost unsettled country. Many of them deserted to our army before and after the surrender, or convention, as it was more tenderly designated at the request of Burgoyne. We have in New England to-day descendants of Hessians for whom the English Government was obliged to pay the agreed price, — being absent from the returning army, they were rated as dead. Descendants of Hoffmaster, Kyar, Patio, and others, have become good citizens of Massachusetts; and no braver soldiers fought for the Union at Gettysburg than some of the representatives of those men who came to this country as Hessians. More of the deserters settled in

New York, and after a full century, a German's cabin was seen at Charlestown, Warren County, of that State. The Hessian officers were equipped with everything for their comfort, as though their trip to America were only an excursion for pleasure. A tobacco-box, which belonged to one of the unfortunate officials, is now seen in a collection of relics in the town of Bedford. The owner fought and died in the northern campaign. This pocket companion was taken to Canada by a British soldier of the king, and at length became the property of an English lady at Halifax, N.S., and was by her presented to a Boston lady, whose interests in the town

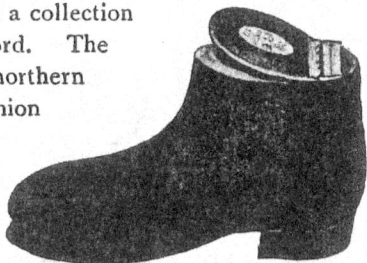

HESSIAN TOBACCO-BOX

of Bedford occasioned it to be finally deposited at her old homestead, and in the house from which the minute-men of Bedford set out for Concord fight on April 19, 1775. In the Salem Institute may be seen a hat which belonged to a Hessian officer who gave up his life in the "Jerseys."

CHAPTER XIII

PRISONERS OF WAR IN AMERICA. — JOURNEY TO
CAMBRIDGE. — PROVINCIAL BARRACKS AGAIN OC-
CUPIED. — HONOR AMONG PRISONERS OF WAR. —
THE BARONESS TELLS HER STORY. — ROUTE FROM
SARATOGA TO CAMBRIDGE. — "TORY ROW"

No foreign king shall give us laws, no British tyrant reign,
For independence made us free, and independence we'll maintain.
We'll charge our foes from post to post, attack their works and lines,
Or by some well-laid stratagem, we'll make them all Burgoynes.

REV. SAMUEL HIDDEN.

THE Germans and Hessians were in a sorry
plight. They came not here voluntarily, but were
caught while in their churches and elsewhere, and
were forced into the service.

The wives who were with them helped make
up the pitiable procession that passed through the
country.

" They had a collection of wild animals in their train — the
only thing American they had captured. Here could be
seen an artillery-man leading a grizzly bear, that every now
and then would rear upon his hind legs as if he were tired of
going upon all fours, or occasionally growl his disapprobation
at being pulled along by a chain. In the same manner a
tame deer would be seen tripping lightly after a grenadier.

Young foxes were also observed looking sagaciously from the top of a baggage-wagon, or a young racoon securely clutched under the arm of a sharp-shooter."

Their advent to Cambridge is thus described by an eye-witness : —

" On Friday we heard the Hessians were to make a procession on the same route. I never had the least idea that the creation produced such a sordid set of creatures in human figure, — poor, dirty, emaciated men ; a great many women, who seemed to be the beasts of burden, having bushel baskets on their backs by which they were bent double. The contents seemed to be pots and kettles, various sorts of furniture, children peeping through gridirons and other utensils, some very young infants who were born on the road. The women were bare-footed, and clothed in dirty rags. Such effluvia filled the air while they were passing, that had they not been smoking all the time, I should have been fearful of disease.

" Among these prisoners were generals of the first order of talent ; young gentlemen of noble and wealthy families aspiring to military renown ; legislators of the British realm ; and a vast concourse of other men, lately confident of victory and of freedom to plunder and destroy, were led captive through the pleasant land they had coveted, to be gazed at with mingled joy and scorn by those whose homes they came to make desolate. Their march was solemn, sullen, and silent."

To many of them the abandoned barracks of
the patriots afforded more comfort than they had
been enjoying, while to some the best quarters
were repulsive in the extreme.

NOTE. — The reader will bear in mind that the German troops
captured and marched as prisoners to Cambridge were only a portion of the whole army hired from that country by the King of
England to subdue the patriots. They were first met in combat at
Long Island in August, 1776, when Washington was defeated with
a loss of one thousand in dead and wounded; but before the year
closed, Washington made that memorable Christmas [1] call upon the
enemy after crossing the Delaware, and captured a full thousand of
the Hessians.

The British soldiers were quartered in the barracks on Prospect Hill, and the Germans on Winter Hill. Cambridge again assumed a warlike
appearance. Besides the almost six thousand prisoners quartered there, a small army of patriots
was required to keep guard over them. Among
the guard were some brave men who had appeared
there under different circumstances in the spring
of 1775. The command of the guard fell to General Glover of Marblehead, although many towns
were represented in the rank and file. In the almost illegible records of the towns may be deci-
phered entries like the following : —

" Men to take and guard the convention troops."

William R. Lee of Marblehead, who had two
years before been prominent as a captain at the

[1] See Story of Marblehead.

Cambridge camp, was again on the ground, but as a colonel, with his troops to form a portion of the guard.

On the day following the arrival of the army, General Burgoyne and his two major-generals, Phillips and Riedesel, dined by invitation with General Heath, the commander of the American forces in and around Boston. The dinner is described as an elegant affair. Whose healths were drunk we do not know. Among the guests were Generals Glover and Whipple, who had conducted the British part of the capitulated army from Saratoga. This fine beginning was too good to last. Many of the prisoners were too base to appreciate favors; as utterly incapable of manifesting a sense of gratitude as they were of understanding the language in which orders were given. They took advantage of the liberty given them, and commenced a wholesale destruction of fences, sheds, barns, fruit, and ornamental-trees, and everything available, under the pretence of necessity for fuel. This led to the enforcement of more rigid measures on the part of the guard, and then to complaints from the prisoners, and a general disturbance.

It is apparent that General Burgoyne entertained no hard feelings against Colonel Lee, for there is credited to him the most remarkable kindness in the following narrative.[1]

[1] See " History of Marblehead " by Roads.

Captain John Lee, brother of Colonel William R., while in the privateer service, was taken prisoner in 1776, and sent to Forton Prison,[1] England. He was there submitted to the most cruel treatment. Three times he attempted, with a few of his companions in misery, to make an escape; but as often failed, and received a worse punishment.

At length he was allowed the range of the larger apartments and yard of the prison. He was informed one day by an officer that there was some one at the gate who had been granted an interview with him. On going to the entrance he found a well but plainly dressed gentleman, who asked, "Are you Captain John Lee of Marblehead?" and being satisfied of his identity, the strange caller presented a purse containing seventy-five guineas.

The prisoner asked in astonishment to whom he was indebted for such a timely and most acceptable present. "No matter," was the answer. And then the gentleman observed, "With a part of the funds, purchase, or procure in some way, a complete suit of uniform like those worn by the soldiers of the guard; and this evening place yourself in some obscure corner or position, whence you can unperceived fall into the ranks when they go the rounds, and come out

[1] Same prison mentioned in "A Romance of War" in "Beneath Old Roof Trees" of this series.

into the yard. But as there are sentinels who
must be passed before you reach the street, the
countersign will be required;" which was then
whispered in his ear, and the unknown gentleman
disappeared.

By using the gold freely and wisely during the
day, Captain Lee was enabled to obtain the needful dress, and following the instructions which he
had so strangely received, he fell into the ranks
as the guard passed through the prison, and soon
reached the yard. Then giving the countersign,
he passed the guard at the outer gate, and found
himself alone in the street. The night was very
dark, and the roads were strange to him, so that
he did not know where to go, or what step to
take next to make sure of success. While he was
endeavoring to reach a decision, the gentleman
who gave him the purse came up, and taking him
by the hand, congratulated him upon his good
fortune. Then conducting him to a carriage
which was waiting at a little distance, the gentleman requested him to enter it, and stated that
the coachman had instructions where to convey
him. As he entered the carriage the strange
gentleman wished him a prosperous and safe return to America, and was about taking his leave,
when Captain Lee again asked to whom he was
indebted for such a humane and generous act.
He answered, " No matter." And after directing
the coachman to move off, he bowed and said,

"Farewell, God bless you !" and was soon out of sight.

On his arrival in America, Captain Lee related the circumstances of his escape to his brother, Colonel William R. Lee, and expressed a strong desire to know who the gentleman could have been, and what were his motives for extending assistance to an utter stranger and a natural enemy. Colonel Lee replied, —

"I can inform you. When General Burgoyne and his army arrived at Cambridge as prisoners of war, I had the command of the troops which were stationed there as guard, and again for several months previous to his departure for England. When I waited upon him to take leave on the day of his departure, he thanked me in the most cordial manner for my attentions, and, as he expressed it, the gentlemanly and honorable manner in which I had treated him and his officers, and wished to know whether there was anything which he could do for me when he reached England. I informed him I had a brother who for more than two years had been confined in Forton Prison; and as he was entirely destitute of funds, I should consider it a great favor if he would take charge of seventy-five guineas, and cause them to be delivered to him on his arrival. He replied, 'Why did you not inform me before that you had a brother a prisoner in England? You shall not send any money to him; I will see that it is supplied, and shall with great pleasure do everything in my power to render his situation as comfortable as possible.' I thanked him for his generous offer of services, but informed him that I could not consent to receive pecuniary aid, and desired as a special favor that he would be so kind as to deliver you the purse which I put into his hand. 'It shall be done,' he said; 'and you may be assured that I shall find him out, and see that he is well provided for in all respects.' Thus, it is evident that you are indebted to General Burgoyne for your fortunate escape from the horrors of a prison."

BARONESS RIEDESEL.

Madam Riedesel gives us some ideas of the journey to Cambridge from the standpoint of a captive.

" As it was already very late in the season, and the weather raw, I had my calash covered with coarse linen, which in turn was varnished over with oil; and in this manner we set out on our journey to Boston, which was very tedious, besides being attended with considerable hardship.

"I know not whether it was my carriage that attracted

the curiosity of the people to it, — for it certainly had the appearance of a wagon in which they carry around rare animals, — but often I was obliged to halt, because the people insisted upon seeing the wife of the German general with her children. For fear that they would tear off the linen covering from the wagon in their eagerness to see me, I very often alighted, and by this means got away more quickly."

On the arrival at Cambridge, Madam Riedesel and family were quartered at a private house, which she describes as follows: "We had only one room under the roof. My women servants slept on the floor, and our men servants in the entry. Some straw, which I placed under our beds, served us for a long time, as I had with me nothing more than my own field-bed."

They were allowed to eat in the room where the whole family ate and slept. It is impossible to imagine the feelings of the baroness when obliged to remain in such quarters. For one used to ordinary living to be thus located it would be hard indeed, and vastly more irksome for one accustomed to the luxury of the Riedesel home.

It is apparent that this was not intentional on the part of the Americans in charge, for after three weeks the family were given lodgings in one of the most beautiful houses of Cambridge. It was the Lechmere House, one of the seven on "Tory Row" (Brattle Street) vacated by the Royalists. It is yet standing, not far from the colleges. Both house and grounds are so changed as to be scarcely recognizable. The Colonial style of the dwelling is utterly destroyed, and many houses now stand on the extensive grounds where richly dressed men and women were often seen before the Revolution.

These noted prisoners enjoyed themselves in their new quarters, and were in full sympathy with the owners who had been obliged to flee. They complained that the town throughout was full of "violent patriots" and "wicked people." They decried the women, who they claimed showed them the greatest indignity.

The kindness of General Schuyler prompted the baroness to pay a visit to his daughter Madam Carter, whose attentions she fully appreciated ; but complained of her husband, who, she said, proposed to the Americans "to chop off the heads of our generals, salt them down in barrels, and send over to the English one of these barrels for every hamlet or little town burned down."

After the abusive measures adopted by General Gage in this locality, it seems remarkable that these prisoners should have been treated with so much lenience, notwithstanding the terms of surrender. It was quite like our more modern way of dealing with our enemies. The family held balls and parties, and even went so far as to celebrate the birthday of the king. When they had become quite contented, expecting to remain in this place until set free, there came an order for a change.

Some of the troops were sent to Rutland in the interior of the State, and others were sent to Virginia.   It fell to the lot of the Riedesels to go to Virginia.

The baroness succeeded in secreting the German colors, and preventing their being captured by the Americans, who were led by her to believe that they were burned at Saratoga, which was not true, the staffs only being destroyed, while the colors were secreted in a mattress.

A daughter born to the family in New York in 1780, while they were prisoners of war, received the name of America, which name she honorably bore through a long life in Germany.

The family spent nearly seven years in this country, it being the autumn of 1783 before they again saw their Brunswick home.   About one-third of General Riedesel's army either perished or voluntarily remained in America.

The record of the Riedesels and the Hessians occupies but a small place in our history, and is passed with but little notice, save as it comes to us occasionally through the lips of one who, like John Colburn of Hollis, N.H., has had it from one of the patriots who faced the foes "who killed for hire."

The poet Longfellow, who became the owner of the house which was the headquarters of Washington during his stay at Cambridge, became interested in the story of the Riedesels, whose home was not unlike his own, and has remembered them in "The Open Window:"—

The old house by the lindens
Stood silent in the shade,
And on the gravelled pathway
The light and shadow played.

I saw the nursery windows
Wide open to the air;
But the faces of the children,
They were no longer there.

The large Newfoundland house-dog
Was standing by the door;
He looked for his little playmates,
Who would return no more.

They walked not under the lindens,
They played not in the hall;
But shadow, and silence, and sadness
Were hanging over all.

The birds sang in the branches,
With sweet, familiar tone;
But the voices of the children
Will be heard in dreams alone!

And the boy that walked beside me,
He could not understand
Why closer in mine, ah! closer,
I pressed his warm, soft hand!

Well authenticated history and tradition prove that Burgoyne and his officers were shown favors seldom granted to prisoners of war. While the

Brunswick general was living in luxury as described, General Burgoyne received the distinction of being located in the Apthorp House, vacated by its Loyalist owner, John Borland, who gave up his beautiful home, rather than forsake the Crown

APTHORP HOUSE, CAMBRIDGE, WHERE BURGOYNE WAS IMPRISONED

and ally himself with the Colonists. With all the softening effect of time and circumstances, one cannot revert to the vacated estates of Brattle Street without arousing the most profound sympathy for that class of people denominated Tories, many of whom had great possessions. These they sacrificed, and much else that was dear to them, rather than espouse the doubtful cause.

These Loyalists were doubtless as conscientious in their course as were their neighbors, the patriots, in their struggle for liberty.

The Apthorp House is one of the notable houses of Cambridge to-day. It is a well-preserved specimen of the Colonial architecture, surrounded by ample grounds, but which have been greatly shorn of their original lawn. In the mellow sunlight of an October afternoon, by the courtesy of the occupant and partial owner, I thoughtfully strolled about that yard, over the turf once trod by the proud general whose glory had departed. I recalled the scene when the general, presuming upon the leniency of the guard, made an attempt to overstep his limits, and, being brought to a halt, gave free expression to his feelings ; so says the daughter of one who was a witness to the scene. The massive door of the mansion, and the large hall in which it swings, are silent reminders of many noted guests who have crossed that threshold. The spacious rooms on either side, where elaborate carvings have withstood the vexing hand of modern architects, and the broad staircase with elegant balustrade, remind one of not only the days when a notable prisoner was the occupant, but of the builder and his successors in possession.

This interesting mansion is familiar to all who have been connected with Harvard University for more than a century, many of whom have dwelt beneath its roof. It was built about 1760 for Rev.

East Apthorp, the first rector of Christ Church, Cambridge. In sentiment and manner of living, Dr. Apthorp may be classed with the Vassal, Lee, Inman, Oliver, Phips, Lechmere, Brattle, and Temple families, who were instrumental in erecting the church edifice and establishing the mission. It was at a time when there was an increasing opposition to the element of aristocracy in the Colonies. Being censured for his high living, etc., Dr. Apthorp became dissatisfied, and returned to England, after advising his parishioners to give less heed to "fashionable imitation and parade in buildings, tables, equipages, etc."

John Borland and family, belonging to the select circle of sympathizers, were occupants of the Apthorp House when the Revolutionary troubles began. They were classed among the "absentees;" but the head of the family having died while in Boston in 1775, the property was not held by the government, and the heirs succeeded to the ownership. During the Borland possession the house was enlarged by adding a story at the top for the use of the negro slaves of the family, there being a growing sentiment in the Bay Colony against the practice of certain New York families, who assigned their cellars for the sleeping apartments of their slaves. Captain Thomas Warland became, through purchase, the next owner of the famous house, and it is still in the possession of his family.

A pair of brass candlesticks, a part of the
travelling equipage or tent ornaments of General
Burgoyne, were presented to Lieutenant Edmund
Monroe of Lexington by a superior officer, after

BURGOYNE'S CANDLESTICKS

the surrender of the northern army.   These are
still in the family, owned by George R. Fessenden,
M.D., of Ashfield, Mass.   They are made so as
to be packed in a compact form, and carried in the
pocket.

NOTE. — To trace the route taken by that part of the capitulated
army which went to Cambridge, the reader should follow it from
Saratoga across the Hudson to Great Barrington, where for the first
time they found shelter in barns.   There they halted for some
time in order to secure a change of teams for the conveyance of
baggage, the sick, etc.   Then they went on to Westfield in a lazy
and shiftless manner.   Two of the Germans perished from expo-
sure before reaching West Springfield, where they crossed the Connecticut River; and finding the people of East Springfield unwilling
to quarter the troops, they were obliged to go on as far as Palmer,
thence to Brookfield, where the Germans overtook their English
fellow-sufferers, who had preceded them a day's journey.   From
Brookfield to Leicester was a march of eleven days, where quarters
for the weary army were obtained.   On November 4 they reached
Worcester, and obtained " deacent quarters."   Generals Burgoyne

and Phillips, with Brigadier Glover, were there at the same time. The next day found them at Marlborough, and on the succeeding day they reached Weston, and one day more was needed to complete the journey to Cambridge, November 7.

One need not study very intently the history of the towns through which the prisoners passed, to find that the patriots on the entire route took pleasure in the panoramic scenes. In many instances, however, they gave relief to the poor bedraggled creatures who fell out by the way, and lay down to die in a strange land.

According to the terms of capitulation, the army was to have a free passage to England under Lieutenant-General Burgoyne. It was to march to Massachusetts Bay by the easiest and most expeditious route, and be quartered as near as possible to Boston. The officers were not to be separated from their men; but they were to be quartered according to rank, and not to be hindered from assembling their men for roll-call and the necessary purposes of regularity. They were to be allowed the privilege of parole, and to wear their side-arms. The terms of agreement signed by Gates in behalf of the Colonies, and Burgoyne on the part of the English Government, were not fully carried out, failing to be indorsed by the Continental Congress.

In times of peace it is hardly fair to impugn the motives of the faithful leaders in times of war; but they were charged with detaining the troops for the purpose of having them desert, and join the American army.

CHAPTER XIV

BARON AND BARONESS RIEDESEL. — GERMAN AL-
LIES. — START FROM GERMANY. — THE BARONESS
AT THE COURT OF KING GEORGE III. — RECEP-
TION IN AMERICA. — WOMEN FOLLOW THE ARMY

EARLY in 1776, when General Gage found he could not have his own way, and Burgoyne had learned that he must fight to have "elbow room," England entered into treaties with the smaller German states to take into her service twenty thousand German troops. The landgrave of Hesse-Cassel furnished the larger share, and hence all the Germans received the appellation "Hessians."

The custom followed by the ruler of this German province of hiring out Hessian soldiers was one of long standing, and one which aided the finances not a little, and sometimes led to the formation of important alliances on the part of the reigning House. It is recorded that the British Government paid £3,000,000 for the services of the army of Hessians who fought against our patriotic ancestors in the Revolution. Of these, four thousand were Brunswickers, natives of the province of Brunswick.

While I will not run the risk of confusing my readers by departing from the appellation Hessians, I desire to have it apparent that the German allies of the king were of different classes, and not all of the grade which we have sometimes contemptuously regarded them, although none of them had any honorable motive for taking up arms against the Provincials.

The Brunswick army was placed under the command of Major-General Riedesel, a man of literary culture and refinement, as well as of military distinction; and the only wonder is that he could be hired to lead an army to come to America "to butcher her children."

If my reader would follow the course taken by this general and his German army from their starting-point to America, let him turn to the map of the German Empire, and find near the centre the province of Brunswick, from which their start was made. They marched across the province of Hanover to Stade, a fortified town about a mile from the mouth of the Schwinge in the Elbe, where they began their journey by water. "The departure of the boats was one of the most beautiful spectacles that can be imagined. All was contentment and happiness." The boat which carried General Riedesel was the Pallas, the same which conveyed General Gage from America to England. The first day's journey was past beautiful villages, plainly seen from the boat on either side of the

Elbe, to Fryburg, and then they were soon out to sea. Touching at Dover, they passed through the Strait to the English Channel, halting at Portsmouth, and passing on to Plymouth, which they left on April 4 for America. The fleet, upon leaving the coast of England, numbered thirty-six sailing-vessels. After a passage of nine weeks, they arrived at Quebec, where the general saw some of our men who had been captured, "Rebel prisoners," he called them. From Quebec they went to Three Rivers, from which place the general wrote to his wife: "We have already conquered the whole of Canada, and shall, as soon as the boats are in readiness, force our way into New England by the way of Lake Champlain, where are all the rebels." After taking Crown Point they went into winter quarters in and near Three Rivers. Here they remained in the full enjoyment of good living, after a time of illness occasioned by the change in climate. The anticipation of a complete subjugation of the patriot army in the spring added to their winter's enjoyment. In May they were made doubly sure of success by the arrival of General John Burgoyne, with a picked army, great stores of ammunition, and the finest brass cannon yet sent over. Good plans were made, but the trouble came in carrying them out.

At first they were successful; and General Riedesel began to win laurels for himself and his army, and Burgoyne thought the way was clear before him. They repulsed Seth Warner and his "Green Mountain Boys" at Hubbardston, Vermont, captured Ticonderoga and the stores at Whitehall. But at length the Germans marched on to Bennington, where General Stark had put in an appearance with some New Hampshire militia. It was their appearance that called forth that oft-repeated remark, "There they are, boys. We shall beat them to-night, or to-morrow morning Molly Stark will be a widow." [1]   They did defeat them, and captured some brass cannon, which they could not turn to a good use until General Stark showed them how to do it.

There soon followed the conditions and experiences which Mr. Colburn described to me, and which have been already recorded in a previous chapter.

The reader recalls the statement of Mr. Colburn, and wonders how the family of the Brunswick general came to be with him at the surrender of October 17. Surprising as it may seem, it was quite the habit of these German soldiers to have

[1] "The morning came — there stood the foe;
    Stark eyed them as they stood;
    Few words he spake — 'twas not a time
    For moralizing mood;
    'See there, the enemy, my boys —
    Now, strong in valor's might,
    Beat them, or Betty Stark will sleep
    In widowhood to-night!'"

their wives along with them. About fourscore women left their homes, and made the journey to America with the army to which their husbands belonged. The peasant women were contented to do the drudgery of the camp, and live in a most disgusting manner. It was in accordance with this custom that the family of General Riedesel was with him at Saratoga ; but their manner of journeying and living was in the greatest contrast to that of the peasants.

The Baroness Riedesel was equally as cultured and refined as her husband the general. She belonged to a distinguished family, and from youth was accustomed to the most cultivated society of her country. Although surrounded with all that wealth and station could provide, the baroness would have accompanied her husband to America had circumstances permitted. At her earliest opportunity, May 4, she set out on her journey to meet him. She took with her three daughters, Gustava, Frederica, and Caroline, aged four years and nine months, two years, and ten weeks, respectively. She was accompanied by a retinue of servants of both sexes, which her wealth and position warranted. They made the journey overland in a coach to Calais, where they took a ship for England, landed at Dover, and were conveyed to London by coach. They arrived in London on June 1, and she immediately received the courtesy from Lord North which her position demanded.

After a few days she went to Bristol, where she met a Captain Fenton, whose wife and a daughter of fourteen years were held as prisoners in Boston, New England. The baroness spent months in making preparations for her ocean voyage, during which time she appeared at Court, and was presented to King George III. and his wife on New Year's Day, 1777.

The baroness thus describes her experience at the Court of England, —

" I found the castle very ugly, and furnished in old-fashioned style. All the ladies and gentlemen were stationed in the audience-room. Into this room came the king, preceded by three cavaliers. The queen followed him, accompanied by a lady who carried her train, and a chamberlain. The king went round to the right, and the queen to the left. Neither passed by any one without saying something. At the end of the drawing-room they met, made each other a profound bow, and then returned to the place whence they had started. I asked Lady Germaine how I should act, and whether the king, as I had heard, kissed all the ladies. 'No,' she replied, 'only English women and marchionesses;' and that all one had to do was to remain quietly standing in her place. When, therefore, the king came up and kissed me, I was greatly amazed, and turned red as fire, since it was so entirely unexpected."

The remarks of the king showed that he was

familiar with the enterprise of General Riedesel, and of the intended journey of the baroness.

She left Portsmouth for America, with her children and servants, on April 15, 1777, and arrived in the harbor of Quebec on the 11th of June. There was a booming of guns from all the ships in the harbor, firing a salute in honor of her arrival, before she realized what it all meant. Presently a boat approached the ship to carry them ashore. The boat was manned by twelve sailors dressed in white, with silver helmets and green sashes. With the boat came letters from General Reidesel, informing his wife that he had been unable to await her arrival at Quebec, and had started on the summer campaign with General Burgoyne. Only remaining long enough at Quebec to dine with the wife of General Carleton, the baroness with her family took a boat, and proceeded up the St. Lawrence, in the hope of overtaking her husband. At midnight they landed, and took calashes for a drive across the country, riding in this way till the following afternoon, when they crossed the river, and reached the village of Three Rivers. Here the Hessians had been in winter quarters, and General Reidesel had left a house prepared for the reception of his family.

The Grand Vicar of the village, seeing the baroness's anxiety to join her husband, loaned her a covered calash, in which she immediately

resumed her journey in pursuit of the advancing
army.   And in this manner this refined lady
and her three young children and servants were
driven over the rough roads of the country.

" How touching a picture is this !   A delicate,
refined woman, accustomed only to the comfort,
luxury, and shelter of an old civilization in a circle
of devoted relations and friends, encountering the
hardships of the wilderness, self-reliant, courageous, persevering, not for one moment forgetting or neglecting the babes who are dependent
on her tenderness, even while her whole soul is
absorbed in that intensity of wifely love and devotion that renders her regardless of fatigue, pain,
and repeated disappointment.   If we are moved
with enthusiasm in recalling the valor and self-
forgetfulness of the patriot in the service of his
country on the wearying march and amid the
carnage of the field, may we not be equally stirred
at a manifestation of heroic endurance and self-
abnegation in an exercise of the most sublime of
human emotions, even though it be on the part of
one who sympathizes with the enemy ? "

After meeting General Riedesel, and spending
a few days, it became necessary for her to return
to Three Rivers with the children.   They spent
some weeks at the village of Three Rivers.   In
the meantime the British and German forces had
met with their successes at Ticonderoga and elsewhere.   Major Ackland had been wounded at

Hubbardston in the encounter with the "Green Mountain Boys," and his wife had been allowed to join him.

This permission led General Burgoyne to turn to General Riedesel and say, —

"Your wife shall come too, General; despatch Captain Willoe to escort her at once."

They left Three Rivers in a boat; and after some strange experiences with rattlesnakes when landing on a small island, and the enjoyment of much charming scenery, they reached Fort Edward, where they were most gladly received by General Riedesel, and warmly welcomed by the commanding officers.

They spent three happy weeks, a reunited family, in the Red House, encircled by the British and German troops.

"The weather was beautiful," said the baroness, "and we often took our meals under the trees."

On the 11th of September the army moved forward; and the little family followed them until the battle of the 19th, when the baroness and her family were obliged to remain at one place, meeting the husband and father as often as circumstances permitted. At length a house was prepared for the family near the camp; and when she was to move into it, an unexpected change took place. Said the baroness, "On my way homeward, I met many savages in their war dress armed with guns. They cried out, 'War! War!'

This completely overwhelmed me; and I had scarcely got back to my quarters, when I heard skirmishing and firing, which by degrees became constantly heavier, until finally the noises were frightful." The baroness was expecting to have a dinner-party that afternoon, at which the generals were to be guests; but instead of the party, she was called upon to care for one of them, General Frazer, who was mortally wounded, and died soon after. The burial of General Frazer, alluded to by my aged friend Mr. Colburn, is here described by the Baroness Riedesel, as she saw it from the standpoint of the enemy, whose leader he was. "Many cannon-balls also flew not far from me; but I had my eyes fixed upon the hill, where I distinctly saw my husband in the midst of the enemy's fire. The clergyman who was officiating was frequently covered with dust, which the shot threw up on all sides of him." Immediately after the funeral a retreat was ordered. Madam Riedesel, with children and servants, travelled all night in the pouring rain, and camped at Old Saratoga. The greatest consternation prevailed in the army; the provisions had failed, and the leading officers were forced from hunger to beg for a morsel from the baroness. Soon the cannonading drove them on, and the family sought refuge in a house. They were detected in entering the house by some of the Americans, who fired at them, and believing that the house was filled with officers, continued a heavy fire. Madam Riedesel and her children escaped by hiding in the cellar, where they sat upon the floor through the entire night, while cannon-balls crashed through the walls above them. Surrounded by the dead and dying, in hourly expectation of attack, this heroic woman cared for her children when servants failed, and also acted the part of a nurse to the suffering about her. After nearly a week of this extremity, the surrender came, and the entire army were prisoners of the Americans.

After the generals of the conquered army had been received by General Gates, and the formalities of surrender had taken place, a messenger was sent to the baroness, asking her to join her husband, who was a prisoner in the American camp. She was met by General Philip Schuyler and General Gates, and also Generals Phillips and Burgoyne of the surrendered army. General Schuyler then took the baroness and her children to his own tent, where he showed them much hospitality, and later sent them to his home in Albany, where they remained three days, when the baroness and her children left to join the General in the trials of the long captivity. They journeyed with the captured army to Cambridge, Mass. This beautiful lady, so recently a guest of the King of England, and during her entire life in Germany surrounded by luxury, was now practically a prisoner of war.

It was in this condition that the Hollis soldier saw the family of the Brunswick general. The station and wealth of the baroness prevented her falling into the condition of the ordinary women who followed the army, yet she was subjected to many trials that she little anticipated when leaving her home at Brunswick.

The Baroness Riedesel had the society of Lady Harriet Ackland during a portion of her camp-life in America. She had left her home of luxury in England, and accompanied her husband, Major Ackland, who was in command of the Grenadiers ; but the English officer was captured before the Saratoga Convention, hence the two ladies were not companions in the prison-life in Massachusetts and Virginia.

The whole number of prisoners was 5,791. Of these 2,412 were Germans and Hessians. The munitions captured consisted of 4,647 muskets, 6,000 dozen cartridges, etc. Among the English prisoners were six members of parliament. The journey of three hundred miles was long and wearisome. There was nothing to inspire the march. On the contrary, it was prison-life for all but the officers, who had special privileges, according to the agreement between Burgoyne and Gates at the surrender.

CHAPTER XV

DANVERS. — FIRST SETTLERS. — HOME OF COLONEL
JEREMIAH PAGE. — OFFICE OF GOVERNOR THOMAS.
GAGE. — FAMILY RECOLLECTIONS OF THE LAST
GOVERNOR UNDER THE CROWN. — ORIGIN OF
LUCY LARCOM'S POEM, "A GAMBREL ROOF." — THE
LEXINGTON ALARM. — BURIAL OF DANVERS HE-
ROES KILLED AT MENOTOMY, APRIL 19, 1775. —
THE BELL TAVERN

My stroll about Danvers in quest of hearth-
stones on which glow the embers of Revolutionary
days was most abundantly rewarded. In fact, I
found many homes in this locality where the
family possession has not been broken from the
early days of the Colonial period of our history.
Essex County is remarkably favored in this particular. The name of Governor Endicott calls our
attention to the very beginning of the settlement
of Salem, and the origin of the Colony of Massachusetts Bay in 1628. Danvers was formerly
known as Salem Village, and includes the Endicott grant.

Wisely directed, I made my way to the Page
house in the centre of Danvers. So well kept is

this home of the Page family that I at first
thought I must have mistaken the direction; but
a glance upward revealed the old-fashioned gambrel
roof, so pleasantly described by Miss Lucy Larcom, and I was fully assured that I had reached
the desired house.   I was at once given a welcome

COLONEL JEREMIAH PAGE HOME, DANVERS

by Miss Annie L. Page, the present owner and
occupant, and by her supplied with the unquestionable data to which I now invite the attention
of my readers.

"This house was built by my grandfather, Colonel Jeremiah Page, about the year 1750, and has
always been in our family possession.   Here my
grandparents spent the greater part of their lives;

my father, John Page, was born here; and it is
still my home. To be sure, there have been some
alterations and additions from time to time; but
the same roof-tree has sheltered the three generations, and we have sat by the same hearth-stone.
The beautiful spreading elms in front of the house
were planted by Jeremiah Page about one hundred and fifty years ago. Scores of his descendants
have enjoyed their gracious shade, and been led to
believe with Emerson, 'God's greatest thought in
nature is a tree.'" Jeremiah Page, the builder of
this well-kept house, was the pioneer of brick-
making in Danvers. He was born in Medford in
1722, and when about twenty-one years of age was
invited by Mr. Daniel Andrews to work the clay-
pits of Danvers. In this way he began the manufacture of bricks, which he continued to the close
of his life in 1806.

Among his large contracts was that of supplying the bricks for Fort William at Salem, in 1794.
The young brickmaker married the only daughter
of Mr. Andrews, who is the heroine of the tea-
party represented in "A Gambrel Roof." Here
Jeremiah Page and Sarah Andrews began their
married life, and for a century and a half the
Pages have made a record most creditable to the
town.

Jeremiah Page early in life acted the part of
a patriot, and possessing peculiar qualifications
for leadership was put in military authority in the

Province. He was commissioned as captain of the militia in the year 1773. This was when the rumblings of the Revolution were all about them, and it required decision of character to fulfil the duties of the office. April 27, 1774, he was ordered to take his company to Trask's Hill in Salem for military exercise. Up to this time the majority of the commissioned officers of the first Essex regiment were in sympathy with the government. Among these Colonel William Brown, a member of the Council Board, refused to resign in accordance with request, and so the subordinate officers withdrew. Then was held a meeting of the members of the Alarm and Training Bands of the third company of Danvers, when Jeremiah Page was chosen as captain. This act was indorsed by a pouplar vote, despite the order from the government officials.

It was at this time that the new governor and Captain-general, Thomas Gage, made his appearance in the Province of Massachusetts Bay, and early announced to the Council and gentlemen of the House of Representatives that after the first of June the seat of government would be transferred to Salem; and consequently, on May 28, he adjourned them to meet there on June 7. This order was in anticipation of the closing of the port of Boston on June 1. It was necessary that the king's agent should be near the seat of government, and the demonstration in Boston on the

first day of the enforcement of the Port Bill may
have hastened his removal. On the following
day the royal governor was driven to Danvers, and
here established his official residence. To be
located a little distance out in the country was
the custom with the officers, and Danvers at the

GOVERNOR GAGE'S OFFICE

beginning of June offered great natural attractions. Then, too, it was the residence of Dr.
Samuel Holton, one of the Council. But the
country home, with its attractions, was too far
out ; and the royal governor applied to Jeremiah
Page for a room in his house to serve him as an
office. Having taken up his abode in the town
in a perfectly peaceable manner, this privilege

was not denied him, and the south front room was set off to his use.

Miss Page told me that her father had often from the windows of this room enjoyed looking at the harbor filled with sail, and this view may have influenced the governor in the selection of his office.

The room, with its present attractions, is a vivid reminder of the summer of 1774, when the last English governor who served the country transacted the king's business and smoked his pipe within its walls. As this dignified tenant sat in his office with sympathizing officials, he had little thought that his landlord was dividing the time between his brick-yard and the patriot cause; for even then Captain Page was attending secret meetings with other patriots, where there was plotting against the king and Parliament.

To one accustomed to hear nothing but evil of the king's troops while quartered in and about Boston, it is a relief to gather from the lips of Danvers people some of their ancestors' personal experiences with the soldiers while quartered in the town and loitering about the highways. "The conduct of the royal troops is said to have been very exemplary; and grandfather enjoyed the company of Governor Gage, although he was not in sympathy with him or the cause which he was here to maintain." Another family report, perhaps somewhat biassed, is, "The governor was as pretty a man in the house as I ever saw."

Mrs. Fowler, a daughter of Archelaus Putnam of Danversport, added her testimony, which is kept as a family tradition.

"In September, 1774, I was in an orchard gathering apples when on looking up, I saw two English officers, one of whom commenced climbing over the fence. The other, seeing that I was alarmed, said to him, 'Wait till the girl goes away; do not frighten her by entering the orchard yet.'"

A thrifty farmer whom I chanced to meet and engage in conversation when driving his stock of cows to the barn, said, "Yes, them soldiers used to relieve our folks of the trouble of milking the cows, though unfortunately for the owners, they appropriated the milk to their own use; but no one could wonder at it. Here they were loafing about with little or nothing to do. I wonder they didn't do a good many more tricks."

Seven of these British soldiers died while encamped here, from July 21 to September 5; and their unmarked graves are still pointed out in a field on the south side of Sylvan Street. Perhaps they thus escaped a more bloody death on the following 19th of April.

It has been thought that Governor Gage provided either a whole or part of the furnishings of this room to suit his own liking, and that in his somewhat hasty departure he failed to take his chairs, which remained in the house for a long

time, and were known as "Governor Gage's chairs."
They had green flag seats, and, being but little
prized, were sold at auction after the death of
Captain Page.

Curiosity prompted me to ask this member of
the Page family for the authenticity of the tea-
party story, to which the genial lady replied, "It

PAGE GARRET, DANVERS

was on my grandfather's return from one of the
meetings with his patriot friends that he told
grandmother he had promised to have no more tea
used in his house, and that she must not have any
made. One day soon after, when he was away
from home, two friends came in to spend the afternoon, as was the good old custom. The tempta-
tion, with plenty of tea in the house, was too great.

Grandmother told her visitors what grandfather had commanded; but as he had said *in* and not *upon* the house, she thought they could enjoy this tea without disobeying him, and they slyly went up and enjoyed some on the roof."

This little ruse, so cunningly executed by Mrs. Page, was lost to the family by the death of the good woman, which occurred within a year before it was prudent to reveal any secrets of this nature. "It is apparent that grandmother was the only member of the family who had a part in the tea-drinking, and it was many years before the secret was revealed which furnished the impulse for writing the well-known centennial poem."

"A GAMBREL ROOF," AND HOW THE SECRET WAS MADE KNOWN.

"It was some time between the years 1845 and '50 that a friend of my mother came to make her a visit. She had recently come to Danvers to live, and had never been in our house before. She begged to go up on the roof, and see the place of the secret tea-drinking, which we now heard of for the first time. Her mother was one of the tea-drinkers, and she had often heard her tell the experience. The return to Danvers had recalled the incident to her mind, in which we were very much interested. I told the story to Miss Larcom, who often visited us, and in 1875, when the centennial anniversaries were noticed as they came around, she wrote a poem upon the tea-drinking, of course making liberal use of poetic license."

It seems that afternoon teas were then in order; and Mrs. Page is represented as remonstrating against the decree of her husband, saying, —

> " ' I've asked a friend or two to sup,
>   And not to offer them a cup
>   Would be a sting'y shame.' "

To which Captain Page replies, —

> " ' Wife, I have promised, so must you,
>   None shall drink tea inside my house,
>   Your gossip elsewhere must carouse.' "

The lady courtesied low, —

> " ' Husband, your word is law,' she said,
>   But archly turned her well-set head
>   With roguish poise toward this old roof,
>   Soon as she heard his martial hoof
>   Along the highway go."

The poem then goes on with a description of preparations for the tea-party, the arrival of guests, and the ascent to the novel place selected for the meal. Having reached the elevation, Mrs. Page remarks, —

> " ' A goodly prospect, as I said,
>   You here may see before you spread.
>   *Upon* a house is not *within* it;
>   But now we must not waste a minute,
>   Neighbors, sit down to tea.'

How madam then her ruse explained,
What mirth arose as sunset waned
In the close covert of these trees
No leaf told the reporter breeze ;
  But when the twilight fell,
And hoof-beats rang down Salem road,
And up the yard the colonel strode,
No soul besides the dame and Dill
Stirred in the mansion dim and still,
  The game was played out well.
Let whoso chooses settle blame
Betwixt the colonel and his dame
Or dame and country. That the view
Is from the house-top fine, is true."

It was while sitting by the hearth-stone in Colonel Page's large armchair, where Governor Gage was wont to sit in meditation, and where his opponents also sat, with the shadow of the second generation upon the wall, that I heard from the lips of the third generation the story of the family's experience on the 19th of April, 1775, —

"On the receipt of the alarm my grandfather made haste to rally his men, and they were early on the road to intercept the enemy. His company was one of three of Danvers militia belonging to the Essex Regiment, under the superior command of Colonel Timothy Pickering of Salem. There were in grandfather's company thirty-seven officers and men. In obedience to the orders of a superior officer, grandfather and a part of his men were not in the thickest of the fight at Menotomy ; but his eldest son, my Uncle Samuel, had a very different experience to report. His father had told him that morning before the start that he must stay at home and take care of his mother. His youthful blood was hot. He had seen Governor Gage walk in and out of this house as if he were here in possession, had watched the movements of the troops which came to town to protect him in his royal authority, and he could not be dissuaded from going. He and other Danvers men stationed themselves in the yard of Jason Russell.[1] In this yard were many bundles of shingles, indicating that the proprietor was about to shingle his house. With these they made a sort of barricade, and inside of the enclosure they prepared to attack the British soldiers. When the main column came down the highway, they began firing without thought of the flanking party, and from this they were great sufferers. As Uncle Samuel was driving a cartridge into his gun, he broke his wooden ramrod, and turning to Perley Putnam, asked him to lend his. At that instant a ball from the rear guard of the British shot Putnam dead. When they saw they were discovered and surrounded, they made a desperate struggle for life, and some of them escaped unharmed, Uncle Samuel being one of the more fortunate ones.

Danvers had eight companies which responded to the Lexington alarm. They numbered fully

[1] See " Beneath Old Roof Trees " for house and story.

three hundred men; but we should bear in mind
that the Danvers of 1775 was a very large town,
including, besides the present town known by
that name, that now set off as Peabody. With
the exception of the militia already mentioned,
these companies were minute-men and Alarm
Lists organized by the authority of the Congress
in anticipation of the difficulty. Some of these
companies seemed to be made up with regard to
the neighborly associations of the members. The
messenger apparently first aroused the people of
the south part of the town, now Peabody, whence
it was carried with great rapidity throughout the
entire territory, and a response was immediately
made. "From field and mill, from farm and shop,
from parsonage and humble dwelling," they set
forth to their country's defence : —

> " Swift as the summons came they left
>   The plough, mid furrow, standing still,
>   The half-ground corn-grist in the mill,
>   The spade in earth, the axe in cleft.
>
> They went where duty seemed to call,
>   They scarcely asked the reason why;
>   They only knew they could but die,
>   And death was not the worst of all."

It was Samuel Epes's[1] company that suffered
the most. They belonged in the south part of

---

[1] For Captain Epes's first service in the Revolution, see page 18
of " Beneath Old Roof Trees."

the town.   When the alarm was given, Captain
Epes made haste to Salem, and obtained from
his Colonel permission to march in advance of his
regiment.   They made the journey to Menotomy,
sixteen miles, in four hours.   Gideon Foster, later
general, who had been a member of this company,
appeared in the capacity of captain over a portion
of Epes's men, acting as a separate company; but
the brave acts of these squads cannot be well separated; five of the young men were killed.

The other losses were from Captain Israel
Hutchinson's company, which numbered fifty-three
officers and privates.   They were from Danversport and Beverly.   Two were killed, and some
were wounded.   Joseph Bell was taken prisoner
and carried to Boston, and kept on an English
frigate for two months.   At the expiration of two
days the Danvers men returned to their homes, to
mingle their tears with those who were saddened
by the day's experience.   The bodies of the slain
were taken to their homes, and later interred with
appropriate ceremonies; those belonging to Israel
Hutchinson's company being first taken to his
house, which stood until a recent date where the
railway station is now located at Danversport.

Israel Hutchinson was nearly fifty years of age
at the opening of the Revolution, and had repeatedly proved his bravery by fighting for the king.
He fought at Lake George and Ticonderoga in
1758.   In the following year was with Wolfe when

he scaled the Heights of Abraham, and routed the
French under Montcalm. Thus, with age and experience on his side, he entered the service of the
patriots to the credit of his native town. He was
early in the Revolution raised to the rank of a
colonel. He was in the siege of Boston, and after
the evacuation occupied Fort Hill, and was sent
to New York in the following October. He was
afterwards in command of Fort Lee and Fort
Washington, and crossed the Delaware with Washington in his retreat through New Jersey, and received the approbation of the father of his country.
His love of country was manifested after the war
in faithful service in the Legislature of his State
and in many positions of honor and trust.

As Danvers was not on the enemy's line of
march, there was no great haste to bury the dead,
so the ordinary funeral rites were observed. Two
companies from Salem performed escort duty.
"With reversed arms, muffled drums, and measured
steps, they led the long procession. On the way
they were met by a band of soldiers from Newbury-
port, Salisbury, and Amesbury, marching to join
the army besieging Boston. These formed in single
ranks on each side of the road, and the mournful
procession passed between them. After the bodies
were deposited, three volleys were fired over their
graves, but they could not rouse the slumberers.
No din of resounding arms, no alarms of war, no
convulsions of nature, can disturb them. Nothing

but the voice of the archangel and the trump of
God —

'Can reach the peaceful sleepers there.'"

Thus Danvers lost seven of her strong, promis-
ing young men, one-seventh of the whole number
of the Americans slain that day,
the largest number of any town,
with the exception of Lexington.
A monument to their memory
was erected in 1835, on the six-
tieth anniversary of the battle.
An address was made by General
Foster, one of the survivors of
the battle, of whom there were
nineteen in attendance.

The inscription is as follows.
On the east side:—

BATTLE OF LEXINGTON, APRIL 19, 1775.

SAMUEL COOK, AGED 33 YEARS; BENJ. DALAND, 25; GEORGE SOUTH-
WICK, 25; JOTHAM WEBB, 22; HENRY JACOBS, 22; EBENR.
GOLDTHWAIT, 22; PERLEY PUTNAM, 21;
CITIZENS OF DANVERS FELL ON THAT DAY.

Dulce et decorum est pro patria mori.

(It is sweet and honorable to die for one's country.)

On the reverse side : —

ERECTED BY CITIZENS OF DANVERS ON THE 60TH ANNIVERSARY,
1835.

By the subsequent division of the town, this
monument is to be seen in Peabody. The granite

shaft seems hardly in keeping with its present sur-
roundings, but more in harmony with the buildings seen on that square sixty years ago. Prominent among them was the Old Bell Tavern, so
called from the wooden representation of a bell
which hung from the sign-post. On this was in-
scribed : —

> I'll toll you in, if you have need,
> And feed you well, and bid you speed.

The house was formerly a place of common resort, being on the great thoroughfare from the
east and north to Boston. Here the Salem Regiment, under Colonel Timothy Pickering, halted
for refreshment on their march to Bunker Hill
on the 17th of June, 1775. Their delay aroused
Mrs. Anna Endicott, a patriotic woman, to repri-
mand the colonel in her characteristic manner,
"Why on earth don't you march? Don't you hear
the guns in Charlestown ? "

"This was the place for the villagers to learn
the news of passing events, for every traveller was
expected to furnish his quota. It was the village
exchange, where prices and every-day gossip were
discussed, and the public affairs of the Colonies and
the mother country settled. Here, too, on Sunday
the more remote villagers dismounted from their
horses at the old block, and walked to the meeting-
house ; again to return, after the two hours' sermon,
and partake, in a snug corner, of a dinner from

their well-filled saddle-bags.   This was also the
place where the people met to celebrate public
events.

"The loyal neighbors here collected to mourn
the demise of the good Queen Anne, and rejoice
in the accession of the first George.   His departure and the rise of his son George II. were here
commemorated over the same bowl of punch.
George III. was also welcomed with a zeal that
was only equalled by that with which they drank
confusion to his ministers.   The odious Stamp
Act and all Parliament taxes on the Colonies were
patriotically denounced."   In fact, all the various
acts of the town of Danvers were freely discussed
in this house, which is still remembered by the
old people.

"Nothing created a greater disturbance there
than the tea-meeting of May 28, 1770, when Dr.
Amos Putnam was moderator, and a committee
was chosen 'upon ye public grievance as to ye
duty on tea.'   Besides agreeing to the non-importation Act, it was also voted not to drink foreign
tea, or to allow their families to indulge in the
beverage until the act of Parliament imposing a
duty upon it was repealed, etc. (cases of sickness
excepted).   A committee was chosen to carry
copies of these votes to every household.   All
persons who refused to sign these copies were to
be branded as enemies to the liberties of the people, and their names were to be registered accord-

ingly. Any one detected selling tea was to be
branded as a Tory, and given a ride on a rail. The
keeper of the tavern, Isaac Wilson, was convicted,
but reprieved from his sentence by furnishing the
villagers with an ample bucket of punch, and publicly repeating a couplet prepared for him." We
can hardly appreciate the condition of society,
when a proud landlord is forced to bow his high
head, and repeat, —

> I, Isaac Wilson, a Tory be,
> I, Isaac Wilson, I sells tea.

But
> " A man convinced against his will
> Is of the same opinion still; "

and I am inclined to the belief that the Danvers
landlord was of that class.

Leaving the site of the Bell Tavern and the old
burying-ground near by, where sleep the brave
who died for their country in 1775, I invite my
readers to seek out with me homes that still exist,
as when grandsires of the present owners gathered
their families about the same hearth-stones, and
there by the light of the pine torch or tallow dip
taught lessons of true patriotism.

CHAPTER XVI

DANVERS CONTINUED. — MOSES PORTER'S HOME-
STEAD. — STORY OF HIS PATRIOTISM. — PATRI-
OTIC WOMEN WORK FOR THE SOLDIERS. — HOME
OF DEACON PUTNAM, WHO LED A COMPANY ON
APRIL 19, 1775. — DANVERS MINISTERS IN THE
FIGHT. — THE PUTNAM HOME AND FAMILY. —
GENERAL ISRAEL PUTNAM. — HIS BAPTISM. —
STORY BY "OLD PUT'S" GREAT-GRANDDAUGHTER

UNDER the escort of Rev. Alfred P. Putnam, a
noted son of Danvers, we leave the centre of the
town by the great road to Topsfield, and soon
come to the birthplace of General Moses Porter.
It stands a little back from the modern highway,
and faces confidently to the south.   In these
rooms we may well linger, and ponder the story
of the Revolution.   Patriots of both sexes have
been cradled here, and have left an indelible impression upon the minds of all who thoughtfully
pass through these great square rooms.   It was
originally the home of the Rea family, one of
whom, Dr. Caleb Rea, was a surgeon in a regiment in the expedition against Ticonderoga.   His
sister Sarah married Benjamin Porter; and they
were the parents of Moses Porter, born in 1756,

who became a distinguished general in both wars with England. Although but nineteen years of age at the opening of the Revolution, this man made an enduring record. At the battle of Bunker Hill, in the artillery company of Captain Trevett, when but nine men stood by the captain, Moses Porter was one of them, and displayed superior skill in the management of one of the field pieces. He served in Captain Thomas Foster's company during the siege of Boston, was made lieutenant in 1780, and received promotions until he was head of that arm of the service. Wounds he received, but they never deterred him from remaining in service until his death in 1822. General Porter was wedded to his country; no other bride ever received his affections; for her he was willing to sacrifice his life, and on her bosom he fell asleep.

> " How sleep the brave who sink to rest
> By all their country's wishes blest ! "

Over his grave, in a secluded spot, stands a modest slab on which is read, —

BRIG.· GEN. MOSES PORTER,

OF THE ARMY OF THE U. S. A.

An ardent and inflexible patriot, a brave and honorable soldier, an unassuming and virtuous citizen, a generous and faithful friend. He served his country with distinguished ability and reputation, from the commencement of the Revolutionary war till he expired, full of years and honors, on the 14th of April, A.D., 1822 Æ. 66.

From the old garret of the Porter house have been gathered many of the general's military papers and private correspondence, and from these it is hoped there will yet be prepared an adequate volume to the memory of a great man. Among these letters is found evidence of the patriotic part taken by his sister Sarah in her knitting and sewing for his comfort, and for that of his soldiers. Sarah Porter was but one of hundreds of her sex who acted well a noble part in the great struggle for the independence which we now enjoy.

Those who claim for Moses Porter a more imposing monument may find it in the great bowlder at the rear of his paternal mansion. Standing upon it, I could see in fancy his tiny bare feet climbing over its rugged sides, and the little group gathered there by the tired mother, who, coming out for rest, had taken the opportunity to impress helpful lessons upon the youthful minds intrusted to her care.

This bowlder, towering above all others, seems to typify the man, who, in his firmness of purpose and inflexibility of character, stood out alone and above others, and when confronted by duty acted as though saying, —

> "Come one, come all, this rock shall fly
> From its firm base as soon as I."

Leaving the Porter House, in which my guide has a family interest, we pass on to the Putman

house, on the paternal homestead of Rev. Alfred
Porter Putnam, the guide for the hour. It is
reached by a drive from the highway through well-
cultivated grounds. The house is typical of its
period, made picturesque by a large tree in front
and a small one at a corner. "From here," said
my guide, "went my great-grandfather, Deacon
Edmund Putman, at the head of his company of
seventeen neighbors on the 19th of April, 1775."

But before tracing out the footprints of these
minute-men, let us consider for a moment the
origin of the house. It is supposed to have been
built by Daniel Rea, the head of that family in
this country ; and after its possession by three
generations of the name it was purchased by Edmund Putman, who carried on the trades of tailor
and farmer. As a testimonial of his honest dealing and good standing with his neighbors, we find
that in 1762 he was chosen deacon of the First
Church, in which position he served twenty-three
years. "My grandsire was chosen captain of the
Alarm List of the third company in this town on
the 6th of March, 1775. Rev. Benjamin Balch
was chairman of the meeting. The vote for
grandfather was unanimous, and also that for lieutenant and sergeant, the former being for Rev.
Mr. Balch, and the latter for Tarrant Putnam."

In this house, now occupied by the sixth generation from Edmund Putnam, though of a different name (Fowler), we catch glimpses of the fading

scenes of the days of trial.   Here met in council
the minister, the deacon, and faithful churchmen,
and from here they went out to act the part of
Christian patriots.

Other ministers of Danvers used their influence
in the patriot cause.   Mr. Holt of the Middle Pre-
cinct (Peabody) was known to say, "I had rather
live on potatoes than submit."   He supplied himself with a musket, and drilled with Captain Epes's
company.   Mr. Wadsworth of the village parish
was very ardent, and was seen at the North River
Bridge, Salem, with his musket in hand ; and to
his words of persuasion more than all else is doubtless due the escape from the first slaughter.

In the March following, Captain Putnam was
unanimously chosen as selectman, and also as an
assessor.   This was at a time when these officers
in any town called for the exercise of the best of
mature judgment.   He was also a member of the
committee in 1778 to consider the report of a form
of government.

But Deacon Edmund was only one of many
Putnams of Danvers who responded to the Lexington alarm.   The returns show that thirty-four
of the name marched from Danvers, and had some
part in that day's struggle.   As we have already
seen, Perley Putnam was killed, and his brother
Nathan was wounded.

NOTE. — A newspaper of those times furnishes evidence of the
efforts made to recover fire-arms lost by the Provincials on April 19,

thus proving the scarcity of munitions of war. From the *New England Chronicle* or the *Essex Gazette* of May 29, 1775, is gathered the following: " Lost in the battle of Menotomy by Nathan Putnam, of Capt. Hutchinson's Company, who was there badly wounded, a French Firelock, marked D. No. 6, with a marking iron, on the Breech. Said Putnam carried it to a Cross Road, near a mill. Whoever has said Gun in Poffeffion is defired to return it to Col. Manffield of Lynn, or to the Selectmen of Danvers, and he shall be rewarded for his trouble."

While this town was the place of the first Putnam settlement, the name was by no means confined to Danvers when Provincial government was overthrown. Eighty-six names, all of Danvers line, are recorded at the State House as turning out on April 19 ; and within two centuries from the time the first John drove his bounds in Danvers, about thirty-five hundred of his descendants were abroad in the land. Coming in to the Putnam headquarters, we are inclined to halt at a modern house on this old farm, better known as "Oak Knoll," the home of the lamented Quaker bard. But it is to the birthplace of General Israel Putnam that we are making our way. Witch houses, Rebecca Nourse and Giles Corey, must not allure us from our course.

What school-boy does not open his eyes and prick up his ears at the mere mention of "Old Put"? But my own confession is, that I had almost fallen into the habit of regarding this man as a sort of monster, struggling in a dim mythical haze ; but when I turned in at the open gate, and stood at the threshold of the birthplace of that hero, I came fully to my senses. Oh, how refreshing it is, in these days of constant changes in ownership of real estate, to find this home still retained by the family.! Our knock at the front door met with a response from one by the name of Putnam, as did that of guests a century and a half ago, when the young man Israel walked in and out the same doorway. The genuine old-school lady, by word and smile, extended a cordial welcome ; and we were at once assured by the words of Miss Susan Putnam that she was of the seventh generation of the family on that farm. The line is John, Thomas, Joseph, David, Israel, Daniel, and Susan, who furnished the information.

The front and more modern part, which first meets the eye of the visitor, was built in 1744; while that in the rear, with its own front door, is supposed to date back to 1650. The part most prominent in the cut was the original house, built by Thomas, grandfather of Israel. It was while the northeast blasts were piling up the January snows of 1718 that in the upper room of this humble home the boy Israel was born. Joseph and Elizabeth (Porter) Putnam were the happy parents. This son was nearly a month old before he was taken to the meeting-house for the rite of baptism. The unusual delay may be accounted for by a desire of the mother to accompany the father to the altar of baptism ; but more likely was

BIRTHPLACE OF GENERAL ISRAEL PUTNAM

the result of the very severe weather of that month, which Cotton Mather describes as follows : —

" Another snow came on which almost buried ye Memory of ye former, with a storm so famous that Heaven laid an Interdict on ye Religious Assemblies throughout ye Country, on this Lord's day, ye like whereunto had never been seen before. The Indians near an hundred years old, affirm that their Fathers never told them of anything that equalled it."

Turning back to that Sabbath morning of early February, we can see the family horse led up to the door of the home, the mother take her seat on the pillion, with the babe carefully wrapped in its bearing-cloth in her arms, and the father mount to his seat in front, take up the reins, and start off to the meeting-house. They make their way slowly, for the path is rough indeed, cut out of the great banks of snow which are piled in heaps on either side.

What a scene is this when the devoted parents, shivering from the ride, enter the cold, barnlike meeting-house, and carry their babe to the altar, their frozen shoes clattering on the rough boards of the broad aisle, telling the measure of each step as they go. While the mother unwraps the babe, the father makes known by gentle whisper the name selected for his last born, and the Rev. Peter Clark cracks the ice in the christening basin, dips his fingers to the water, and laying them upon the innocent brow, says, " Israel, I

baptize thee in the name of the Father, and of the
Son, and of the Holy Ghost, Amen." Surely with
the treatment of the babes of those days there
was a continuous example of the survival of the
fittest.   Born of the best of New England stock,
and of parents accustomed to hardships, and enduring this early test, the boy Israel grew and developed a marvellous physical activity and power
of endurance, which served him well, and enabled
him to do at the age of threescore what the ordinary man of forty years would quail beneath.

Desirous of entering the house by the door of
Israel's day, we made our way out and around to
the front door of long ago, and crossed the threshold familiar to his restless feet.   Up the narrow
staircase we went, and into the room where the
child first saw the light.   A board partition makes
two apartments of the original room, but there
can be no mistake as to the part in question;
for there is the open fireplace, with its smutty
back, and the rude fire-dogs, as when the flames
crackled on the hearth, and rolled up the chimney
to mingle with the wintry blast of 1718.   There
are the rough-hewn posts at the corners, and thick
projecting beams overhead, with no attempt at
disguise.   There is little else here that is tangible
to remind us of him whom we delight to honor as
Major-General Israel Putnam; but as we love the
hard-handed yeomanry who formed the real back-
bone of the Revolution, so we love to linger on

the ground which their feet have trodden, and
hear from the lips of one of the seventh generation the stories confirmed which we have often
heard before.

"Robust and full of energy, he was a boy given
to sports, and to feats of strength and daring,
often the champion of courageous exploits, all of
which were somewhat prophetic of his more extraordinary powers and achievements in maturer
years."

Much of Israel's boyhood was spent in Boxford,
at the home of his stepfather, where perhaps the
school advantages were no better than those of
Danvers, and the boy's education was defective.
When he had reached the age proper for him to
set up for himself, he returned to the old homestead, and settled on a portion of the farm, and
built a small house, the cellar of which still
remains. He married, July 19, 1739, Hannah,
daughter of Joseph and Mehitable (Putnam) Pope,
and the young couple established a home for themselves, adding another to the then almost score of
Putnam homes. After the birth of a son Israel,
the young couple, seized with the spirit of adventure, with many others set out for broader fields ;
and the remainder of the story of "Old Put" will
be found in another connection in this series.

The great willow-tree standing in the yard reminds us of many changes since Israel Putnam
left the homestead. It was planted by a slave of

the family, who is still remembered for her faithfulness, although she has been sleeping for many years with those whom she served.

The Putnams who remain at the old home are descendants of David, brother of General Israel, and none of his line of the family have ever settled in Danvers; but they are numerous in the world, a large group of them being found in Bedford, Mass. We will now make a digression to hear the story by a great-granddaughter of General Israel Putnam, Mrs. Mary (Waldo) Webber.

She was born at Pomfret, Conn., August 15, 1807. She is the daughter of John Augustus Gleason and Elizabeth Waldo, and granddaughter of Samuel Waldo and Mary (Molly) daughter of General Israel Putnam.

A large part of Mrs. Webber's life has been spent in Bedford,— the town where Israel, a cousin of the general, settled about the time that the Connecticut home was established, the same spirit of adventure having actuated both this one who settled in Bedford and the one who went to Connecticut to leave the Danvers settlement. The Bedford people remember their Israel Putnam with pride; for he was a selectman at the beginning of the town, and one of the first deacons of the church, and a benefactor of the new settlement.

It was early in the present century that the Gleason branch of the Putnam family made its way to Bedford, Lewis Putnam Gleason being the pioneer at this time.

Mrs. Webber spent some of her girlhood with her grandmother, Elizabeth Waldo.   Her longing

MARY (WALDO) WEBBER, GREAT GRANDDAUGHTER OF "OLD PUT"

for amusement was gratified, when sitting at the old hearth-stone with her grandmother, by listening to the stories treasured in the family of the wolf-hunter, the Indian fighter, and the hero of Bunker Hill.

A GREAT-GRANDDAUGHTER'S STORY OF GENERAL
ISRAEL PUTNAM

As Told on Her Eighty-Ninth Birthday.

" Yes, I keep old grandfather's picture hanging
in my room. It seems but yesterday that I sat by
the side of Grandmother Waldo, for whom I was
named, and heard her tell of the trials of Grandfather Putnam. Those of the Indian wars and
the wolves charmed me much; and I often found
the tears running down my cheeks, as I hid my
head beneath her apron, when she told of the hair-
breadth escapes from the savages. I suppose he
had the fight born in him; for when but a boy he
first displayed it in Boston, whither he had gone
on a visit. He was doubtless dressed in the coarse
cloth spun and woven at the old home in Danvers,
and probably looked rather queer in the eyes of
those sons of wealthy merchants and office-holders
of the Province. They began to pick upon him.
He bore it for a while, but at length challenged
one of the brilliantly attired youths, twice his size,
and vanquished him, to the great amusement of a
crowd of people who looked on to see the rustic's
performance.

" My ancestor's Connecticut home was at Pomfret, known as Brooklyn since 1783. He had just
started in as a pioneer, and was laboring hard to
clear some land bought of Governor Jonathan

1. Harold Augustus Gleason.
2. Clifford Raymond Gleason.
3. Carrie Putnam Webber.
4. Paul Baron Webber.
5. Marcus Bernard Webber.
6. Lewis Gleason Webber.
7. Ruth Isabel Gleason.
8. Jennie Frances Gleason.
9. Lewis Edward Pierce.
10. Bertha Gleason Pierce.
11. Marie Withington Gleason.
12. Dorothy Stearns Gleason.
13. Gertrude Evelyn Gleason.
14. Arthur Lewis Gleason.
15. Prudence Markham.
16. Waldo Wood Gleason.

Belcher. He had a family to care for, and it was
annoying to have his sheep continually carried
off by wolves. In one night he had a large flock
of sheep and goats killed, besides many lambs and
kids wounded. This was done by a she-wolf,
which, with her whelps, had for several years in-
fested the locality. The young were commonly
destroyed by hunters, but the old one was too
cunning for them.

"At length grandfather and others formed a
company to hunt in turns until they should kill
the old enemy. It was known that, having lost
the toes from one foot by a steel trap, she made
one track shorter than the other. This betrayed
her route on the snow. She was driven into a
den a little distance from grandfather's house.
The folks came together with dogs, guns, straw,
fire, and sulphur to attack her. The hounds went
in, and came out in a bleeding condition. The
smoke of burning straw did not start her, and the
fumes of brimstone were to no purpose.

"At length, tired of all this, grandfather proposed to his negro man to go down in and shoot
her; but he refused to comply, so grandfather decided to go, and went regardless of the protests of
his companions. He knew wild animals did not
like a close contact with fire, so he stocked himself with birch bark, and prepared for the attack.
He threw off his coat and waistcoat, and having
a long rope fastened around his legs, by which he

might be pulled back, he entered head foremost, with blazing torch in hand.

" He went in, and down, and soon saw the eyes of the beast glaring at him. Startled at the approach of the flaming torch, she gnashed her teeth and growled. He then gave a signal to the men at the end of the rope, who pulled him out so rapidly as to strip off his garments, and some flesh as well. But with his gun loaded with nine buckshots, and torch in hand, he retraced the course. He fired and killed the animal, was pulled out, and after reviving from almost suffocation, he went in a third time, and the creature was taken out.

"Grandfather had some trying experiences in the French and Indian wars, but he awed the savages so they dared not kill him. They thought he had a charmed life, and called him 'a god or a devil,' they could not tell which. By his services against the French and their Canadian and Indian allies, he acquired a good reputation as a soldier and a hero ; and so he had gained many honors from the authorities of Connecticut, and entered the service of the Revolution with his well-earned popularity."

CHAPTER XVII

DANVERS CONTINUED. — KING HOOPER AND GOV-
ERNOR GAGE. — CAMP OF THE ENEMY. — HOLTON
FAMILY. — SAMUEL HOLTON'S LETTER TO DANIEL
PUTNAM. — KING GEORGE'S WHIPPING–POST. —
WASHINGTON'S LETTER TO MAJOR LOWE. —
MAJOR–GENERAL GIDEON FOSTER. — LIST OF
EIGHT DANVERS COMPANIES

AFTER the digression of the previous chapter,
made in order to follow the life of Israel Putnam,
we now turn again to listen to Rev. Alfred P. Putnam, our Danvers guide, and learn of the King
Hooper house.

"The Hon. Robert Hooper was a wealthy merchant and acknowledged autocrat of Marblehead.
He had become weary of his limited surround-
ings, pushed out into the country, and spent
a portion of his rapidly accumulating wealth in
building a princely residence. The site is a part
of the twenty acres formerly laid out to Governor
Endicott, who, like Governor John Winthrop, always was on the lookout for desirable lands, and
became the possessor of thousands of acres. This
house was built about 1770, and here the merchant

set up his home with the expectation of spending his last years in the quiet of Danvers, and in the full enjoyment of his abundance. This is the home to which reference has already been made, where Governor Gage found a cordial welcome when moving out of Boston in June, 1774. The patriotic people of this town were not well pleased with the coming of the governor, yet there was something interesting to them in the splendor which attended his presence among them."

Mr. Putnam resumed by saying, " At the time of the coming of this Marblehead merchant into our midst, there was little affinity between our grandparents and any one who favored the Stamp Act.   But Robert Hooper was rated as very honest and kind-hearted, and they received him with becoming grace.   When he opened his doors to the royal governor, who was here to force our people to submit to the obnoxious acts of Parliament, the farmers began to look upon their new neighbor as a Loyalist, which he proved to be ; and his name was reported to the town as one of those inimical to the cause of their country."

According to Drake, this mansion is one of the best specimens of later Colonial architecture in existence, and we readily accept the decision.   The massive building has an elegant front door leading into the hall.   This extends the whole length of the house, with doors on either side into extensive apartments.   The house is surmounted by a gam-

KING HOOPER HOUSE, DANVERS

brel roof with an ornamental balustrade at the top. It is of wood; but the front is set off in panelling so as to represent stone, and painted a cold gray, which adds to the deception. In fact, the old mansion bears a strong resemblance to the stone Hancock house which formerly stood on Beacon Street, Boston. The Hooper house is set back from the highway, surrounded by spacious, well-kept grounds, and approached by shaded avenues. The beautiful trees have already afforded a name for the historic place, "The Lindens." If, as the Slavonians imagined, the goddess of love ever dwelt in this variety of tree, we fancy she was not in power at this place during the stay of Governor Gage.

The public is indebted to the Peabody family for the restoration and preservation of this Colonial mansion, which the proud builder never enjoyed after the Revolution. Even a public renunciation of his Loyalist principles did not fully reinstate him in the confidence of his neighbors. His business was ruined, and his fortune wasted, so that he died a poor man.

Through the courtesy of Mr. and Mrs. Francis Peabody, we were given a welcome to the house, and roamed about under the direction of our guide, familiar to each well-kept apartment. The elaborate carvings and adornments remind one of other houses of the time, where once dwelt those proud families derisively spoken of as Tories; yet they were doubtless conscientious in their adherence to the Crown, but were, nevertheless, ruthlessly driven from their homes. While the furnishings of each apartment call forth our admiration, they cannot blind us to those memories which now become a greater reality than ever before.

At this hearth-stone we see the clear flame of loyalty fade away to smouldering embers, and at length become entirely extinguished. Through the spacious hall below and above, and over the gently ascending staircase, we trace the footsteps of · Governor Thomas Gage. We see him in the drawing-room surrounded by his admirers, among whom is his private secretary, Thomas Flucker, father-in-law of General Henry Knox. We watch him as, with anxiety stamped upon his brow, he paces these rooms in waiting for the troops ordered from Castle William in Boston Harbor. It must be that he has detected signs of dissatisfaction, and concludes that his personal safety depends upon an armed force. He has heard that the General Court in session has appointed five delegates to Philadelphia, taken steps to aid the suffering people in Boston, and also determined to cut off all importations of British goods. He has sent his secretary with a proclamation dissolving the Court, but to his surprise he finds that Samuel Adams and his associates had already dissolved it without the governor's aid; and thus ended the last General Court under a royal governor in the Massachusetts Bay Colony. How much of this Governor Gage apprehended while pacing these rooms we do not know; but from the press of that time we learn: "Last Thursday two companies of the 64th Regiment arrived here from Castle William. The next day they landed, and marched through the town on the way to his Excellency's seat, near which they are now encamped."

As we leave the mansion, and pass down the avenue, we see in front of us, on the opposite side of the road, the camping-ground of the redcoats, who were there as the governor's guard. King Hooper's neighbors were not entirely ignorant of military life; but when they saw the sentinels pacing back and forth on their own highway, and saw the camp-fires of an enemy kindled within view of their own homes, they began more earnestly to stock up with bullets and cartridges, clean up the old muskets, and sharpen the rusty swords which for a time had been turned into pruning-hooks.

But it was the people over at Salem who caused Gage the greatest anxiety. They utterly disregarded his proclamation, and, in fact, ordered him to leave the town. Strange conduct, we may say, for a people towards their governor: but we must bear in mind that they had no voice in his appointment; and while there was nothing disagreeable or despotic in him personally, he was the local representative of the despised king across the water. The governor's stay in the country was cut short ; and on Saturday, August 27, 1774, he left his Danvers home, soon followed by the guard, who broke camp, and marched over the road to Boston.

The most vivid reminder of the days of Governor Gage at the Hooper mansion is the bullet-hole in the now abandoned front door. The good people of Danvers have different stories in regard to this ; but the more common belief is that when Provincial troops were marching by the mansion, some of the boys in homespun seized upon the lead ornaments of the gate-posts, when the master of the house opened the door, and remonstrated in plain language, to which they replied with a reckless shot, which left its mark in the door, and there still remains.

In leaving the temporary abode of Governor Gage and the camping-ground of his guard, we instinctively turn to the home of Judge Samuel Holton,[1] who, although an undoubted Whig, did much to prevent an outbreak among his neighbors when the royal governor was in the town of Danvers. How different are the feelings of the visitor when crossing the threshold of the Holton house from those experienced at the Hooper mansion. No one can doubt the patriotism of the oc-

[1] Joseph Holton was the first of the family to settle in Salem Village, Danvers. He was succeeded by Henry, Samuel Sr., and Samuel Jr., who was better known as Doctor or Judge Holton.

cupants here from the earliest days of the family possession. The house is thought to have been built about the year 1650, and passing in family succession was the home of Samuel of the fourth generation, who was born here in 1738, and was a practising physician in the town when troubles with the mother country began to take form. He was their representative in the General Court for the year 1768, and was chosen to join a convention of delegates from the towns of the Province, to be held in Fanueil Hall on the twenty-second day of September. This lasted several days, during which the difficulties between the Colonies and the mother country were freely discussed. Dr. Holton had an active part in this convention, called by vote of a Boston town meeting without authority of the royal government. We find him also on the town's Committee of Correspondence, and may well conclude that this old house was the scene of many interesting discussions, where none but patriots gathered familiarly about this hearthstone.

The discipline which was undertaken to be maintained by Governor Gage's guard is inferred from the record that " near the encampment was a large oak-tree, afterwards known as King George's whipping-post. When the frigate Essex was built in Salem, the tree was felled ; and on hewing the timber the iron staple to which the soldiers had been confined for punishment was found inbedded in the wood. King George's whipping-post was converted into the stern-post of the Essex frigate."

Very soon after the departure of Gage and his troops from this neighborhood, the people of the town assembled and instructed their representative, Dr. Holton, as follows : —

Sir, — As we have now chosen you to Represent us in the Great and General Court to be holden in Salem on Wednesday the 5th day of October next ensuing : we do hereby Instruct you that in all your doings as a member of the House of Representatives, you adhere firmly to the Charter of this Province granted by their Majesties King William and Queen Mary, and that you do no act which can be possibly construed into an Acknowledgment of the Act of the British Parliament for Altering the government of Massachusetts Bay, more especially that you acknowledge the Honorable Board of Counsellors Elected by the General Court at their session in May last, as the only rightful and constitutional Council of this Province. And as we have Reason to believe that a Conscientious Discharge of your Duty will produce your Dissolution as an House of Representatives, we do hereby impower and Instruct you to join with the Members who may be sent from this and the neighboring Towns in the Province, and meet with them at a time to be agreed on, in a General Provincial Congress, to act upon such matters as may come before you, in such a manner as shall appear to be most conducive to the true Interest of this Town and Province, and most likely to preserve the liberties of America

It was on November 21, 1774, that the government of England was here practically repudiated; for the town voted to adhere strictly to all the resolves and recommendations of the Provincial Congress, and Dr. Holton was their unanimous choice as representative. It was about this time that Dr. Holton relinquished his profession and private business, and devoted himself to the service of his country. He was chosen first major of the first regiment in Essex. When serving in the Provincial Congress he wrote a letter to Mr. Daniel Putnam, from which we gather much of interest : —

> COUNCIL CHAMBER,
> *Monday, July* 15, 1776.

Sir, — When I arrived on Saturday last at Watertown the Court was about rising, and I had no opportunity to converse with the members about the town giving so large a bounty. Therefore I can give no advice about what sum is proper to give the men that are willing to go. But in general I advise that the Resolves of the Court be complied with as far as possible, and as soon as possible. What sum of money Captain Flint, yourself, and Lieut. Putnam shall think I ought to pay towards raising the men, I shall endeavor to comply with, but I do not doubt you will consider I spend all my time in the public service, and have greatly hurt my constitution by close application to public business, and an aged father sick, and no help but what I am obliged to give a great price for, which makes it very difficult for me ; but I am ready to spend my estate and life for my bleeding country if called to it. The Court was prorogued on Saturday last to the last Wednesday of August, but last evening an Express arrived here from the Honorable Congress, and another Express from Gen. Washington. The Congress have sent us their Declaration, declaring the Colonies independent States ; and the General informs us of his ordering three of the Regiments of the Continental troops at or near Boston to march immediately to Ticonderoga, so that I suppose the Court must be called together again immediately. Give my kind regards to Capt. Flint and Lieut. Putnam, and let them know from me that I desire them to 'xert themselves for their distressed country, for we have everything to get or everything to lose. We have not a day to lose, no, not even an hour. Independency is the best news I ever heard, and as I trust our cause is just, we ought to put our trust in the God of Armies, and not fear what man can do in an unjust cause. I am, Sir, with great regard,

Your humble Servant,

S. HOLTON, JR.

MR. DANIEL PUTNAM.

We see by this letter that Samuel Holton was ready to redeem the pledge to give life and fortune if needful. We find him in the Continental Congress for a period of five years ; a member of the Constitutional Convention ; two years in the United States Congress ; Representative to the General Court eight years ; five years a senator, and twelve years a councillor, and twice presidential elector. He was for thirty-two years Judge of the Court of Common Pleas ; thirty-five years Judge of the Court of General Sessions ; fifteen years Chief Justice ; nineteen years Judge of the Probate Court for Essex County ; and twenty-four years town treasurer.

It is indeed becoming for us to make this halt at the home of a man who served his town and country so well, and while passing through the rooms sacred to his memory make anew our resolutions for good citizenship.

Simple indeed is the slab erected on the grave of this faithful man, who lived to fully enjoy that freedom for which he labored and sacrificed. He died January 2, 1816, aged seventy-eight years.

"Peace to the Memory of a Man of Peace.'

On October 19, 1895, the sons of the American Revolution of Massachusetts, together with the children of the American Revolution of Danvers, gathered about the grave of "Hon. Samuel Holton," and there placed the marker of the "S. A. R," and held a patriotic service. Holton Street and high school are reminders of this noted son of the town of Danvers.

We have thus far traced the footprints of four of the Danvers companies to the homes of their captains, and we naturally desire to locate the remaining four. South Danvers, near Salem, was the home of Captain Caleb Lowe, who with twenty-two neighbors marched to Menotomy and Cambridge on April 19. They are credited with fifty miles of travel, and two days' service on the Lexington Alarm List. Captain Lowe became major, and was in command under Washington on the Hudson River. It is apparent that he had the confidence of the commander-in-chief, who on his return from Connecticut in September, 1780, ad-

dressed a letter to him.   The circumstances were
briefly as follows : Washington, accompanied by
General Knox, Lafayette, and other officers of
his suite, made a visit to the Count Rochambeau
and the Chevalier de Ternay at Hartford, where
they arranged plans for their next campaign ; and
on their return discovered that General Arnold,
in command at West Point, had plotted treason
with Major André, adjutant-general of the British army.   The plans had failed ; André was captured, but Arnold escaped, and there was not a
little confusion in the army.   When such a man
as Arnold, a hero of Ticonderoga in the first of
the war, had proved false, Washington must have
been in doubt as to who was worthy of confidence, but found in Caleb Lowe a faithful officer.
The original letter, now in possession of the Danvers Historical Society, reads as follows : —

Sir, You will be pleased to march early to-morrow morning with all the militia under your command and proceed to
the landing at West Point.   You will send an officer on to
this place, by whom you will receive further orders.   Colonel
Gouvior the bearer of this will apply to you for an officer
and a small party of men.   These you will furnish.
     I am sir with esteem   Yr mo ob'et Servt,
                                        GO. WASHINGTON.
HEAD QUARTERS, ROBINSON'S HOUSE,
     25th Sept., 1780, 1–2 after 7 o'clock P.M.
                    MAJOR LOW, at Fishkill.

With the original letter in my hand, there came
to me as never before a realizing sense of the sor-

row that burdened the heart of Washington when penning the lines, and later when on October 2, 1780, the rules of war were carried out, and the handsome, amiable young British officer suffered death by hanging at Tappan in the State of New York.

Samuel Flint, another of the Danvers captains, with forty-five men, is credited with forty miles of travel. An officer once asked Captain Flint where he could be found on a certain occasion. His reply was, "Where the enemy is, there will you meet me." Captain Flint was in the army at the siege of Boston, and was later killed at the head of his company at Stillwater, October 7, 1777. He was the only officer from Danvers who perished in the Revolution.

Asa Prince, with thirty-five men, was at Lexington; and his company is credited with fifty miles of travel. He was also at Bunker Hill and at Lake George. On June 17, when attempting to cross the Neck when the cannon-balls were flying from a British frigate, he dislocated his ankle, but hastily put the bone back into the socket, and went on his way.

Captain John Putnam was at the head of an Alarm Company consisting of thirty-five men, seven of whom were Putnams. They travelled forty miles, and served like the rest two days. On the grave-stone erected to the memory of a Danvers patriot we read: —

IN MEMORY OF

CAPT. JEREMIAH PUTNAM,

WHO DIED SEPT. 16, 1799. AGED 63 YEARS.

AN OFFICER UNDER THE IMMORTAL WASHINGTON.

This modest stone, what few vain mortals can,
May truly say: Here lies an Honest man.

Gideon Foster, who reached the rank of major-general, lived until 1845. There are those in Danvers to-day who with pride recall their many conversations with General Foster, the comrade of Warren and Prescott and Stark, and one who had held official intercourse with Ward, Putnam, and Washington. They repeat the story of General Foster as he gave it on the occasion of laying the cornerstone of the Revolutionary monument in Danvers.

"I was then twenty-six years of age. About ten days before I had been chosen to command a company of minute-men, who were at all times to be in readiness at a moment's warning. They were so ready. They all assembled on the very spot where we are this day assembled; they all went; and in about four hours from the time of meeting, they travelled on foot (full half the way upon the run) sixteen miles, and saluted the enemy. This they did most effectually, as the records of that day most clearly prove. I discharged my musket at the enemy a number of times (I think eleven), with two balls each time, and with well-directed aim. My comrade, Mr. Cleaves of Beverly, who was then standing by my side, had his finger and ramrod cut away by a shot from the enemy. Whether my shots took effect I cannot say ; but this I can say, if they did not, it was not for the want of determined purpose in him who sent them."

Captain Gideon Foster's company was stationed at Little Cambridge (Brighton) at the time of the battle of Bunker Hill. He was ordered by General Ward to escort a load of ammunition to Charlestown. He met the Americans when on their retreat, and supplied them with powder for one more attempt. This is the account, " We took the ammunition in casks, and conveyed it in wagons, and delivered it freely, with our hands and our dippers, to their horns, their pockets, their hats, and whatever else they had that would hold it. I well remember the blackened appearance of those busy in this work, not unlike those engaged in the delivery of coal on a hot summer's day. At the same time we were thus occupied, the enemy's shot were continually whistling by ; but we had no time to examine their character or dimensions."

CHAPTER XVIII

THE STORY OF DILL, A NEGRO SLAVE IN THE REVOLUTION

THE willows had put forth their downy catkins, the blue-birds and robins were abroad in the fields, and all nature had said farewell to grim winter. The spring of 1766 was so far advanced that in early April Mrs. Jeremiah Page ventured to allow her group of little ones to play out in the garden a few hours each sunny day. What a merry group they were, six bright-eyed little children! and what a relief to the mother when she could safely allow them to be out-of-doors, after the long winter, when amusement had to be furnished in the limited apartments of the home, which, however, compared favorably with any of the farmhouses of the day. To be sure, Sarah, the eldest and namesake of the mother, now fifteen years of age, assumed not a little of the care; but with the opening spring came her opportunity for attending school, and neither Jeremiah Page nor his wife would allow anything to keep her from the few weeks of schooling furnished for the girls of the town. The girls must be able to read and write;

and the Pages, who were in advance of some of the people, were desirous that their daughters should know a little "reckoning." "It won't come amiss," said the father, when being charged with trying "to tiptoe" his girls above the neighbors. Hannah, the baby, was less than a year and a half, while the birthdays of the other four ranged between 1751 and this spring-time.

The fond parents stood one day at the south window of the best room looking at the merry group, while, like so many samples of perpetual motion, they were amusing themselves around the trunk of the elm whose buds were already swollen to bursting.

Just then there came a cry of alarm. Lydia, who had been too ambitious, stumbled, and was trampled upon by her eager pursuer. There was no one but mother who had the balm for every wound of flesh or mind, and she was as prompt to respond as were the children to give the alarm. Having effectually applied the remedy and set all to rights, she rejoined her husband, who now began to realize as never before the cares which each day brought to his faithful wife. The illness which had detained Mr. Page from his brick-yard for that one day had afforded an opportunity which the early morning and late evening hours had not granted him.

"Wife, you must have more assistance," said Jeremiah Page. "I see these burdens are wear-

ing upon you.   We need a younger slave.   Dinah
is too old and clumsy to keep an eye out for those
children, and catch them when they run away
from the house as they are bound to do."

At this serious moment of parental discussion,
black Dinah came rolling into the room.   She had
overheard the charge as to her abilities, and lost
no time to vindicate herself.

"Lor's sake, Massa Page," exclaimed Dinah,
"I car for dem ar chillen jest as well as ever I
did. I lubs every one on 'em, specially Hannah;" at the same time stooping to the babe,
whom she grabbed up, and covering its little rosy
cheeks with audible kisses from her great lips,
she waddled away.

"Dinah is willing and faithful as far as she can
be," said Mr. Page, standing in the centre of the
room, and looking towards the door which Dinah
had just closed behind her and the youngest of
the group; "but she would be of more use in
some family where she could sit in the chimney-
corner and knit. She's become too large for us.
I must trade her off. The first day I'm down to
Salem I'm going to see if Tapley has any fresh
stock on hand. It's time for some spring black-
birds from Guinea to be in." Mrs. Page agreed
with her husband as to her needs, though she
rather disliked to part with her good cook; but
like a dutiful wife (particularly of those times)
listened to the reasoning of her husband, the

head of the family, and quietly assented to his
further remarks in regard to domestic service.
"These black women depreciate in value very
rapidly after they reach middle life. Dinah is
as large as two now, and takes up lots of room.
I know the children are attached to her, but
they'll soon learn to like a young and lively girl."

It is evident that Jeremiah Page ruled in his
family affairs as well as in his brick-yards, but he
had a most tender regard for the wife of his youth
and mother of his children. Now that he had
learned from personal observation what her daily
cares were, he was bent upon relieving her.

Had this family been the only one in the possession of slaves, here would be a time to pause
and interject a series of execrations; but the
course pursued in this family was such as the
customs of the time approved. The families in
the highest walks of society were the most thoroughly equipped with colored slaves, or servants
as they were sometimes called. Slaves of both
sexes were generally found in the families of
the clergy, and it was no uncommon thing for a
people to present a slave to their pastor as an
act of tender regard.

The Rev. John Hancock of Lexington, grandfather of John Hancock the patriot, received such
a gift from his church; Rev. Joseph Sewall of the
Old South Church, Boston, was similarly remembered; Rev. Joseph Emerson of Malden, father of

Rev. William Emerson of Concord, had his slave, but whether acquired by purchase or gift is not known. Rev. Samuel Moody of York, Maine, says by letter to his granddaughter Hannah, daughter of Rev. Joseph Emerson, —

" My love to your brothers and sisters, not forgetting Dinah ; she also is espoused to Christ in her Baptism, and she must love, honor, and obey ye Lord."

Colonel Page made repeated trips to Salem, but found no negroes on sale who gave promise of what he needed ; so he left his order with John Tapley, who agreed to notify him of the arrival of the first freight from Africa in which there were any negroes likely to answer his purpose.

It was on the morning of April 19, 1766, that the colonel rose from the breakfast-table, lathered and shaved, called for his surtout, and said by way of explanation, " Tapley has sent up word by Putnam that he's got some fresh African stock that'll just suit me ; so I'm going down before I go over to the yard. If any one calls, tell 'em I'll be home before noon," with this he mounted his horse and galloped off.

Mr. Page was a business man, and not long about a trade when he found what he wanted. " In bonds yet, are they ? " he asked, as he strode about the storehouse at Tapley's wharf among the casks of wine, molasses, rum, and an occasional negro. " Yes ; but I'll have off the duties quick enough, if you want them. Fine family, I tell you ; young to be sure, but they'll improve every day, and not be going the other way like that old wench of yours," replied Tapley, as he hustled his human goods about to make them show off in a favorable manner. " It's a trade," said Page, with an air of business such as characterized all his proceedings at the market. " Make out your bill. Here's your money, and Putnam will make the exchange." While Tapley's bookkeeper was making out the receipt, Colonel Page counted out the cash. The business done, Jeremiah Page mounted his restless steed, and would have been off, had not the merchant called him to a halt by saying, " What do you suppose they'll try on us next, another Stamp Act, or what ?" The proceedings of Parliament affected every business man ; and Colonel Page was not without an interest in them, although he was engaged in the manufacture of bricks. " Things look a little cloudy. If his Majesty expects to make us pay the expense of the French wars, besides fighting and sacrificing as we did, I'm afraid he'll find we shall protest pretty strongly." With these words, uttered with a deal of emphasis, the customer mounted his horse, and was off towards his Danvers home.

It was a full hour before noon that he drove into the yard, dismounted, entered the house, laid aside his surtout, took from his waistcoat pocket the legal evidence of his trade, and announced to Mrs. Page that he had made a swap, saying, " You'll soon have *three* instead of *one*, and altogether they won't take up as much room as Dinah does." And he read aloud the following : —

DANVERS, *Apr.* 19, 1766.

Rec'd of Mr. Jeremiah Page, Fifty eight pounds thirteen shillings and four pence lawfull money and a negro woman called Dinah, which is in full for a negro woman called Combo and a negro girl called Cate, and a negro child called Deliverance or Dill, which I now sell and Deliver to ye said Jeremiah Page.

JOHN TAPLEY.

JONᴬ BANCROFT,
EZEKᴸ MARSH.

The prospect of more assistance in her family was cheering to the over-burdened housekeeper, yet she disliked to part with Dinah. But before she had time to reconcile her mind to the thought, Putnam stopped his ox-team at the door, and shouted, "Here's your slaves!" And with the same breath said to the living portion of his load, "Get off, ye darkies ! here's your new home." The farmer's words were unintelligible to the family ; but his gestures, with ox-whip in hand, were understood by the trio, and they were soon at the threshold of the Page mansion.

Dinah was at once sent to the loft to locate the new-comers, and manifested much pleasure upon having in her apartment of the Page home an ad-

dition of three from her own country. It was with
difficulty that she could make them understand
her words, for she had been so long with English-
speaking people that she had lost her native
tongue.

As Tapley allowed but little for Dinah, he was
not particular to have her sent down at once; and
she remained for some days before Putnam called
to take her to the merchant's office.

"How do you like them, wife?" inquired Jeremiah Page, when returning at night from the
brick-yard. "Rather awkward, surely. Still, I
think Combo is tractable, and as for Cate, she's
only a girl, but Dill is so young she is little more
than a bother at present." — "I know that," replied the head of the family, as he drew up to the
tea-table; "but these will improve with age, while
Dinah is too old for that, you know. I thought
I'd take the little one — I didn't want to see them
separated; and then, she'll be a good thing for
our children to play with till she gets old enough
for service. I made a good trade with Tapley.
He didn't want the youngster round."

"If they are just from Africa, there is a good
deal of uncertainty about their living until they
become useful. We do not know what effect our
climate will have on them," remarked Mrs. Page,
who did not regard the trade as favorably as her
husband represented, but she resolved to make
the best of it.

Combo, the mother, soon learned, through the patience of Mrs. Page, to do many things; and Cate was useful in watching the children and looking after her little sister Deliverance, who for short was called Dill.   They promised well through the heated season; but when the cold weather of winter settled down upon them, it was more than their constitutions could endure, and before another spring Combo and Cate were charged off to the profit-and-loss account on Jeremiah Page's ledger.

The family were now in a more unfortunate condition than when Mr. Page decided to make a change.   Dinah could not be traced, or she would have been brought back, if money could do it.   As for Dill, she was too young to be of any help, but had proved to be uncommonly tractable; and Mrs. Page was bent upon giving her a good training in culinary matters.   "I sha'n't try any more of them unless they are acclimated," said Jeremiah Page one day, half aloud, as he sat balancing his accounts.   Thoughtfully folding the bill of sale, and placing it in his great file for the year 1766, he added, "Poor investment that."

New cares now began to engross the attention of the brickmaker.   The Stamp Act had been passed and repealed.   The people of Danvers, like all the patriots, were filled with anxiety.   Jeremiah Page was as bitter against taxation without representation as were any of his neighbors, and he feared that something would be done to injure his business. He heartily indorsed the non-importation agreement, and strongly forbade the use of tea in his house. But Mrs. Page, who lacked nothing in the way of patriotism as she regarded it, saw no harm in using the supply she had in the house, and decided to have a social sip without violating the letter of the family edict.

Dill became accustomed to the New England climate, and developed into a useful servant by the time the Revolution began to absorb the attention of the people; but it is doubtful if she played the part in the tea-party on the roof which Miss Larcom assigns to her. The minor duties so early allotted to Dill no doubt included that of polishing her master's buttons, when in 1773 he was made a captain of the militia. With what pride she must have looked upon her master, dressed in his military garments, set off with the white ruffles that she had so deftly crimped, when all ready to start to a meeting of the patriots down at Salem! And how much greater her pride must have been when "Massa Gage" occupied the front room, and passed in and out attired in the brilliant costume befitting the king's governor of the Province.

It was on the ninth anniversary of the coming of Combo, Cate, and Dill to the Page home that Captain Jeremiah Page responded to a hasty alarm, and marched off to intercept the army of the king.

From that time forth there were heated discussions in the home ; and Dill's interest in the family caused her no little anxiety, although she had no adequate appreciation of the occasion of the disturbance. She met her first real grief when her mistress died on March 1, 1776, and she was subjected to a new mistress.

Dill heard much talk about the Declaration of Independence, but was far from comprehending its significance. Her lot had fortunately been cast among good people, and she had no thought of any liberty which she had not always enjoyed. The younger children of the family clung to her more closely now that their mother was gone. Dill manifested an interest in those under her charge only surpassed by a mother's affection : she romped with them in the garden, fondled them in her arms by the family hearth-stone, dried their innocent tears, and seemed like one of them. And Dill was contented in her ignorance until she was shown that the Declaration of Independence, which brought cheer to her master, and to maintain which he fought and sacrificed, had a meaning for her, although she was black and had been purchased by Jeremiah Page's money.

She was yet in her "teens" when the Constitution of the State was adopted, and the people said, " All men are born free and equal, etc."

It was some years before Dill left the Page family, and then her going was more like that of a daughter, who having attained her majority and reciprocated the affections of a worthy man, exchanged the paternal home for that of one of her own choice in which she was to preside as mistress.

Slaves who took their freedom, and others who remained with their masters and mistresses, were very numerous in Salem, and Dill naturally cast in her lot with the people at the seaport. There were many Cæsars among them, and to prevent confusion they were known by the surname of their respective masters. It was Cæsar Symonds who won the affections of "Deliverance Page" the marriage records of Salem attest.

DILL'S DAUGHTER, ANSTISS

The new responsibilities assumed by Dill were not so absorbing as to cause her to forget the people and the home which she had left, neither was she forgotten by the Page family. Seldom did they visit the port without seeking out the little black house in North Salem where their old servant presided as mistress. Bundles and baskets were continually left at the cottage door, and each recurring Thanksgiving brought cheer to the Page family as they carried cheer to the hearts of Dill and her children. As each of the children of Jeremiah Page established homes for themselves, a

St. Peter's Church at Salem

new channel of supply was created for the increasing family at Salem. The visiting children took delight with those of black faces, and in listening to the chatter of a parrot, which in summer was kept in a green cage hanging from a limb of a willow-tree near the door of the humble home of the Symonds family. Dill never failed to make regular visits to the Page home until old age settled down upon her.

She was tall and erect in stature, and when dressed as her taste directed, with bright yellow turban, gold ear-hoops, and bright plaid shawl, had every appearance of an African princess. Her presence, together with that of her daughters Hannah and Anstiss, brought pleasure to the Danvers home, where the grandchildren of Jeremiah Page kept up the family interest.

In the great company assembled on a June day of 1805 to honor the memory of a noted man, there were seen no faces more tearful than those of Deliverance Symonds and her daughters. All the words of eulogy from eloquent lips over the remains of Colonel Jeremiah Page could not outweigh the half-audible sentence, " He was a good man," uttered by the black woman who lingered by the bier of her master and benefactor.

It was nearly a half century later when in Salem a little company of people, chiefly colored, bore the form of a nonagenarian through the aisle of St. Peter's Church; and among all who gave reverent heed to the rector's words, " I am the resurrection and the life," were noticed members of the Page family of Danvers, who had seen in the departed an innocent slave, an honest servant, a faithful wife, a devoted mother, and a sincere Christian.

CHAPTER XIX

CHELMSFORD.[1] — EARLY PATRIOTS. — EARLY MEANS
OF PROTECTION FROM THE ENEMY. — OLD GAR-
RISONS. — THE PATRIOT PREACHER. — STORY OF
HENRY S. PERHAM. — POSITIVE ACTS OF THE
CHELMSFORD PATRIOTS. — RELIEF TO BOSTON
SUFFERERS. — LEXINGTON ALARM. — MR. GEORGE
SPAULDING TELLS HIS GRANDFATHER'S STORY.
— PATRIOTS TOO MUCH IN HASTE TO STOP FOR
PRAYER. — JOURNAL OF REVEREND EBENEZER
BRIDGE

CHELMSFORD is one of the trio of towns which
received the seal of incorporation on May 29, 1655;
Concord had preceded them by twenty years, and
Woburn by thirteen years. Previous to this date
Woburn and Concord were the nearest to this settlement; but subsequently Billerica was the nearest neighbor, and Groton, the other of the three,
was not far away. But civilization had pushed its
way into this wilderness before the towns were
granted a corporate existence. The men who first
took action towards a settlement of the tract "ly-

---

[1] This town included Lowell for many years after the Revolution, and the footprints of the early patriots in that now busy city
will be traced in this connection.

ing on the other [west] side of Concord River"
were from Concord and Woburn ; and their names
have been continued in the town through all the
years of the history of Chelmsford, and they are
honored among the early and later patriots.

As it was a frontier settlement, it was soon
found expedient to take precautions against Indian attacks, although they had lived at peace for
a score of years with the Wamesits, or Pawtuckets,
who were their near neighbors. But during that
general uprising, King Philip's war, the settlers
in Chelmsford were not entirely exempt from trouble, yet they suffered much less than many frontier towns. Some years before these hostilities
had begun, the Chelmsford men took precautions
peculiar to the time. Divine worship was their
chief concern, and they naturally adopted measures to prevent being attacked and overcome while
assembled at the meeting-house on the Sabbath.
The following appears upon the records : —

25 the 5 moth, 1671. It is ordered by the selectmen For
Severall Considerations espetialy for the preseruation of peace,
That with in one month after the Date hear of Eury every
malle person with in our towne above the Age of fiveteen years
shall provid a good Clube of fouer or five foote in lingth with
a Knobe in the end, and to bring the same to the metting
house ther to leave the Same vntill vntill ocation fore use of
it be (found, etc.)

The name of the Rest By

SAMUEL ADAMS,

Clerke.

Other precautions followed, such as the erection
of a strong house on an eminence now known
as Robins Hill. Several garrisons were built in
1675 ; and their identity is not entirely obliterated,
as we shall see in our circuit of the town in quest
of the footprints of Chelmsford patriots.

This town had been making a noteworthy record for one hundred and twenty years before the
Revolution burst upon the Colonies. During the
greater portion of this time the people had been
in more or less military service, and were not unprepared for the struggle for independence. New
people had joined the first settlers ; and their descendants, with those of the pioneers, had been
wisely guided by devout pastors, three of whom
had done their work and been laid to rest, and a
fourth, Rev. Ebenezer Bridge, was settled as the
pastor in 1741. These clergymen had been closely
identified with the military interests of the town,
according to the custom throughout the Colonies.
The fourth minister's journal bears witness to his
faithfulness in this direction ; and his Artillery
Election Sermon of June 1, 1752, is largely devoted to showing the consistency of military life
with the profession and practice of Christianity.

Rev. Mr. Bridge had been in service in the
town thirty-four years when he was called upon to
take a stand with the king or against him. This
must have occasioned many a severe struggle in
his honest breast ; for he was intimately associated

with the government officials, and enjoyed their society in Boston as well as at his own hearth-stone. His love for the king may be inferred from the following entry : —

Dec. 31, 1760. Heard with certainty of the death of King George the 2nd and of the accession of George the 3rd. The king was proclaimed at Boston yesterday, sermon and procession, etc., to-morrow.

January 4, 1761. Preached sermon on the death of King George 2nd, and the accession of George 3rd to the British throne.

Every act of the Chelmsford minister evinced his patriotism and proves his social standing. He notes under date of

June 24, 1763. Dined at Col. Stoddard's with his Excellency, the Governor, and Hon. Mr. Bowdoin and others and their ladies.

He records : —

May 15, 1765. Dined at Capt. Barrons with Col. Phipps, Mr. Lechmere, Major Vassal, and their ladies, upon invitation, supped at Col. Stoddard's with Secretary Oliver and lady. They lodged at my house by reason of Col. Stoddard having plastered his chamber.

With what awe the common people must have viewed these scenes, when the gilded coaches arrived from Boston and Cambridge, and rolled up to the Colonel's door, and from them alighted the officials of the king, in rich and brilliant costumes, together with their puffed and powdered ladies !

In April, 1771, he notes : —

Fast Day. Lieut. Governor Oliver attended service with us.

and in the same year he records a visit to Dr. Ellis and Governor Hutchinson, the latter of whom received him " very graciously."

Had we no other evidence than the parson's own diary, we should be convinced that he at first was inclined to favor the existing institutions, and adhere to the Crown. This appears in his entry at the time of the riotous opposition excited by the passage of the Stamp Act. No doubt his indignation was strengthened by the severe treatment of his personal friend Oliver. His entry on August 30, 1765, is —

Every day we hear ye news from Boston of ye mobish doings there in which first insurrection they hanged Secretary Oliver in effigy, and then burned him ; burned the Stamp Office, etc., rifled his dwelling. . . . All this is owing to ye Stamp Act.

September 1, 1766, the pastor makes record of a town meeting, in which it was voted that the damage to the sufferers in the late insurrection on account of the Stamp Act should not by their consent be paid by the Province.

The sympathies of the Chelmsford minister being with Francis Bernard, the governor, he was invited to preach the election sermon, and did so on May 27, 1767. The country parson, doubtless flattered by the honor, expressed himself strongly in his attachment to the mother country, and was duly complimented by the friends of the government who sat at meat with the officials. Entertainment at the Province House at this time must have been an agreeable change from the Parson's burdens in his parish, where he found it difficult to live within his limited salary. · He was not unused to seeing negro slaves in his parish, but not such a retinue of both sexes as waited and tended in the governor's family.

The Chelmsford minister makes a record of having

Visited Col. Stoddard & discoursed with his mulatto servant, Hagar, who seemed to feign herself ill.

He frequently recorded baptisms of negro infants, and funeral services over some of the race then family slaves.

What influences may have been brought to bear to convince the Chelmsford minister of his duty as a patriot when the king proved unfaithful to his subjects may not be known ; but his journal shows him to have been intimately associated with the patriot preachers, Revs. Daniel Emerson of Hollis, N.H., Joseph Emerson of Pepperell, and William Emerson of Concord, Mass. He was also associated with Rev. Jonas Clark of Lexington, and other ministers of the same standing. It is sufficient that Rev. Mr. Bridge, after the publication of the Hutchinson letters in this country, became an ardent supporter of the liberties of the Colonies.[1]

Says Mr. Perham, the town historian, "The position of the people of the town in respect to the grievances under which the Colonies suffered was in the highest degree creditable to them. While they firmly adhered to their rights as Englishmen, there is not the remotest suggestion of a desire to sever their connection with the existing government."

They did not hesitate to instruct their representative, Colonel Stoddard, after the passing of the Stamp Act, —

" This being a time when, by reason of several acts of parliament, not only in this province, but all the English Colonies of this Continent, are thrown into the utmost confusion and perplexity ; the stamp act as we apprehend not only lays an unconstitutional, but also an insupportable, tax upon us,

---

[1] In 1772 a number of Hutchinson's letters written to the British Cabinet were found. They revealed the fact that he was urging them to enforce their plans against the liberties of the American Colonies. The General Court, upon knowledge of this, voted to impeach him, and requested his Majesty to remove the governor from office. Hutchinson, when informed of this, dissolved the assembly, and at length became so obnoxious that he was superseded by Governor Gage, whose name is familiar to every patriot. Hutchinson died in England in 1780.

and deprives us, as we humbly conceive, of those rights and privileges to which we are entitled as free born subjects of Great Britain by the royal charter ; wherefore we think it our duty and interest at this critical conjuncture of our public affairs, to direct you, sir, our representative, to be so far from countenancing the execution of the aforesaid stamp act, that you use your best endeavors that such measures may be taken and such remonstrances made to the King and Parliament, as may obtain a speedy repeal of the aforesaid act, and a removal of the burden upon trade."

Says Mr. Perham, "Our people continued to thus firmly adhere to their principles, and on January 22, 1773, instructed their representative, Mr. Simeon Spaulding, at some length."

" Sir, as the present aspect of the times is dark and difficult, we do not doubt but you will cheerfully know the sentiments and receive the assistance of those you represent. The matters that may now come under your cognizance are of great importance. The highest wisdom, therefore, prudence and decision, are evidently necessary. We would earnestly caution you by no means to consent to any rash, passionate plan of action, which will not only sully the dignity, but finally prove the utter destruction of the cause we pretend to support. We hope those little animosities that involve persons, not things, may be utterly banished, and that every determination will be found in the nature of a free state, and that therefore every   annexed to each part may be religiously preserved.

"Of course, you will be careful not to trample on majesty, while you are firmly but deacently pleading the liberties of the subject. In fine, we wish you that wisdom which is from above, and we pray you that your conduct in this important crisis may be such as the coolest reflection will ever justify."

The act for closing the port of Boston brought out the people ; and in a town meeting on May 30, 1774, they again put themselves on record against the act, and in sympathy with the people of Boston. They chose a Committee of Correspondence, — Jonathan William Austin, who had come from the office of John Adams in Boston, and settled as a lawyer in town ; Captain Oliver Barron ; Mr. Samuel Perham, who was tilling the acres now cultivated by his great-grandson ; David Spaulding ; Benjamin Walker ; Deacon Aaron Chamberlin ; Captain Moses Parker ; Samuel Stevens, Jr. ; and Simeon Spaulding.

They concluded their action of that May day by declaring, " In freedom we're born, and in freedom we'll die."   Each onward step was carefully taken by the Chelmsford patriots, and there were no halting or backward movements.   In September, 1774, they sent Simeon Spaulding to represent them at Salem, while Mr. Austin and Samuel Perham were made delegates to the first Provincial meeting at Concord.   They had their Committee of Inspection to prevent the purchase and sale of goods imported from Great Britain ; and they also voted to equip the Alarm List with implements of war, and to raise and discipline fifty minute-men.

While their hearts and hands were full at home, they did not forget the suffering people in the blockaded port.   The following letter affords unmistakable evidence of this fact : —

BOSTON, *Octo.* 3d, 1774.

Sir, — To commiserate the Afflicted, to sympathize with the oppressed Sufferers, to reach out the bountious hand for the Comfort, Relief & Support of the Distressed, are sacrifices well-pleasing and acceptable to God thro Christ our Savior.

Our Worthy Friends and Brethren of Chelmsford have in this way done honour to the Gospel of our divine Redeemer and by so doing have greatly honour'd themselves. We have an evidence hereof in the very kind Donation of Forty Bushels of Rye from the patriotic Inhabitants of that Town : it has been received and housed at the Granary and shall be disposed of agreeable to the benevolent Intent of the generous Donors.

It affords us great satisfaction to find that the Conduct of this much abused Town meets with their approbation; we greatly value it; and trust that by the same gracious directing and supporting hand. Hand, which hath brought us hitherto, we shall not be left to do anything which may incur a forfeiture of that Affection and esteem. How can ye help us at such a time as this more effectually than by carrying our Cause daily to the God of all Grace and imploring his Mercy and Favour for Us. They are inclusive of all Good.

Your Invitation to make your Houses our Homes is very engaging should we at length be forced out of these once peaceful Habitations, we think ourselves very happy that we are like to be so well provided for; but should we be obliged even to remove off fifteen times the distance of Chelmsford, yet the Consciousness of a Cordial Attachment to the invaluable civil and religious Liberties of our Country, which we believe to be the Cause of truth and Righteousness, would yield us content and Satisfaction far superior to that which those can experience who are ungratefully seeking to " build their greatness on the Country's Ruin." With grateful Acknowledgements, I am, Sir,

Your truly obliged Friend, & Servt.,

DAVID JEFFRIES,

Per Order of the Committee of Donations.

MR. JONATHAN WILLIAM AUSTIN.

In addition to this donation of the autumn of 1774, together with the offer of their homes to any who desired to move to the town, this patriotic people gathered a flock of sheep from the various farms, and sent them during the winter of 1774–5 to the relief of the sufferers who remained in Boston. In my journey about this town I met several people, who, at the same hearth-stones where they gather their families, have heard their grandparents tell of making their contributions from their flocks to the sufferers.

Mr. Simeon Spaulding was the town's agent for delivering contributions. He was a yeoman of prominence and influence, living on a portion of the ancestral homestead. He never shrank from duty, and was ever ready for patriotic service. Besides representing the town in various legislatures and congresses, he was the colonel of a regiment commissioned February 14, 1776. He was succeeded on the farm by his son, Deacon Noah Spaulding, whose daughter, Julia Ann, married John C. Dalton. Their son, Charles H. Dalton of Boston, while at the old home, rescued many valuable papers from a destructive hand, among them the letter already quoted. Through the courtesy of Mr. Dalton I am enabled to give these facts to my readers.

Weekly drillings and ordinary cares so absorbed the farmers of this town that the early spring of 1775 was upon them before they hardly realized it. They not only kept an eye out to their country's interest, but plied themselves with all diligence to the welfare of their families, and the distressed from Boston who had accepted their invitations. The musket, well scoured, stood at the bedside, or hung over the fireplace, and the well-filled cartridge-box had a convenient place near by. A bountiful wood-pile had been prepared at the door. The sheep and cows, "well wintered," were cropping the early sprouts, and the plough was turning the fresh soil.

Suddenly an alarm was heard. A familiar voice shouted, "The Regulars are coming!" In a moment the scene changed. The husband, father, and son, with a few hasty farewells, are gone; the munitions of war are not to be seen in the home; the plough is still in the furrow; and the wife, mother, and daughter, more than double their burden in assuming the care of the farm.

" From these farms came more than a hundred resolute, determined men. Theirs were not acts of men eager for war, nor did they display the caution of timidity. Their language was not the language of men eager to achieve glory by deeds of arms; but the time for words had passed, the time for action had come."

Mr. George Spaulding said, in repeating his grandfather's story, "We rallied at the alarm-post, a bowlder agreed upon by previous arrangement, and made hasty preparations for our march.

Parson Bridge was on hand, and wanted us to go into the meeting-house and have prayers before we left town; but some were on horseback, and some on foot, and all more or less anxious to get started. In fact, Sergeant [later Captain] Ford, who came from East Chelmsford [now Lowell] in charge of a squad, replied to the good parson, that he had more urgent business on hand, and hastened on with his men. There was but little military order observed by us. We went off in squads as soon as convenient. One company of sixty-one men was under the command of Captain Oliver Barron, and the other of forty-three men was under the command of Colonel Moses Parker. We reached Concord in time to have a part in the pursuit of the retreating redcoats. We had our first shot at them at Merriam's Corner, and more at Hardy's Hill. Captain Ford, who was at this time sergeant in Captain Barron's company, was prominent on the Hill. He was an old fighter of the French and Indians, and knew how to handle his musket to an advantage. He claimed to have caused the death of five of the enemy on Lincoln soil. [See "Beneath Old Roof Trees."] We continued in the pursuit, determined on redressing our wrongs. Captain Oliver Barron and Deacon Aaron Chamberlin were wounded that day."

Doubtless my young patriot readers are anxious to know the attitude of Rev. Mr. Bridge as revealed in his own journal. A few entries are

introduced to show the pastor's course of proceed-
ing when patriotism was evinced by adhering to
the king : —

1755, *Sept.* 15. A general muster of companies through
the Provinces to raise men to reinforce army at Crown Point.
Spent evening at Parker's with officers, & this day the news
came of the engagement between Gen. Johnson's army &
the French & Indians, in which Johnson's army came off
conquerors, having taken the French General, & killed 700
officers & men, & taken and wounded many. The battle
was on the 8 Sept. instant — a signal mercy. Though at the
same time we are called to mourn the loss of divers brave
officers and soldiers to the number of about 120 or 130.

Sept. 25. Visited the wife of Jona. Barron, as I did yesterday towards night, upon a flying report of her husband
being killed in the battle agt. the enemy on the way to Crown
Point.

26. Visited Mrs. Barron this morning upon the acct. of
her hearing more news of her husband being killed, & discoursed with her. Prayed at Parker's with a company going
off to Crown Point, Captain Butterfield of Dunstable.

27. Visited Widow Parker upon a flying report of her
son being killed in the fight under Gen. Johnson, so upon
the same acct. visited wife of Jacob Parker.

30. Visited Mrs. Barron, who this day is certified of the
death of her husband in the late battle with our enemies in
the way toward Crown Point, by an extract of a letter of
Maj. Nichols (to his wife), who also was wounded in the
same engagement. I discoursed with her again, & endeavored to comfort her.

Lieutenant Barron was in the successful siege
of Quebec, and upon his return presented his
minister with a silver cup, a trophy brought from

there ; but he lost his life in the campaign against Crown Point in 1755. Two other Chelmsford soldiers perished at the same time, viz., Jacob Parker and James Emery.

In the following year came the unsuccessful campaign against the same place, when four men of Chelmsford lost their lives, viz., Nathaniel Butterfield, Simeon Corey, James Dutton, and Isaac Parker. Clergymen were required to be furnished with military equipments. The Chelmsford pastor makes record on July 8, 1757, of a call from Colonel Stoddard, who asked him if he was furnished with arms and ammunition according to law.

Through all these sorrows we find the pastor having a personal interest in the sufferers, and in the general results. In 1758, Rev. Mr. Bridge records : —

Spent the evening at Parker's, whose company met to appoint Bayonet men under the new law.

He also gives an account of Benjamin Byham and others going to the war. It seems that it was customary for troops passing through a town to halt for prayers, etc. Mr. Bridge has recorded : —

Prayed with troops which came from Newbury, Rowley, &c., on their way to the Forts ; also at Lieut. Proctor's with the same.

The rejoicing at the completion of the French war is seen in the following : —

Col. Stoddard's whole house was illuminated on account of the taking of Quebec. 16 Oct., 1759, was the day appointed by the government to be observed.

25th *Oct.*, 1759. Thanksgiving on acct. of the reduction of Quebec. Preached from Psalm 98–1. At night Col. Stoddard and others visited me; also brother John from Boston, who fired us a half doz. Sky Rockets.

August, 1760. Visited Lieut. Jona. Spaulding and Ensign Jona. Harwood, each of them lately bereaved of a son in the army at Crown Point.

This faithful pastor's journal is evidence of his service on occasions more cheerful, such as "raisings," "huskings," and the like, in his own parish, also "barbecues," "ordinations," etc., in other towns. While weeping with his sorrowing neighbors, he is called to marry a couple, and receives as his fee, "a guinea & a pair of kid gloves for self & wife."

After the King Street massacre of 1770, Reverend Mr. Bridge wrote : —

Bad news this day or two from Boston, the soldiers having killed four persons and wounded others.

Under date of April 19, 1775, he wrote : —

The Civil war was begun at Concord this morning! Lord direct all things for his glory, the good of his church and people, and preservation of the British Colonies, and to the shame and confusion of our oppressors.

April 20. In a terrible state, by reason of ye news from our army. The onset of ye British was begun at Lexington, was carried on at Concord, where some were killed on both sides. They ingloriously retreated soon and were followed by our men down to Cambridge, before night. Five captives were carried through this town for Amherst. A constant marching of soldiers from ye towns above toward ye army as there were yesterday from this town and the neighboring towns. We are now involved in a war which Lord only knows what will be the issue of, but I will hope in His mercy, and wait to see His salvation.

April 21. I sent provisions to the army as did many more. 'Tis a very distressing day, soldiers passing all day and all night.

Sergeant Ford, upon returning from service in response to the Lexington alarm, proceeded immediately to raise a company. His patriotic zeal inspired others ; and in ten days he was joined by fifty-seven men, and on May 19 he received his commission as captain.

The part taken by the Chelmsford soldiers in the battle of Bunker Hill was most creditable. The companies belonged to the Twenty-seventh Regiment, of which their former townsman, Ebenezer Bridge, was colonel. John Ford, captain of one of the companies, distinguished himself in this connection.

" He volunteered to carry from Cambridge to Bunker Hill a message from General Ward. To do this he must pass over Charlestown Neck in the range of British guns, at the imminent peril of his life. He had orders from General Ward to dismount from his horse at the Neck and cross on foot, in order to escape observation. But he ran

the risk, and passed and repassed on horseback.
While at Bunker Hill he warned General Prescott
that from the movements of the enemy it was
evident that they were preparing to attack the
Americans upon the hill, and urged the necessity
of immediately casting up breastworks and redoubts.

"When the preparation for the battle began,
the gallant captain, who had no taste for inactiv-
ity, obtained permission from General Ward at
Cambridge to withdraw his company privately, and
march directly to the scene of action to re-enforce
the troops. They marched across Charlestown
Neck, which was being raked by cannon from the
British ships, and proceeded down Bunker Hill,
where they were met by General Putnam, who ordered Captain Ford, with his company, to draw
into the line the cannon which had been deserted
by General Callender, and left at the foot of the
hill after the first attack. The captain at first remonstrated on the ground that his company were
ignorant of the management of artillery, many having never seen a cannon before ; but finally obeyed,
and moved with the cannon and the general himself to the rail fence, which they reached just before the battle began.

"Captain Knowlton with Connecticut troops,
and Colonel Stark with New Hampshire troops,
were also stationed at this part of the defence.
The right wing of the British army, under Gen-

eral Howe, was directed against this point for the purpose of turning the American flank, and cutting off a retreat from the redoubt. As the enemy advanced to the attack, the artillery, manned by a portion of Captain Ford's company, opened upon them with great effect, some of the shots being directed by General Putnam himself. The muskets were ordered to reserve their fire till the enemy were within eight rods."

An old grave-stone in the burying-ground at Chelmsford tells how a soldier from that town disobeyed orders.

SACRED TO THE MEMORY OF
MR. JOSEPH SPAULDING,
WHO DIED JULY 31, 1820, Æt. 64.

IN HOPE OF ETERNAL LIFE WHICH GOD WHO CANNOT LIE HATH
PROMISED TO BELIEVERS IN CHRIST.

He was among the brave asserters and defenders of the liberties of his
country at Bunker Hill, where he opened the battle by firing
upon the enemy before orders were given & after enjoying for many years the blessings of civil &
religious liberty in common with others

He sank to rest
With all his country's honors blest.

The Chelmsford men were among those who used their fowling-pieces with deadly effect; and the enemy were obliged to retreat for a time, " leaving on the ground," as General Stark related, " where but the day before the mowers had swung the scythe in peace, the dead, as thick as sheep in a fold." During the entire engagement, Captain Ford and his men bore an honorable part. Thirteen of the company were wounded. Ten Chelmsford men were in Captain Benjamin Walker's company, and did good service. Captain Walker was wounded, taken prisoner, and died of his wounds in a jail in Boston. Lieutenant-Colonel Moses Parker met a similar fate.[1]

The first report of this battle was received in Chelmsford by way of Billerica on the evening of the 17th. The alarm-guns were fired, great excitement prevailed, and before morning some of the wounded returned to their distressed families. Under that date, Rev. Mr. Bridge writes : —

"A terrible time this in relation to our army, in battle with our oppressors at Charlestown. The whole town on fire. The armies engaged on Bunker's Hill. At night we saw a fire from Chelmsford."

On the following day the parson writes : —

"The armies at Charlestown still engaged, and news flying with respect to the slain and wounded. This is a day big with distress and trouble. Our enemies are those who were our brethren of the same nation, and subjects of the same king, and all for the sake of a wicked and corrupt ministry, a deluded, a devilish, a venal parliament."

[1] "During the evening and night after the battle, the air trembled with the groans of the wounded, as they were borne over the Charles, and through the streets of Boston to hospitals, where they were to waste away from the summer heat, and the scarcity of proper food." — BANCROFT.

Rev. Mr. Bridge's journal furnishes us with glimpses of later service of Chelmsford soldiers, and of his own patriotic acts.

CHELMSFORD MONUMENT (REVOLUTIONARY)

June 30, 1776.   Read a resolve of the General Court relative to raising men to go to Canada, and notified the people to appear with arms, etc.

July 2.   The town again in confusion.   Companies met to draw out men for Canada.

July 5.   More hurry about raising soldiers.   Col. Cummings appointed General but resigned.

July 22.   Two of the British officers, prisoners at Dunstable, visited me. (They may have expected sympathy from the parson, formerly known to be a loyalist.)

July 23. Capt. Ford and his company marched off in order to join our northern army. At his desire I went to the meeting-house previous to their marching, sang the 18 Psalm, and prayed with them and gave them a word of exhortation. Part of two other companies of soldiers on their march from the lower towns came into town towards night and lodged in town.

Capt. Ford was again out with his company to re-enforce the northern army in Sept. of 1777, and was present at the surrender of Burgoyne and the northern army in the following month.

July 25. Much company and much confusion by reason of the soldiers passing through.

July 26. Early in the morning I prayed in the meeting-house with Capts. Fay and Bancroft of Woburn and Reading and their respective companies upon their march to join the northern army.

Sept. 1. Read the Declaration of Independence of the U. States of America in public congregation agreeable to the order of the council of this State, and when I had done added ' Zion heard and was glad, and the daughter of Judah rejoiced because of the judgment of the Lord.'

Sept. 8. Was sent for and went to Parker, Bills, or Wm. Parkers, his child sick, he in the war, prayed with them.

Sept. 19. Visited David Spaulding upon his receiving the news of his son David in the army at Ticonderoga — he dies of small pox.

Sept. 24. Visited Willard Byam ill at his fathers. Jonas Dutton ill at his mothers, both came home from the army, prayed with each family.

In the morning went to the meeting-house and prayed with a company of soldiers going off toward New York. They are to go under command of Zach. Wright of Westford.

Opposite the burying-ground, and on an attractive common, stands a unique granite monument on which is read : —

IN HONOR OF THE TOWNSMEN OF CHELMSFORD WHO SERVED THEIR COUNTRY IN THE WAR OF THE REVOLUTION, THIS MONUMENT IS ERECTED BY A GRATEFUL POSTERITY.

ERECTED 1859.

Let the children guard what the sires have won.

JOHN BATES, Died in Army at Cambridge

DAVID SPALDING, JR., Died in Army at Ticonderoga ;

PELATIAH ADAMS, killed at Cherry Valley;

NOAH FOSTER, shot at capture of Burgoyne;

HENRY FLETCHER, killed at White Plains;

LT. COL. MOSES PARKER and CAPT. BENJ. WALKER, Wounded at Bunker Hill, June 17, 1775. Died Prisoners in Boston, July 4, and Aug. 1, '75;

LT. ROBERT SPALDING, Died at Milford, Ct., '76.

CHAPTER XX

FOOTPRINTS OF THE PATRIOTS OF THE REVOLUTION
IN LOWELL. — BOWERS FAMILY HOMESTEAD OF
TWO HUNDRED YEARS. — STORY OF FORD HOME-
STEAD. — CAPTAIN JOHN FORD'S DESCENDANT
TELLS THE STORY OF THE PATRIOT MILLER. —
CAPTAIN FORD'S JOURNAL IN THE NORTHERN
CAMPAIGN OF 1776. — LIST OF PATRIOTS PRE-
SERVED BY CAPTAIN FORD. — STORY OF FATHER
OF PRESIDENT FRANKLIN PIERCE

Man loves the soil that gave him birth as the child loves the mother,
and from the same inherent impulses. — B. J. LOSSING.

THOSE who are accustomed to think of Lowell
as a city of comparatively recent origin will hardly
expect to find the footprints of the patriots of the
Revolution along its busy streets ; but a careful
search will reveal them, and also bring to mind
the faithful service of much earlier patriots.

Nature, through the distribution of her water-
ways, had determined that East Chelmsford should
be a city ; but long before the white settlers found
a use for the bountiful waters, there lived and
loved another race of beings. The red man of the
forest, with his dusky mate, was early attracted to

the place.   In 1653 the Legislature of Massachusetts granted the Indians a reservation about the
falls, and they were peaceable through the influence of the Christian patriot, Eliot.   Yet other
tribes were of hostile intent ; and the good citizen

BOWERS HOMESTEAD, LOWELL

was he who kept a vigilant watch for the lurking
enemy, and took steps to protect himself and
family against the foe.

Of those who early did service in the interest of
the white settlers of this locality, we can readily
trace one to the Bowers farm.   " This estate,"

says Mr. Perham, " has been in the family possession as long as its history is known.   The dwelling
is the oldest standing in Lowell, and has doubtless
served the Bowers family for two centuries.   The
first to settle here was Jerathmell Bowers, who
was a son of George, who was in Plymouth in
1639.   Jerathmell was born May 2, 1650.   He
doubtless came to Chelmsford, now Lowell, with
the family of Henry Boutell, who was his stepfather.   He was a man of wealth and influence,
was early chosen representative to the General
Court, and was captain in the military organization
doing good service."   In proof of this I quote
from the diary of Chief Justice Samuel Sewall,
who, with all his cares, found time to make a tour
of inspection through Middlesex County.   In his
diary he wrote : —

" *Monday, Oct.* 26, 1702.   Went to Chelmsford, by that
time got there 'twas almost dark ; saw Capt. Bowers and his
company ; gave a volley and Huzzas ; sup'd at Mr. Clark's [1]
I and Col. Pierce in his study."

The document reproduced on page 297 is of
interest in this connection for the signature of
Thomas Hinchman, a patriot of the time, whose
name is indelibly stamped on the pages of the
early history of Massachusetts.

[1] Mr. Clark was the minister, Rev. Thomas Clark, whose daughter married Rev. John Hancock of Lexington, and hence became
the grandmother of Governor John Hancock.

Jerathmell Bowers removed from this homestead to Groton, where he died in 1724, at the age of seventy-eight years. Probably he was not long away from his home, as we find in Chelmsford burying-ground a stone to the memory of " Mrs. Elizabeth Bowers, wife to Capt. Jerathmell Bowers who died, March 4th 1721, in ye 76 year of Her age." Captain Bowers was a man of influence in his time, and on this old homestead conducted business according to the demands of the time. October 5, 1686, Jerathmell Bowers and John Fisk were licensed by the court to sell "strong waters." Two years later Bowers and Cornelius Waldo were licensed to carry on the same business. Fisk was a son of the minister, and Waldo was the deacon of the church. No harm was thought to arise from the sale of intoxicants to the white people, but it was bad for the Indians with whom Captain Bowers had to do.

Six children were objects of Captain Bowers's solicitude at this old homestead, and he was doubtless succeeded by his son Jerathmell, and perhaps Jonathan, at the old home; and it is certain that William, Joseph, and Sewall have each tilled the ancestral acres and gone to their reward, and two generations are still living there. The hearthstone around which the family gathered when the red men were their enemies was the place where anxious mothers and children gathered on the morning of April 19, 1775, when the men fell in with Captain Ford's company and hastened on towards Concord.

At some distance from the Bowers homestead was the home and mill of John Ford. He was a son of Robert Ford, born in Haverhill in 1738, and early settled in East Chelmsford (Lowell), near

CAPTAIN FORD HOMESTEAD, LOWELL

the Pawtucket Falls. He was a strong man, of an adventurous spirit, and was led to this locality by the advantages which it afforded for milling. He obtained the land bordering on the Merrimack, either whole or in part, from the Indians. He erected a mill near the falls, and a house not far away for the comfort of his family. Here he took up his abode, and was recognized as an influential

citizen of Chelmsford long before any one thought
of rebelling against the king, whose faithful subjects they were.   In the bustling city of Lowell,
where so little remains to remind us of the pioneers, it is refreshing to turn aside from the hum
of the many spindles, follow the course of the
river a short distance, and come to the Ford estate, where the descendants of the brave captain
still live, and with most commendable pride cherish the old homestead of the founder.

To be sure changes have come.   The rude dwelling which sheltered the brave miller and patriot
has given way to two commodious residences, both
occupied by Ford descendants.   The roof-tree set
up by Captain John Ford after the Revolution is
that which shelters the fourth generation.   Here
I received a most cordial welcome from Mrs.
Henry G. Lambert, to whom I am indebted for
the following story : —

" The first of our family here was John Ford.
He was succeeded by a son, Elisha Ford, and
daughters ; of the latter, Sally married John Corliss of Haverhill, N.H.   Their son, John L. Corliss, was succeeded by daughters.   Sarah Corliss
married Henry A. Lambert of New York, and
Helen married William D. Earl of North Attle-
boro, Mass.   I am a great-granddaughter of Captain John Ford, and there are seven of the next
generation who cherish these ancestral acres.
Grandfather Ford was at work in his mill when

the alarm-gun sounded from the hill not far away. But the miller was so well posted on the state of affairs that he knew what that meant, and he lost no time in adjusting his saw, and making things ready to leave. He refreshed himself with a bowl of bread and milk, which he ate when standing by a window seen in the cut, the one-story part of the dwelling being his home at that time. He mounted his horse, and made haste to the centre of the town of Chelmsford. Hè was joined by neighbors on the way, and as you have already learned, was in so great haste as to decline the thoughtful invitation of the good pastor to go into the meeting-house for prayers."

" Grandfather Ford," continued my informant, " was familiar with military life long before the call to arms on the morning of April 19, 1775. He had been obliged in his early days here at the mill to keep a close watch for the Indians, who were inclined to make some trouble at times ; and on one occasion he had an experience which resulted in putting an end to the annoying party. While such incidents are not altogether pleasant to recall, they serve to show the nature of the preparation which Captain Ford had for the service of a true patriot in 1775."

The family story around the old hearth-stone becomes doubly real through the presence of the sword carried by Captain Ford from this place to the battle of Bunker Hill, also his musket and powder-horn used in the Continental army. Among numerous papers that belonged to the patriot are two commissions. The first is to John Ford as "captain of a company, raised by this Colony as a temporary re-enforcement to the American army, until the first day of April next, at Watertown, 7th day of February, 1776, in the 16th year of the reign of his Majesty, King George the third. By command of the major part of the council."

The other is to appoint John Ford as "captain of the First company in the Regiment of Foot, whereof Ebenezer Bridge is colonel, raised by the Continental Congress aforesaid for the Defence of the Colony. By order of the Congress, Jos. Warren, President, P. T."

Among other papers which these descendants cherish with a genuine spirit of patriotism are the following : —

CHELMSFORD, *Jan.* 26, 1776.

Received of Philip Parkis three pounds, twelve shillings, lawful money, in full for doing a turn for him in the Continental army, this present year.

SYLAS PARKER.

Attested: FRANCIS SOUTHACK.

CAMP AT CAMBRIDGE, *June* 27, 1775.

Received of Eben Bridge Fifteen pounds in Province notes for my company.

£15.   JOHN FORD.

In the summer of 1776 another company was raised in Chelmsford, and stationed at Ticonderoga

under command of Captain Ford. While there
the captain kept a regimental order-book, which
is still in the family. In this book, now one hundred and twenty years old, are recorded regimental orders, trials by courts-martial, promotions of
officers, punishments of disorderly soldiers, and
other matters pertaining to a military encampment. Every day are recorded the parole and
countersign of the camp. From this book I quote
a few orders, being careful to preserve the exact
form and spelling.

August 24, 1776.

Ensign Lee of Capt. Spauldings company, Col. Reed's
Regt. tryed at the Court-Marshal for bying a Gun belonging to Col. Marshfield Regt. & Defacing the name New
Gersey & the No that was mark^t on it. Pleading Guilty —
the Court Sentenced him to Return to Col. Marshfield &
to be Repromanded by the Commander of the Regt. at the
H. D. of the Regt. Richard Buck of Col. Patisons Regt.
tryed at the same g^l Court Marshal for Refusing his Duty &
striking his officer. The Court finds him Guilty & Sentences
him to Receive 39 Lashes on his Bare Back for Each Crime.

James Conner of Capt. Osgoods Company in the Regt.
Commanded by Lt. Col Ward is tryed by the same g^l
Court Marshal for Desertion & pleads Guilty, & is Sentenced
to Receive 39 Lashes on his Bare Back & ware a with on
his neck for 14 Days for a mark of Igno-minion, & if he is
seen without it is to Receive 100 Lashes, he is to return to
his Duty in his Battalion, the Gel approves all the a bove &
orders the Execution's to-morrow morning at guard mount-
ing. — JOHN FORD.

Town records, old grave-stones, and family tra-
ditions prove to us that many young patriots, the

pride of New England homes, perished from disease during this northern campaign, in the same locality where other patriots from the same towns had given up their lives in the service of the king in the earlier wars. We have an intimation of this in an entry of Captain Ford, under date of August 26, 1776 : —

"After order the commanding officer of each Reg^{t}m is to send a subbordinate officer to-morrow morning at sunrise to Fort George to Bring the Arms of the *Dead & Discharged* of their Respective Reg^{t}ms to this Place, officer will Receipt to the Director at Fort George for the Arms they Receive, and on their arrival at this Place Deliver them to the commanding of their Respective Corps."

HEAD QUARTERS, *August* 31st, 1776.

GENERAL ORDERS.

The Officers & Soldiers may be satisfied that the General has left no means in his Power untry'd to procure medicines and every Comfort for the Sick of this Army which the Station & Circumstances of this place will admit. The Director of this Department Dr. Stringer was sent to N. York three and thirty Days ago with positive orders to return the instant he had provided the drugs and medicines so much wanted ; since this, repeated Letters have been wrote to N. York and Philadelphia setting forth in the strongest terms the pressing necessity of an immediate supply of those articles. The General is credibly informed that a principal Surgeon is dispatched from N. York above a Fortnight ago with a supply of medicines & apprehends that the Badness of the weather and Road has alone prevented his Arrival. It is the Soldiers Duty to maintain the part he is ordered to defend. The same climate affects them, our enemies, that effects us, & the favor of the Almighty to whom we have appealed will, if we trust in him preserve us from Slavery & Death. The General recommends it to the Surgeons of the Different Reg^ts to communicate to each other the state of the sick in their ranks, and their different Diseases, the Remedies principally wanted & the comforts which are most in request, for he will have nothing unattempted in his power to provide what ever he can command for their Recovery. The General also desires the medical Gentlemen will consult upon and adopt the most proper measures for obtaining those salutary purposes.

HEAD QUARTERS, *Oct.* 8th, 1776.

PAROLE MADRID, CT. SN. WALL.

The Commissary to issue four sheep to each Regt., 3 to the Corps of Artillery, & 3 to the Artificers, at their usual time of Drawing Provisions. The Commanding Officers will direct the sick & weak Soldiers be supply'd with this Refreshment. The Commissary is to recon the Sheep in their Allowance to the Regt. at their estimated weight.

HEAD QUARTERS, *Oct.* 12, 1776.

Discharged soldiers are to return in to the commanding officers of the Regt., to which they belong, the arms, ammunitions, accoutrements, &c, which they may have in Possession belonging to the public. The commanding officers are to see that this order is comply'd with. A Return of the names, companies & Regiments of soldiers who have been discharged the Service from the first Day of Oct. is to be given in to the Deputy Adjutant Genl., to-morrow at orderly-Time, afterwards to be given in on Saturdays.

We have an intimation of the condition of the army by a return of Captain Ford's company, made on September 27, 1776 : —

Capt., 2 Lieuts., 1 Ensign, 4 Sargts., 2 Trumpeters, 33 fit for duty, 11 on command, 4 sick absent, 34 sick present, 82 total rank and file.

HEAD QUARTERS, *Oct.* 15, 1776.

The Fleet have acted a noble part. Let it not be said hereafter that the cause of all America was injured by the supineness of the northern army. Capt. Lt. Jones of the Artillery will return to the side of Ticonderoga and Major Bigelow, being recovered from his late Indisposition, will return to the Command of the Artillery on Mount Independence.

HEAD QUARTERS, *Octr.* 19, 1776.

Lt. Col⁰. Baldwin 1st Engineer will take the Direction of the works upon the side of Ticonderoga with the following assistants under him, Major Paine, Capt. Newland, Lt. Dallis, and Ensign Parrett. Lt. Col⁰. Pallifor, 2nd Engineer will take Direction of the works upon Mount Independence with the following assistants under him, Capt. Patterson, Mr. Delezenne and two other gentlemen that the Colᵒˢ. on that side may command. This arrangement being settled & the particular works to be completed, determined upon, the General has no doubt but the necessary preparations for a vigorous Defence will be made with that animated zeal becoming soldiers who are also citizens of America. Soldiers whose arms have been wet by the late bad weather and cannot be drawn, are to be drawn up in squads in proper places half an hour before sunset, and there discharge their arms. The Regts. who want ammunition may be supplyed by applying to Col⁰. Trumbull D. A. G. The troops have two days provisions ready dress'd until further orders. All the spears that can be spared from the vessels to be delivered for the Defence of the French Lines & Redoubts.

As this campaign was drawing to a close, an effort was made to induce the soldiers to enlist for the war. Of this Captain Ford makes the following record : —

HEAD QUARTERS, *Oct.* 24, 1776.

The Commanding Officers of the Regt^s. are directed to ¼ lb. of buck shott for every man fit for Duty in their respective Camps. The honorable, the Congress of the United States of America have for the Reward & encouragement of each non commissioned Officer & Soldier who shall engage to serve during the War, further resolved to give every above the Bounty of 20 Dollars to each man annually with one complete suit of clothing which for the present year is to consist of two linen hunting shirts, two pair stockings, 2 pair of shoes, two pair of Overhalls, a leather or woolen jackett with sleeves, one pair of Breeches, one leather cap or hat amounting to 20 Dollars in the whole or that sum to be paid each soldier who shall procure those Articles for himself & produce a certificate thereof from the Capt. of the Company to the Paymaster of the Reg^{mt}."

It was in this campaign that Rev. William Emerson was taken ill and died. (See Chap. XXIV.)

The names of the patriots of Chelmsford who responded to the Lexington alarm, preserved by Captain Ford, are here given, together with the number of days each was in service, in order that the reader may more clearly understand the confused state of the country at that time : —

Oliver Barron, Capt., 16.
Samuel Stevens, Lieut., 10.
John Ford, Sergt., 6.
Benjamin Warren, Sergt., 9.
Silas Spaulding, Sergt., 16.
Jonas Pierce, Corl., 6.
John Spaulding, Drummer, 10.

Jacob Howard, Private, 10.
Benjamin Spaulding, 11.
David Burge, 11.
Ephraim Parkhurst, 11.
Oliver Richardson, 7.
Daniel Dammon, 18.
Daniel Sillaway, 9.

Willard Howard, 2.

William Bowers, 13.

Josiah Richardson, 3.

John Dunn, 3.

John Twiss, 3.

Henry Spaulding, Jr., 7.

Joseph Marshall, 5.

Stephen Pierce, Jr., 5.

Samuel Fletcher, 4.

Joshua Davis, 8.

Oliver Fletcher, 8.

Jonathan Peirce, 11.

Nathaniel Farrar, 9.

Joseph Taylor, 10.

Thomas Marshall, Jr., 9.

William Mears, 4.

John Roby, 17.

Benjamin Parkhurst, 3.

Moses Barron, 15.

John Mears, 5.

Jeremiah Abbott, 5.

Reuben Parker, 13.

David Danforth, 4.

Benjamin Parker, 3.

Amos Mastes, 7.

Isaac Kent, Jr., 6.

David Marshall, 5.

Benjamin ———, 5.

Samuel Marshall, 9.

Daniel Keyes, 6.

John Keyes, 6.

William Dunn, 4.

Benjamin Barrett, 6.

James Dunn, Jr., 8.

Francis Daverson, 7.

Moses Esterbrooks, 8.

William Cambel, 6.

David Chambers, 8.

John Chambers, 7.

Jonathan Sprague, 6.

Isaiah Foster, Jr., 6.

Samuel Britton, 6.

William Chambers, 3.

Benjamin Parker, Jr., 8.

Benjamin Pierce, 7.

Josiah Fletcher, Jr., 9.

Joseph Spaulding, 6.

It was on the 22d of April, 1775, that the Provincial Congress voted to raise thirty thousand men, and on the 25th John Ford had enlisted fifty-seven men — a company of which he was made captain. Nineteen of these were on the roll of those who turned out on April 19, and several continued through later campaigns with their trusted leader, Captain John Ford. In the burying-ground near Pawtucket Bridge, a plain headstone records : —

CAPT. JOHN FORD
DIED NOV. 6, 1822, Æ 84.

Benjamin Pierce, afterward General Pierce and the father of President Franklin Pierce, was a member of Captain Ford's company. Of him Joshua Merrill, Esq., of Lowell says, —

" He was born in Chelmsford, now Lowell, December 25, 1767. He was bereft of his father at the age of six years, and was taken by his uncle, Robert Pierce, a farmer. . . . He remained with his uncle until April 19, 1775. He was then ploughing in a field on Powell Street. He heard the firing of guns, and soon messengers arrived notifying the inhabitants of the battles of Lexington and Concord. Young Pierce was then in his eighteenth year. He chained his steers, as he called them, to a stump, went to the house, took his uncle's gun and equipments, and started for Concord on foot. The British had retreated before he reached Concord. He enlisted in Captain Ford's company, and was in service till the close of the war.

" In one of the battles, when the bearer of the colors was shot, young Pierce seized the colors, and bore them to the front during the conflict. In subsequent years, Governor Pierce, when he came from his home in Hillsborough, N.H., to Lowell to visit his old friends, took delight in pointing out to them the stump to which, on April 19, 1775, he hitched his steers."

CHAPTER XXI

OLD HEARTH-STONES IN CHELMSFORD. — PERHAM
HOMESTEAD, WHERE NINE GENERATIONS OF THE
FAMILY HAVE LIVED. — TEN GENERATIONS OF
SPAULDINGS ON THE OLD FARM. — THE OLD GAR-
RET OF THE SPAULDING HOUSE. — ELEVEN GEN-
ERATIONS OF FLETCHERS ON THE OLD FARM. —
HAYWARD HOME THE OLD GARRISON. — OLD
HOME OF THE BYAMS SINCE 1655. — THOMAS
HENCHMAN AND THE WARREN FAMILY. — THE
BURYING-GROUND

CHELMSFORD is peculiarly favored in the unbroken family possession of its old farms. The
first visited in my circuit of this ancient settlement is the Perham homestead.

The first white settler on this farm was John
Perham. He married in 1664 Lydia Shepley,
who had come with her parents in the Wenham
Colony.

When the Perham pioneer began to subdue
these acres, the apostle Eliot was looking after
the interests of the Indians here; and a company
of Mr. Perham's neighbors were trustees for the
aboriginal owners of the soil, of what is now the

town of Chelmsford and the city of Lowell, and even beyond their limits. "The first dwelling," says Mr. Perham, the present thrifty owner and occupant, "was doubtless one of the rudely constructed houses of the times, but compared favorably with that erected by him and the other settlers for their minister, Rev. John Fisk, who had come from Wenham. The plan for the minister's house

PERHAM HOMESTEAD, CHELMSFORD

is thus indicated; 'And we do agree and order that he shall have a house built for him, thirty-eight feet in length, and twenty-four in breadth, with three fire rooms. The chimney built with brick or stone.'"

After enduring the hardships of pioneer life, and struggling nobly for existence for more than a half century in this locality, Mrs. Lydia Perham died in 1710, and was followed by her husband in 1721. They were succeeded on the farm by a son,

Benoni Perham, who with Sarah Robbins, his wife, was contented in the original house until their son Samuel erected a more comfortable dwelling, which, with modern improvements, has sheltered seven generations. The two who succeed the present owner make nine who have dwelt there. "Our family had been located here a full century," said the present owner, "when the drum beat to arms on April 19, 1775." The hero of the family at that distressing time was Samuel, senior, who served the patriot cause on the Committee of Safety and in the Provincial convention at Concord. His sons Samuel and Oliver were among those who shouldered their muskets, and served in the company from this town.

Another old homestead visited was the Spaulding farm. The Spauldings were in the town among the first settlers. Edward Spaulding was there before the incorporation in 1655, and was among those selected in November, 1654, "by the consent of the major part of the town for ordering the Public affairs." He belonged to that colony, who, with their minister, left Wenham in Essex County, and did good service in establishing the church and town that have made a most commendable record for two hundred and forty years. Ten generations of the Spaulding family are recorded as having resided in Chelmsford, and figured in the history of the town. I met, among others of the family, Mr. George Spaulding, busily occupied in tilling his acres. He said, " My father was Alpheus, and his father was Joseph Spaulding, who left this farm in response to the call of April 19, 1775, and who gained some notoriety in the battle of Bunker Hill. You have read the inscription on the slab at his grave, which gives

SPAULDING HOME, CHELMSFORD

only a part of my grandfather's story. His own report of it was, 'I fired ahead of time, and Putnam rushed up and struck at me for violating orders. I suppose I deserved it, but I was anxious to get another good shot at Gage's men ever since our affair at Concord. The blow from " Old Put " hit me on the head, made a hole in my hat, and left this scar ;' and," said the grandson, "it was an honorable scar. Grandfather was proud of it, and carried it to his grave." Mr. George Spaulding, who is of the eighth generation, continued his story, " My grandfather was living at that time in an old house on this farm, and had just raised the frame of this dwelling when he was called to do a patriot's duty away from these acres. When the house was completed he moved into it with grandmother and the children, one of whom was my father; and the Revolutionary roof has already sheltered five generations of Spauldings."

SPAULDING WATCH, USED AT
BUNKER HILL

To make his grandfather's part at Bunker Hill more vivid, Mr. Spaulding brought from the house a silver watch, ticking with as much regularity as it was on the morning of June 17, 1775, when Joseph Spaulding aimed his fowling-piece at Major Pitcairn. Said the proud descendant, "My grandfather brought the watch to this house; and here it has been kept ever since, often proving more reliable than some modern timepieces."

In confirmation of Mr. Spaulding's story of the cocked hat, Mrs. Luther Faulkner of Billerica says, "It was one of the delights of my childhood to play in that old garret with my companions, the grandchildren of Joseph Spaulding. It was the storeroom of scores of articles that dated back to the early generations of the family. There were the rude implements of the farm, the cast-off utensils of the kitchen, and many articles of husbandry that time had relegated to that lumber-room. Oh, what a pleasure it was for us children, on a rainy day, to amuse ourselves among those relics! The flax cards, the hatchel, the reel, the wheels great and small, were all put to our childish service. Then a season was spent in playing soldier, but the boys thought the girls had no part in that. 'Grandsir's' cocked hat was brought from its hiding-place; and each boy in turn, crowned with the tattered relic, marched up and down the garret floor. 'Just as Grandsir Spaulding marched at Bunker Hill,' was the childish order. It had received holes through the crown, and 'grandsir' was proud of them; but the old soldier of 1775 was gone, and I am afraid we were rough with his hat. The hat and all else in that ancient garret were consumed by fire; yet the memory of those days, and particularly of the old cocked hat, will remain as long as life lasts."

Another most interesting representative of the Spaulding family is Mrs. Mary (Spaulding) Shedd, who, at the age of ninety-three years, delights in repeating the stories heard from the lips of her grandfather, Zebulon Spaulding, who was one of the minute-men of the town. The story of the opening Revolution, as she tells it, confirms that already given, and her personal recollections of the second war with England are as vivid as are those of the Civil War. Said this venerable member of the family, "My father was Sherebiah Spaulding." In regard to the second trouble with England, she said, "The early spirit of patriotism was quickly kindled in his breast, as in others of Chelmsford. He presented a most charming appearance to my youthful eyes, when he was equipped in his brilliant uniform, and ready to march to Boston. I

MRS. SHEDD

was too young to fully realize what the war-cry meant; but there were those in our family who recalled the sufferings of Concord, Bunker Hill, and Valley Forge, and with tearful faces stood by as the soldiers went away, while the old fire of patriotism was rekindled in their breasts; but their forms were too much bowed with age to again face the enemy."

This delightful lady of the old school, on her ninety-third birthday, remarked, "'I have known eight generations of my family, and have seen an entire change in the manner of conducting domestic matters, as well as business affairs. I have seen the loom and wheel, which were kept in action in each family, give way to the innumerable looms and spindles of the city of Lowell, which has sprung into existence since I came to maturity."

I was next conducted to the Hayward farm, where five generations of the family have flourished, Miss Adelia Hayward being the present owner. Miss Hayward said that her great-grandfather came to this house in 1726. Here in the walls are unmistakable evidences of the garrison of the early wars; and the chimney of stone, such as the settlers agreed to build in the minister's house in 1654, is suggestive of a stronghold. There is the hollow passage-way by the side of the rough stone, allowing free passage from the bottom of the cellar to the chimney top. It was

to be used for concealment, and for an outlook
whereby to discern the approach of danger.	This
place, and all such in old houses, are always de-
lightfully suggestive and interesting.	Here the
rude ladder, over which generations of Haywards
have climbed, adds to the interest of the place.

HAYWARD GARRISON, CHELMSFORD

An aged neighbor is a frequent visitor at this
house, who says her mother often told her that
it is the place where the women went for safety
when the Indians were out.

The Hayward family has flourished here for one
hundred and seventy years; yet they are modern
in the town in comparison with the Adams family,

of whom the farm was purchased a half century before the Revolution. The name of Thomas Adams is seen in connection with the settlement in 1653, and Samuel Adams was early chosen as the town clerk. The descendants have been among those who have made a record as good patriots through all these years, both in Chelmsford and elsewhere.

BYAM HOME, CHELMSFORD

The Byam estate is one that has been in the family since the first settlement of the town. The name of George Byam appears in the list of those who came from Wenham in 1655. He located on the farm where the ninth generation is met to-day. The pioneer wisely selected his land where there was an abundant supply of running water; and Beaver Brook, that wound on its course through his meadows, has continued of service to each of the generations in their time. How early the stream was given that name does not appear; but in January, 1659, we find: —

> "George Biam and Thomas Barrett are appointed a committee to state a Highway that gos to Tadmuck before Thomas Chamberlain's hous. The tree at his Hog's Coat is concluded one bound, and so to Run his due bredth acording to order, towards the Broak Cold Beaver broak."

George Byam, the first, had three sons, whom he named for the Jewish patriarchs, Abraham, Isaac, and Jacob. But instead of representing three successive generations, they were of one and the same; yct the promise to Abraham of old was verified here, and there has not been wanting a son to continue the family name and possession. We find Amos, of the fifth generation, with his wife, Sarah Pierce, located in the original dwelling of only two rooms, one above the other. This house has been preserved; and there are pointed out to-day the four corners where the loom, fireplace, wheel, and bed were located.

WARREN HOMESTEAD.

Very near the centre of Chelmsford is the Warren homestead. This estate belonged to Thomas Hinchman, who was an influential man in the early days. In the year 1699 he deeded it to the first

Joseph Warren. A portion of the original house, more than two hundred years old, is disguised in a more modern dwelling, which identifies the spot where the first hearth-stone was placed. So large was the original farm that it admitted of divisions and subdivisions, and several families of the name or blood are settled there in the enjoyment of a competency. For nearly two centuries there has been a Joseph Warren on the farm. The donor of the farm is pleasantly remembered in the name of one of the present generation, who is Edwin Henchman Warren. The family has ever enjoyed the confidence of its contemporaries, each generation doing the part of true patriotic citizens. Among the treasures of early military service held by the family at the old homestead are a musket and a halberd, which doubtless date back to the time when Jeduthan Warren served in the northern campaign in 1776, with a large company, under Captain John Ford. The Lexington alarm called Sergeant Benjamin Warren from the old home. He was in Captain Oliver Barron's company, and actively engaged in the running fight of April 19, 1775.

The first Joseph Warren, born in 1670, possessed a copy of "The General Laws of the Massachusetts Colony, Revised and published by order of the General Court, in October 1658." This volume has been kept by the successive Josephs, and is now one of the family treasures. It is believed to have been the property of Jacob Warren, the pioneer of the family.

THE RICHARDSON HOME

About two miles north of the centre of Chelmsford is the early home of the Richardson family, where I met Mr. Edward F. Richardson, who modestly said, " I am of the seventh generation in a direct line of our family in possession of this farm.   The first was Josiah, who, with the other male inhabitants, petitioned on May 17, 1658, the ' honored Court Assembled at Boston ' for the privilege of trading with the Indians.   They represent themselves as located ' into this Remoat Corner of the wilderness.' "   Says the present owner, " My pioneer ancestor built his log house in the south side of this great sand-bank, and here located with his family.   He was succeeded by John, Eleazer, and Samuel, who represented as many successive generations.   Each in turn, with his family, enjoyed and improved the homestead, doing manfully their part in church and government.   It was Oliver, son of Samuel, my grandfather, who responded from this place to the Lexington alarm.   He was but sixteen years of age when he was found in Captain Barron's company in pursuit of the Regulars.   He was among those who fought down by the rail fence on June 17, at Charlestown.   He had a great powder-horn ; and he always said, ' I had a plenty of ammunition

when the others had none; for my horn was well
filled with my own stock from home, and I used it
to the best advantage possible on that morning at
Charlestown.' Oliver was not disheartened by
these early experiences, but was found with the
Chelmsford men in the campaign at the north
when Burgoyne was obliged to give up his enterprise. Oliver, the young soldier, was succeeded
by his son Francis, from whom the present generation received the estate."

The Adams family early made a record in
Chelmsford; and many of that name to-day
revert to the mother town as the place of their
origin, while the patriotic deeds of their ancestors for two centuries are an inspiration to them.

" The family of Adam or Adams (meaning red; adamah,
red earth) can claim the distinction of having the oldest
individual name on record." — *Adams Genealogy.*

Two sons of Henry Adams, the immigrant
leader who settled in Braintree, were among the
founders of Chelmsford. Thomas, born in 1612,
was well established with a large family when he
was received as a member of the Chelmsford
Church, "27th of 2d '56." Samuel, born 1617, was
the father of a family when he appears as town
clerk of Chelmsford.

They did a grand work here during the remainder of their lives. The former died in 1666,
and the latter in 1676.

Samuel Adams was the first miller of the town. On July 3, 1656, he was granted four hundred acres of land to encourage him to set up a saw-mill, and later he had one hundred acres more for erecting a corn-mill. These mills marked a new era in the building of houses, as well as the preparation of grains for food. It was on a commanding site just beyond the brook that the miller erected his dwelling. Seven generations occupied the farm, and presided at the mill; but it has now passed into other hands, as have homesteads of other branches of the family. It is apparent that the Adams family of Chelmsford was connected with Samuel Adams the patriot, and it is interesting that the two branches should have been so positive in espousing the cause of the patriots in the Revolution. Pelatiah Adams from this town, who died in the service of his country at Cherry Valley, is remembered by the monument on the Common in his native town; while Samuel, the leader in the Revolution, sleeps in Granary Burying-Ground in Boston, with no slab to remind the passing stranger of the brave patriot. The Adams Library at Chelmsford is a fitting memorial of not only the donor, but of all the descendants of the early settlers at Chelmsford by the name of Adams.

The name of Parkhurst first appeared in this town in 1658, and the family is one of the most numerously represented to-day. Joseph, from Water-

town, was the founder here. He married Mary
Read, and settled on his share of the "New
Field." He was succeeded by his son Ebenezer.
Then came Jonathan, who was born in 1701,
married Hannah Richardson in 1724, and died in
1737, leaving a widow and seven children. Of
these Josiah continued the family line in the
town. He married Elizabeth King. Samuel, one
of the four children, was a noted patriot among
the many of the town, acted well his part in the
various campaigns, and lived to a great age. He
was fond of fighting over his battles by the fireside, to the delight of not only his own descendants, but of the many who were inspired by his
patriotic zeal to do valiant service for town and
country. A sword captured by the patriot Samuel, together with his musket, are treasured relics
of the family.

FLETCHER HOMESTEAD.

TWO HUNDRED AND FORTY-THREE YEARS OLD.

A most peculiar interest centres at the Fletcher
farm. The first pulsations of civilized life in the
town are traced to this homestead. The name of
William Fletcher is seen with others on the petition of May, 1653, for a grant of six miles square
"which bordereth upon Merrimack River near to
Pautucket, which we do find a very comfortable
place to accommodate a company of God's people

upon ; that may with God's blessing and assistance live comfortably upon and do good in that place for church and commonwealth." The petition was granted eight days later, May 18, 1653, on conditions that a reservation should be made for the Indians, through the intercession of the apostle Eliot.

"CAPTAIN BILL FLETCHER'S" HOUSE

The common lands were allotted to the settlers, William Fletcher being one of them. He was a son of Robert of Concord, born in England, and made a freeman in the Colony in 1643. He married Lydia Bates of Concord, and they set up their home in this wilderness in 1653. Tradition tells us that the house to which William Fletcher conducted his trustful bride was the first in the settlement having the pretensions of a frame, and was distinguished as having been the place of the first town meeting.

The 22d: the 9th: month: 1654.

At a meeting then at William Fletcher's Hous there was chosen to officiate in Ordering the Publick affairs of the Place, by the Consent of the Major part of the Town for this present year ensuing are as followeth: — Esdras Read; Edward Spaulding; William Fletcher; Isaac Lerned; Simon Thompson; William Underwood; Thomas Adams. They also set apart thirty acres of land for the minister, and provided for his house.

William the pioneer was of the second generation in the country, and acted a prominent part in the affairs of town and Colony until his death in November, 1677. He was succeeded on this farm by a son William, born four years after the first settlement; but he was not made a freeman until twelve years after his father, William, died. Governor Dudley commissioned him a lieutenant in 1704, which position he honorably filled until his death in 1713. Although the pioneer here was not honored with military titles, yet his record is with the faithful patriots of the early days of the Colony. Josiah of the fourth generation was the next in order on the farm; and he was succeeded by a son Josiah, born October 30, 1719.

While each generation has continued the name of William, other names have appeared in the line of possession of the farm. In the sixth generation

William asserts his birthright. He was born December 22, 1754. His cradle lullaby was of the conquered French, and in his maturity a military spirit actuated him. He was one of four Fletchers to respond to the Lexington alarm. His family story repeated by his great-great-grandson William is : —

"I was one of those who stepped over the body of the first British soldier killed at Concord Bridge, when was made 'the first forcible resistance to British aggression.'"

The musket carried in the war by one of the family is still treasured at the old home by William of the tenth generation. This musket has never been robbed of the old flint-lock and the primitive arrangements of Colonial days. Oliver Fletcher, the famous town clerk, was of the fifth generation ; and his record is among those who did faithful service for his native town.

William, the hero of April 19, '75, married, during the years of the Revolution, Lucy Hildrith ; and thus the two old and influential families were united. William of the seventh generation, their son, was born May 18, 1782, and married in 1815 to Orpha Spaulding, thus making a connection with another of the oldest families of the town. This William died in 1846, and was gathered to the grave with his fathers on the hill. His successor was William, born in 1819. He brought as a helpmeet to the old home, Diantha

E. Dustin of New Hampshire, and second, Eliza A. Warren of Chelmsford. Having made a good record in the town, State legislature, etc., he resigned the family home in 1893 to Charles Frederic of the ninth generation, who was born on Independence Day, 1846, in time to receive his grandfather's parting blessing. He dedicated himself to the cause of preserving the Union early in the War of the Rebellion, and kept good the record of patriotism begun by his ancestors.

The next in line of this family is William of the tenth generation, who was born in 1872, and married to Jenny A. Fulton on New Year's Day of 1893. A representative of the eleventh generation in the country, and the tenth on this farm, is Rachel Fulton Fletcher. This babe is cradled within a few rods of the site of the first house built by William Fletcher in 1653. Different branches of the family have set up homes on the paternal acres, the oldest of which is a red house with a gambrel roof. It is in much the same condition as when "Uncle Bill" Fletcher, at ninety years of age, used to gather his children and grandchildren about the old hearth-stone, and tell his story of personal experience at Concord, and in the other events of the 19th of April, '75, and of his service with Captain Ford in the northern campaign of 1777.

> Not " a man is now alive,
> Who remembers that famous day and year;"

but it comes to us with double reality when told
on such homesteads, and from lips first taught to
lisp the word patriot by those who fought for independence at Concord and Bunker Hill.

Having traced the footprints of early and later
patriots at the old homesteads, we naturally turn
to the old burial-ground where —

> "Their names, their years, spelt by the unlettered muse,
>   The place of fame and elegy supply."

Chelmsford proper has but one burying-place;
and in this ground, a gracefully sloping enclosure
hard by the meeting-house, has been gathered the
dust of many generations.   " Quaint inscriptions,
the traditional death's head and hour-glass, greet
you on every hand."

The oldest stone is —

> HERE LYES Y^R BODY OF GRACE
> LIUERMOAR WIFE TO IHON
> LIUERMOAR AGED 75 YEARS
> DIED THE 14TH OF IANUARY
>   1690.

This and other stones in that enclosure show
that the town had among its brave founders those
who were born before the Pilgrims landed at
Plymouth.

A rudely carved and sunken stone, standing in
its fastness with but little regard for its more

MAJOR THOMAS HINCHMAN'S MILITARY ORDER

(Original owned by the author.)

modern companions, recalls to mind a patriot in
deed, who did great service for town and country.
One can barely decipher the following : —

HERE LYETH Yᴱ BODY OF

MAJOR THOMAS HINCHMAN

AGED 74 YEARS

DECᴰ JULY Yᴱ 17 1703.

He was not mighty with the sword, but through
his skilful management the barbarities
of the savages were averted.

" Peace hath her victories no less renowned than war." — MILTON.

HINCHMAN STONE, CHELMSFORD

Some of Major Thomas Hinchman's military orders are still preserved by a grateful people ; one
from which the plate is made was found in a garret of the old town.

Near by is another small but suggestive stone
on which is read : —

HERE LYES Yᴱ BODY OF
DEACON CORNELIUS WALDO
AGED 75 YEARS
DIED JAN. 3 1700.

The memory of the Just is Blessed.

CORNELIUS WALDO STONE

His daughter Re-
becca married Ed-
ward Emerson, a
teacher for a time
in Chelmsford. This
shows us how the
name of Waldo was
introduced into the
Emerson family.

Evidence of the
youthfulness of sol-
diers in the Revolu-
tion is gathered from
a stone on which is chiselled : —

ERECTED TO THE MEMORY OF
JOB SPAULDING
BORN MARCH 1762,
DIED NOVEMBER 15, 1835.

A Revolutionary Pensioner, Honorably discharged, from
the first three years service of his Country
May 1780, at the early age of
18 yrs. & 2 mos.

An honest man.

This man enlisted to the credit of the town of Westford. But among his descendants is Mrs. Parkhurst of Chelmsford, who treasures not only her grandfather's stories of the war, but also a fork made by the young soldier when in service, and a small volume brought from the army, which was printed in Dublin in 1776.

On a stone to the memory of Mrs. Hannah Foster is read : —

ALSO OF MR. NOAH FOSTER
SON OF MR. WILLIAM AND MRS. HANNAH FOSTER
WHO DIED AT STILLWATER IN THE SERVICE OF HIS
COUNTRY, OCTR. YE 7TH 1777,
AGED 20 YEARS.

Among the six generations of Perhams, the patriot Samuel has an honored place. He died March 2, 1788, aged 31 years and 6 months.

At the grave of the pioneer of the family is read : —

HERE LYES YE BODY OF
MR. JOHN PERHAM
WHO DECEASED JANU^{RY} YE 21ST 1721
AGED 88 YEARS.

The pioneer pastor, Rev. John Fisk, sleeps in an unmarked grave, unless a large table-stone without inscription was intended to mark his place of sepulture. But he is remembered for his unselfish patriotic acts.

The second minister, Rev. Thomas Clark, who

died in 1704, is memorialized by a tablet on which is read an extended Latin inscription. The stone was purchased by "a gift of fifty shillings from sundry persons in Chelmsford," as appears by a receipt from Rev. John Hancock of Lexington, who married a daughter of Rev. Thomas Clark.

We here get a hint of the manner in which the families of the clergymen of early New England were joined in marriage, and a sort of literary aristocracy created. The second wife of Rev. Thomas Clark was a daughter of Rev. Samuel Whiting of Billerica. In following down the line from Chelmsford, we find that a daughter of Rev. John Hancock and grandaughter of Rev. Thomas Clark became the wife of Rev. Nicholas Bowes of Bedford, and that a daughter from the Bedford parsonage became the wife of Rev. Jonas Clark of Lexington, and so was mistress of the Lexington parsonage during the Revolution. A second daughter from the Bedford parsonage became the wife of Rev. Phinehas Whitney of Shirley, and served that people from 1770 to 1805.

MINISTER'S TABLE, CHELMSFORD

The fourth minister of Chelmsford, Rev. Ebenezer Bridge, married a daughter of his immediate predecessor in office, Rev. Samson Stoddard ; and their daughter Sarah married Rev. Henry Cummings of Billerica. Among the scores of stones at the graves of the patriots of 1775 which afford no hint of their peculiar service is one —

TO THE MEMORY OF THEIR MINISTER
DURING THAT TRYING PERIOD.

BY THE CHURCH OF CHRIST IN CHELMSFORD.

In testimony of their esteem and veneration this sepultrial stone was erected to stand as a sacred memorial of their late
worthy Pastor

THE REV. EBENEZER BRIDGE,

who after having officiated among them in the service of the sanctuary for more than a year above half a century, the strength of nature being exhausted, sunk under the burden of age and joined the congregation of the dead.

OCT. 1, 1792. Æ. 78.

Chelmsford's patriotic minister was represented by his son and namesake, Ebenezer Bridge, a graduate of Harvard University, who did good service on April 19th and June 17th.[1] The minister was faithful in looking out for the comfort of the poor of Boston, of whom forty-nine were consigned to Chelmsford at one time. There were also among his parishioners those who had come out on their own account to seek a place of safety.

April 9, 1775. Capt. Symmes came from Boston to secure a place of retreat in the present troublesome season at Boston.

---

[1] See " Beneath Old Roof Trees," page 240.

The pastor records the death of Mr. Fitzgerald, who lived in town since the siege of Boston. Rev. Mr. Bridge was among the faithful ministers who went to camp to look after their townsmen during the siege of Boston. He records : —

May 29, 1775. Rode to Cambridge and lodged with ensign Hastings at the headquarters of the army.

May 30. Visited our soldiers, dined at Capt. Steadman's by invitation. Met and delighted with the appearance and order. Saw the spoils taken at Chelsea from the Regulars.

The sculptor did his best work in the execution of customary emblems on a stone to the memory of a clerk of the

To the Memory of the Town Clerk, Chelmsford .

town, whose records are a source of delight to every one who has an occasion to study them.

" Memento Mori."

OLIVER FLETCHER ESQ.

Departed this Life Nov. 30, 1771, in the 63d Year of his Age, and his Remains are here Interred.

There are two memorial stones in this ancient burying-ground, which for position, design, execution, and preservation prompt a stranger to a diligent inquiry. They mark the graves of Colonel and Mrs. Jonas Clark, and serve to recall a most notable couple to the scene of action. Jonas Clark was the eldest son of Rev. Thomas Clark, born in 1684, and was early trained to walk in the strait and narrow way by a genuine New England clergyman. He doubtless disappointed his father in not following him in a

CLARK STONES, CHELMSFORD

profession ; but he was a man of affairs, and became notable in that direction.   He kept a tavern
in what is now known as Middlesex Village, Lowell.
It was near the ferry, and a resort for all fashionable people.   He was foremost in civil and military
affairs, and withal " a good Christian."   Around
him gathered the leaders of all branches of society.
The coaches of Lowell's most wealthy and distinguished citizens of to-day are inferior to those with
the armorial bearings of the Colonial times, which
rolled up to that hospitable door where the stately
Colonel received his relatives and guests, among
them the Hancocks of mercantile and clerical life,
and scores of like noted families.   Of no less importance were the Colonel's associates in military
affairs who also congregated at this house.   The
most timid rustic could not pass the tavern without turning to catch a glimpse of the spangle
and glitter within ; while the more brave presented
themselves at the bar, drank from the common
decanter, backed up to the flaming hearth, and
witnessed such displays of Colonial grandeur as
could be observed from their standpoint.   The
brilliancy of a dinner-party of those days has no
parallel for the eyes of this generation.

   With the class of guests who sat at the Colonel's
board, he might have been excused if he had kept
silent on the great questions that exercised the
minds of the Colonists during the latter part of
his life ; but he was bold in his declaration for the

rights of the Colonies, yet did not live to see the clash of arms. Wrapped in his scarlet cloak, he was laid to rest with military honors in the spring of 1770; and it was truthfully recorded, " He was honored in his day, and was the glory of his times."

CLARK TAVERN, LOWELL

As ancient is this hostelry
As any in the land may be.
Built in the old Colonial day,
When men lived in a grander way
With ampler hospitality.

LONGFELLOW.

The Parker homestead is another estate within the limits of Lowell which belonged to Old Chelmsford. While it is apparent that no other family has been in possession of the estate since the Indians quit their claim to Wamesit, it is impossible to decide when the first Parker set up his home on the present attractive site. A petition of 1653 for a grant of a tract six miles square, "which bordereth upon Merrimack near Pautucket," bears the names of twenty-nine men, four of whom are Parkers. The first recorded birth, in 1653, was that of Joseph Parker. A well-founded tradition says that the wife of Abraham Parker was the first woman who "baked and brewed in Chelmsford." The first town clerk of the settlement was Jacob Parker, who, we believe, at this time was intending to become a permanent settler, but later removed, with Sarah his wife, to Malden. Some of their children, however, remained, and perhaps took up the work at this homestead relinquished by the parents. Benjamin Parker, born in 1663, is the first family proprietor known to have been located here on Chelmsford Neck. He married Sarah Howard, granddaughter of Major Simon Willard, one of the founders of Concord. They were succeeded by a son Benjamin, born in 1699, whose son Benjamin, born in 1723, continued the family possession. The next in order of descent is Jeduthan, born in 1763, succeeded by Benjamin, born in 1803, whose son Henry E. is the present owner. He has two sons, who represent the eighth generation on the homestead.

This family, prominent and thrifty for more than

two hundred and forty years, has not failed of
a representative in each generation whose filial relations prompted him to a full appreciation of the
work of those who have preceded him. There is
now treasured in this home in the city of Lowell
an accumulation of papers, among which are reminders of several changes in government from

PARKER HOMESTEAD, LOWELL

the days of the Indians to that of the present.
Through the courtesy of Mr. Henry E. Parker, I
am able to invite my readers to share in the consideration of some of them.

The most attractive are two deeds written on
skins of animals, so badly dressed as to be a poor
apology for vellum. A hole in one was doubtless
made by the bullet which killed the animal. The
deeds are attached to rollers of primitive make.

They bear date of December 14, 1686, and convey
five hundred acres of land to forty-six white proprietors of Chelmsford. The land was a part of
the Indian reservation granted for the benefit of
the tribe through the interposition of John Eliot.
There were five hundred acres on the north side
of the river, and a much larger quantity on the
south side. The chief of these Indians was Pas-
saconnaway, who died in 1662, and was succeeded
by his son Wannalancet, who, in following the in-
junction of his father, was peaceable and friendly
with the white people. At the opening of King
Philip's war he withdrew to the northward rather
than join in the general attempt to exterminate
the English settlers.

As the natives abandoned the Wamesit grant,
the lands were gradually occupied by individuals
from Chelmsford and elsewhere; and in 1686 they
sold the unoccupied tract of five hundred acres to
Jonathan Tyng and Thomas Henchman, who conveyed it to the early proprietors. Among them
was Benjamin Parker, then twenty-three years of
age. This conveyance was in the "second year
of the reign of our sovereign lord, King James
the Second." It was before the union of the
Plymouth and Bay Colonies, when the first charter
was in force, and Simon Bradstreet was Colonial
governor.

The Wamesit purchase took place in the very
month of the arrival of Sir Edmund Andros, who

soon began to question the titles to all the lands
held by the settlers, and especially declared that
deeds from the Indians were no better than
"scratches of a bear's paw." But the insurrection begun in Boston resulted in the expulsion of
the tyrant, and the people had no trouble from
that source as to the possession of their lands.

COMMISSION TO BENJAMIN PARKER, CHELMSFORD

The next of these papers to hold our attention
is a commission granted by Governor Shirley in
1654 to the third Benjamin Parker as lieutenant
in the first foot company of Chelmsford, of which
Ebenezer Parker is captain. It is in the twenty-
eighth year of the reign of his Majesty, King
George the Second.

This paper, bearing the autograph of "W. Shirley," reminds us that Lieutenant Benjamin Parker was active during that expedition under Sir William Pepperell which resulted in despoiling the thrifty Acadians of their homes and property, and scattered seven thousand of the exiles throughout the Provinces. Twenty-three of the Chelmsford men were engaged in that service. A good number of the victims of that questionable measure of war were soon found at the doors of the Chelmsford farmers, to be provided with the necessaries of life.

Benjamin Parker continued to exercise the authority of his position through the remainder of the term of William Shirley, and also through the administration of Governors Phips, Pownal, and Bernard, and died soon after Thomas Hutchinson became governor. His death in May, 1771, called together a notable company, who were treated with all the courtesies of the age.

The next paper to enlist our attention is the bill for the funeral supplies. Among the items purchased of Samson Stoddard are: "seventeen pairs of men's black gloves ; twenty-two pairs of women's gloves ; 3 black Handkerchiefs ; 3 Veils ; 1 piece of Black Ribband ; 1 Black Fan ; 3 yds. of Hat-band crape." Another paper shows that nine pairs of the men's and two pairs of the women's gloves were purple ; one pair was white, and others were black. Other items were, " Rum & Shougar."

The religious service at this funeral, according to Rev. Mr. Bridge's journal, was confined to a prayer by him. He noted that at the funeral of Mrs. Parker, a few years before, the prayer was offered in the parson's absence by the " squire," the functionary next in order of dignity and importance in the town. We can see in fancy the large company of comrades and neighbors gathered on this day in the last of the spring month to do honor to the memory of Lieutenant Benjamin Parker. " The names of those who are to receive the gloves " is a paper which aids our imagination ; and we see the long procession form in the yard, some with black, some with purple, gloves, and the clergyman with white ones. They present an imposing appearance as they take up the body of their neighbor, and bear it all the long way to Chelmsford Centre. There were doubtless those who compared the outlay at this funeral with that of other similar occasions ; for the funeral customs had reached an extreme from which there soon came a decided reaction.

The mourning customs of this time in the Bay Colony were such as the early settlers had brought from Europe to New England. Black was the color worn in the mother country by the people in general, but kings and cardinals appeared in purple.

Rings were also an additional badge of mourning. The extremes to which this custom was often carried gave rise to legislation in 1721, and again in 1741, but with little effect. In 1743, at the death of Rev. Mr. Cooper, the amount of eight hundred and ninety-five pounds was collected in his congregation to meet the expense of the funeral, and to put his family, consisting of ten persons, and Dr. Colman into mourning. Among the items are twenty-nine rings for the ministers, and twelve dozen pairs of gloves.

Isaac Royal of Medford in 1743 advertised, —

"A handsome mourning coach and a pair of good horses to let to any funeral, at ten shillings old tenor, each funeral."

It was the custom to hang the escutcheon of the deceased head of a family from a window, or over the entrance to the house from which a funeral took place. The last instance in Boston was that of the funeral of Thomas Hancock in 1764, when the family arms appeared over the entrance to the famous house on Beacon Hill. Scarfs were frequently added to the gifts on these occasions.

The great and most decided change in funeral customs came during the contention with the mother country. The non-importation act had its effect, for imported garments had been more commonly used. In order to render the act more effective, the Grand American Continental Congress assembled at Philadelphia in the autumn of

1774 passed resolutions. The eighth article was
as follows : —

" We will, in our several stations encourage frugality,
economy and industry . . . and on the death of any relation, or friend, none of us, or any of our families will go
into any further mourning dress, than a black crape or ribbon on the arm or hat, for gentlemen, and a black ribbon
and necklace for ladies, and we will discountenance the giving of gloves and scarfs at funerals."

The act generally adopted by a vote of the
towns, coming soon after the funeral of Lieutenant Parker, leads to the conclusion that it was
among the last occasions of the kind when this
custom was practised to an extreme.

Another suggestive paper of the collection recalls the time of peculiar trial in the Provinces,
and reads : —

" Permit Benj^{a.} Parker to pass the Guards from Head
Quarters, May 23, 1775. J. WARD, *Secretary.*

The Chelmsford men were among those who
had left all in response to the Lexington alarm,
and were a part of the army holding the soldiers
of the king pent up in Boston. Benjamin Parker,
either as soldier, or as one who had come to bring
supplies, was given this pass, which served its purpose, and was added to the collection of earlier
papers.

An old wallet comes next to view, and its contents remind us that among the many questions

involved in our Revolution was that of the currency. There was none more difficult to meet. Each colony had its paper money, current within its own borders, but passing, if at all, at a depreciated rate in the sister colonies. This gave rise to peculiar difficulties soon after the beginning of open hostility.

The men who had come from beyond the limits of the Bay Colony had with them paper currency,

PARKER GARRET TREASURES, LOWELL

which was not accepted in exchange for the necessaries of life. This seemed hard in the extreme. They had left their peaceful abodes to succor their neighbors in distress, and when trying to pay their own expenses, found their money questionable. Our Provincial Congress made an early effort to remedy the difficulty by having the currency of Rhode Island and Connecticut pass in Massachusetts. They soon empowered the treasurer to borrow one hundred thousand pounds lawful money, secured by notes of the Province at six per cent, and made payable June 1, 1777. They also desired the other colonies to give currency to their securities. In June the Continental Congress ordered an emission of notes to the amount of two millions of dollars. Similar acts repeatedly followed as the war advanced. But a lurking sentiment of Toryism with some pretended patriots, as well as ordinary caution on the part of friends of the Provincial cause, usually commendable, had a depressing effect upon public confidence in paper currency. This prompted the Legislature to pass an act branding individuals as enemies to the country who declined to receive it for any pecuniary obligation. They all knew that a failure of the Provincial cause meant ruin to them, and that success might bring redemption of the doubtful currency. In the extremity they took the objectionable paper, and realized but little, if anything, upon it. That which remained in their hands was at length relegated to the old red chest, as in the Parker family, where the eighth generation brought it forth from the garret hiding-place, and patiently listened to the story of its intended purpose by the hearth-stone of early days.

CHAPTER XXII

CHELMSFORD CONTINUED. — CONTAGION FROM THE
ARMY. — FORMATION OF THE GOVERNMENT BY
THE PATRIOTS. — STORY OF A PATRIOT SPINNER.
— PETER BROWN WRITES TO HIS MOTHER FROM
CAMBRIDGE CAMP. — MISS SUSAN BROWN TELLS
THE STORY OF HER GRANDFATHER. — THE FIRST
BLOOD AT BUNKER HILL

ALTHOUGH far removed from the seat of war, the
town of Chelmsford was not exempt from the contagion which frequently visited the camp of the
army.   In the year 1776, a soldier returning from
the army called at the home of Dr. Marshall for
refreshment, as was the necessity of many weary
men when making their journey on foot with
empty purses.   The physician was away during
the call of the soldier, but upon his return detected
evidence of the contagion in the atmosphere,
which filled him with forebodings of evil.   The
worst was realized.   The entire family took the
smallpox, and Mrs. Marshall and two children died
from the loathsome disease.   In the following
year Samuel Lufkin and his wife and Solomon
Keyes died of the same disease, contracted in a
similar way.

The old burying-ground of Chelmsford reminds one of this entailment of war. On one stone we read of Mrs. Hannah Fletcher, wife of Lieutenant Benj. Fletcher, who, with four children, perished within the space of two weeks in the autumn of 1778.

FLETCHER STONE IN CHELMSFORD

While in the full enjoyment of our wisely instituted government, we hardly pause to think that our patriotic ancestors hesitated in its formation, and trembled at the experiment, even after they had fought to be free from the control of the mother country. It was easier to find the faults in the existing government than to point out the reliable remedy.

Probably no period of our national history has been more perilous than that which intervened between the close of the Revolutionary war and the adoption of the Constitution.

The Continental Congress, which was the result of an emergency, had done its work. The Articles of Confederation which followed were not sufficient; and it became apparent that a constitution must be formed by which the rights of each State would be protected, and also the interests of the whole be maintained. Then it was that every patriot so situated as to mould public opinion set to work to inform himself on governmental affairs. The patriotic ministers were looked to as guides; and it can be said to the honor of Rev. Mr. Bridge, that he made use of all light at his command, in order to be a wise counsellor to his people.

He records, December 28, 1787, "Spent part of the day, as I have done several days, in reading Adams' book on government." In February, 1788, he records, "Much talk about Constitution of the government, its being adopted by the vote of the Convention which has been sitting in Boston just 4 weeks."

We can but fancy the relief of the people, when, on March 4, 1789, the new government went into operation, and on the 30th of April following, when General George Washington, on the balcony of Federal Hall, New York, took the oath of office as the first president of the United States.

It was by these hearth-stones, and others long since demolished, that the patriotic women of the towns kept busy during the years of the Revolution, in preparing the town's complement of blankets, stockings, etc., while thinking of the husband, father, brother, son, or lover who was away in service of his country.

On January 4, 1776, the House of Representatives passed an order that four thousand blankets be provided by the selectmen of the respective towns in the Province, and be paid for out of the Province treasury. Chelmsford's portion was twelve. This was in the midst of that winter when the army was in camp at Cambridge, Medford, and Dorchester; and soldiers from the town were so near home that friends kept posted on their condition, and were continually going to camp with supplies. We can imagine with what earnestness the patriotic women went to work with their wheels and looms to prepare the garments ordered. Threads were saturated with tears from the eyes of those who had seen their loved ones go forth in response to the April alarm, and who never returned after the battle of Bunker Hill, but languished and died in Boston — so near and yet so far from those who longed to smooth their pillows and soothe their pains.

We can see in fancy the patriotic minister, Rev.

Mr. Bridge, going from house to house in his
parish with his reports from camp, after returning from a visit to absent members of his flock.
We can catch his words of cheer dropped here
and there, and hear him in prayer commending
them individually and collectively to the care of
Him who notes the sparrow's fall.

This service seemed to be for their own people;
but in the following year, when the seat of war
was removed from Massachusetts, there was a call
for five thousand blankets, and Chelmsford's share
was nineteen.   There was no slackness on the part
of the people, although they knew not who were to
be protected from the severity of winter by their
productions.   It mattered not as long as they
were acting in the patriot cause.   Independence
had been declared; and having pledged their sacred
honor to maintain it, they had no inclination to
halt, although the calls were often repeated.

Only a few of the implements of domestic
manufacture are retained in the old town, yet I
chanced to meet with one which bears a suggestive inscription.   It is a reel made of wood, and
on it is read : —

> " Miss Poley Carter Her Real
> March yᵉ 6th 1777
> Count your Threads Right
> If you real in the night."

With this rude implement in my hand, seated
by the hearth-stone where nine generations have

sat, I gazed into the blazing fire on the hearth
until there rose up before me the graceful figure
of Polly Carter, dressed in her homespun frock,
with a plaid kerchief neatly folded over her bosom.
She is turning off the threads on the great wheel
by the fire, while a stalwart young man from a
neighboring farm stands by, thoughtfully carving
with his jackknife the rude letters which, to his
untutored mind, spell out the name of her in
whom he has a tender interest. ·These he hopes

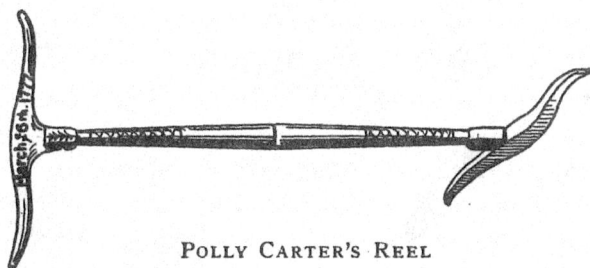

POLLY CARTER'S REEL

will serve to remind Polly of him when he is far
away in the service of his country.

The scene changes to the following year, 1778,
when the town was called upon for forty-seven
shirts and as many pairs of shoes and stockings.
The same gentle face appears, but with the lines
of anxious care more plainly seen. She has reeled
off her day's work of spinning, and is casting up
the stitches for a stocking. Her eyes rest on the
simple figures, which remind her of an evening
less than a twelvemonth ago, but seems like years

to her whose thoughts are of the bare and bleeding feet pacing the rough and frozen ground of Valley Forge.   No stitch is dropped ; and with each round of the needles there is breathed a prayer for the success of the patriot cause, and for the safe return of one whom she loves.

The extremity to which the patriot army was reduced at times is evidenced by the course taken by the Chelmsford people to procure supplies [1] for the men in camp.   A document purporting to be a subscription paper was found in the collection of Mr. Henry E. Parker.   It reads as follows : —

"We, the Inhabitants of the town of Chelmsford, Taking into consideration the Dificulties and Hardships which our Brethren endured and undergo that are in the service of the United States of America and in the defence of the United States of America and in the defence of the Rights & Priviliges of the people of said States, do agree to provide the articles set against our names."

The name of Captain John Ford heads the list with the promise of " 1 pr. shoes."   Others follow with promise of shoes, stockings, shirts, jackets, and other articles of clothing.

We have a most thrilling description of the battle of Bunker Hill, together with earlier and later experiences, in the letter written by Peter Brown to his mother.

[1] The absence of a date renders it uncertain as to time, but our inference is that the supplies were for the army at Valley Forge during the winter of 1777–8:

CAMBRIDGE, *June* 25, 1775.

Dear and Hon'd Mother, — After my duty to you, I would inform you of my present state and employment, being rather scrupulous whether you may receive these lines, shall give but a short sketch of affairs which if otherwise I would. Before these long threat'ned difficulties began among us, I had plan'd out to go to Connecticut, where I expected to work the summer, but the Allwise in His providence hath very differently plann'd my summer's work, which I hope may turn to His Glory and my good. I suppose I need not acquaint you of the manner in which the enemy first approached us at Concord. It is more than probable you have had it in print long since. When I was first alarm'd I was at Westford, whither I went to take leave of my friends and settle some affairs that I had in hand. Was call'd about Daylight, or a little after, and rode as post that afternoon before I could get to Concord, after which I pursu'd with the rest and fought that day, tarried at Cambridge that night being forbid to go home. Soon after this there was an army establish'd, all business being stagnated, and a great deal wholly broke up. I did not know what I could do better than to enlist therefore being hearty in the Cause. I did it directly (and listed) under Captain Oliver Bates, in Collo. Prescott's regiment with whom I tarried awhile till he, our Captain, was taken sick and went home, when Mr. Joshua Parker, by succession, took his place, and makes his ground good, in whose company I remain yet, where I do a Clerk or Orderly Sergants business, which requires much care, but the Duty is easier and the pay higher than a private soldiers. Friday the 16th of June we were order'd on parade at six o'clock with one days provisions and Blankets ready for a march somewhere, but we knew not where, but we readily and cheerfully obey'd; the whole that were called for were these three: Collo. Prescott's, Fry's and Nickson's Regiments; after tarrying on parade till Nine at Night we march'd down on to Charleston Hill against Copts hill in Boston, where we entrench'd and made a Fort ten rod long and eight wide with a Breastwork of about eight more; we worked there undiscover'd till about five in the morning when we saw our danger being against Ships of the Line and all Boston fortified against us. The danger we were in made us think there was treachery and that we were brought there to be all slain, and I must and will say that there was treachery, oversight or presumption in the Conduct of our officers, for about 5 in the morning we not having more than half our fort done, they began to fire (I suppose as soon as they had orders) pretty briskly for a few minutes then ceas'd, but soon begun again, and fir'd to the number of twenty minutes (they kill'd but one of our men[1]) then ceas'd to fire till about eleven o'clock when they began to fire as brisk as ever, which caus'd many of our young Country people to desert, apprehending the danger in a clearer manner than others who were more diligent in digging & fortifying ourselves against them. We began to be almost beat out, being fatigued by our Labour, having no sleep the night before, very little to eat, no drink but rum, but what we hazarded our lives to get. We grew faint, thirsty, hungry and weary. The enemy fir'd very warm from Boston, and from on board their ships that lay in Ferryway and from a ship that lay in the river against us to stop our re-enforcement which they did in some measure; one cannon cut three men in two on the Neck. Our officers sent time after time for Cannon from Cambridge in the morning & could get but four, the Capt'n of which fir'd a few times then swung his Hat three times round to the enemy and ceased to fire, then about three o'clock there was a cessation of the Cannons roaring. Soon after we espied as many as 40 boats or barges coming over full of troops it is supposed there were about 3,000 of them, and about 700 of us left, not deserted, besides 500 re-enforcements that could not get nigh enough to us to do us any good till they saw that we must all be cut off, or some of them, they ventured to ad-

[1] Asa Pollard of Billerica. See " First Blood at Bunker Hill."

vance. When our officers perceiv'd that the enemy intended to land, they ordered the Artillery to go out of the fort and prevent it if possible, from whence the Artillery Capt'n took his pieces and returned home to Cambridge with much haste, for which he is now confin'd, and it is expected must suffer death. The enemy landed fronted before us and form'd themselves in an oblong square in order to surround, which they did in part. After they were well form'd they advanc'd toward us in order to swallow us up, but they found a Choaky mouthful of us, 'tho we could do nothing with our small arms as yet for distance and had but two Cannon and no Gunner, and they from Boston and from the shipping firing and throwing Bombs Keeping us down till they almost surrounded us. But God in Mercy to us fought our battle and tho' we were but few in number and suffer'd to be defeated by our enemy yet we were preserved in a most wonderful manner far beyond our expectation and to our admiration for out of our Regiment there were but 37 killed, 4 or 5 taken captive, about forty-seven wounded & oh may I never forget God's distinguishing mercy to me in sparing my Life when they fell on my right hand and on my left, and close by me, they were, to the eye of reason, no more expos'd than myself. When the arrows of death flew thick round me I was preserv'd while others were suffer'd to fall a prey to our Cruel enemies. O may that God whose mercy was so far extended in my preservation grant me his grace to devote my future Life to his divine service. Nor do I conclude that the danger is yet over unless God in his mercy either remove our enemy or heal the breach — but if we should be called again to action, I hope to have courage and strength to act my part valiantly in defence of our Liberties & Country trusting in him who hath hitherto kept me and hath covered my head in the day of battle, and altho' we have lost four out of our Company & several taken captive by the enemy of America, I was not suffer'd to be touch'd.

I was in the fort when the enemy came in, jumped over

the wall and ran half a mile when balls flew like hailstones and Cannon roar'd like thunder, but tho' I escap'd then it may be my turn next.   After asking your Prayers must conclude wishing you the best of blessings, still remain your Dutiful son

PETER BROWN.

P. S.   I wish very much to come and see you, 'tis in vain to think of that now.   I desire you to write to me, direct to Peter Brown Cambridge, to be left at Colo. Prescott's Chambers in the South Colledge [1] and send by way of Providence to Roxbury, from whence it will be likely to come safe; my love to Polly, Sally & Patty, have not leisure to write to them in particular, and Conveyance very uncertain, hope they will excuse me this time.

> To-day at Cambridge, to-morrow —
> To-morrow the Lord only Knows where.

P. B.[2]

A bronze tablet recently placed on the westerly side of South College has the following : —

MASSACHUSETTS

HALL

BUILT BY THE PROVINCE, 1720.

OCCUPIED BY

THE AMERICAN ARMY

1775-1776.

USED FOR STUDENTS' ROOMS UNTIL

1870-1871.

[1] Massachusetts Hall.

[2] The above letter from Peter Brown to his mother, now given for the first time in enduring form, confirms a tradition in regard to the first victim of the British guns on June 17, 1775.

It was my good fortune to meet at her home in Lunenburg Miss Susan Brown, who related the following facts : —

" Peter Brown was my grandfather. He was born in Newport, R.I., in 1753. He was a son of

SOUTH COLLEGE (MASSACHUSETTS HALL)

William Brown, and a descendant of Peter Brown, who came in the Mayflower in 1620, and settled in Plymouth, and whose son Peter, a non-conformist, went to Rhode Island with Roger Williams. My grandfather, Peter, removed to Massachusetts,

and, as the letter shows, was living at or near
Concord at the beginning of hostilities. After
his service in the Revolution he had a temporary
residence at Boylston, Mass., where he married
Olive Dinsmore, October 24, 1781. They settled
in the part of Lunenburg known as Flat Hill,
at a beautiful situation now occupied by their
descendants."

"My grandfather was an influential man. He
was for several years one of the school committee,
a selectman and coroner. He was chosen deacon, but declined on account of age, and distance
from the meeting-house. Peter's son William was
my father. He lived at the old home, and there I
was born. My grandfather followed the trade of
a blacksmith in connection with the care of his
farm."

Miss Susan Brown was quite young when her
patriot grandfather died ; but she has vivid recollections of him as a man small in stature, and
busy in making his children and grandchildren
happy.

"I am the only living grandchild of Peter Brown
who bears the family name," said Miss Brown, as
standing at her door in Lunenburg she pointed
out the old homestead, and directed her guest to
the delightful locality where the soldier set up his
home. She then guided me to the burying-ground
near by, where is read on a slate tablet, chiselled
out by William, son of Peter, the following : —

IN MEMORY OF
MR. PETER BROWN,
WHO DIED JULY 15th, 1829,
Æ. 76 YEARS.

He was a soldier in the Revolution; was one of those who pursued
the British in their retreat from Concord to Boston. Was in
the Battle on Bunkers Hill. He was an honest
man and a devoted Christian.

THE FIRST BLOOD AT BUNKER HILL.

I learned the story of the first blood at Bunker Hill from the lips of the venerable officer of the town of Billerica, Mr. Dudley Foster, while sitting with him by his family hearth-stone.

Mr. Foster said, "I am a descendant from Thomas Foster, who appeared in this country as early as 1659. My grandfather was Joseph Foster, the clerk of the town of Beverly in the early days. My father, Samuel Foster, came to Billerica and settled more than a century ago.

"It was through the Pollard family, to which my wife belonged, that we have the kinship with Asa Pollard, the first to fall at Bunker Hill."

Asa Pollard was the fourth son of John Pollard and Mary, daughter of Isaac Stearns, born November 15, 1735, at a farm located in North Billerica. The family first appeared in possession of the land in 1692. Its members were inured to hardship, the devastations of the Indians having set their teeth on edge at an early age. Asa served in the French war, was a scout, and well trained in military tactics when the Lexington alarm called him from the old home. It is said that the musket which he took from the pegs above the family hearth-stone on April 19, 1775, carried to Concord and to Bunker Hill, was one that he had received from the Provincial Government as a bounty for a certain number of Indian scalps brought in by him after that questionable means was adopted for exterminating the race. The scarcity of fire-arms at the opening of the Revolution tends to support the family tradition, while the recorded votes of the town give added testimony.

Asa Pollard and his comrades were more than glad of an opportunity to shoot at Gage's men ; for they had vividly in mind the coat of tar and feathers given to one of their neighbors while in Boston a little more than a year before the opening of the war. (See "Beneath Old Roof Trees.") When the town voted "to look up the old bayonets," Asa Pollard looked up his, and all that went with it, and used it like a trained soldier. He and his brother Solomon were at Concord on April 19, and the latter was in command of the minute-men of Billerica at Bunker Hill. The records fail to tell us when the company went to join the forces under General Artemas Ward — possibly they did not all go at one time. Billerica was in the line of march of many of the up-country troops, and companies were seen passing along the highway at various times. A company from New Hampshire reached the town at nightfall; and being weary, it was decided to camp in a farm-yard until the following morning. This was done; and the combined hospitality and patriotism of the farmer's wife were manifested in a substantial manner. She made haste to prepare for them a genuine New England meal, and in the early morning hot beans and rye bread were brought forth from the great brick oven fo the delight of the soldiers. The wooden shovel on which the balls of spungy dough were committed to the heated bricks by the hands of Mrs. Sarah Manning[1] is still in existence, as a reminder of that act of a patriot of the town, who like many another did valiant service beneath her own roof.

Asa Pollard was of the number of men who went over on the evening of the 16th of June, and labored through the night throwing up earth-works.

Said Mr. Foster, "My wife's uncle, Edward Pollard, lived in her father's family during her girlhood; and having served four years in the Continental army, he had a large store of anec-dotes of those days, with which he used to enter-tain the young people, who never tired of the

---

[1] Sarah Heywood of Burlington married William Manning of Billerica in 1769. She died in 1838, aged 91 years. Her husband was commissioned Second Lieutenant in Captain Kidder's com-pany, Seventh Regiment, May 31, 1776.

veteran's stories, among which was that of Asa's
death.   It was about noon, and they were taking
their lunch brought over from camp on the previous evening.   An occasional cannon-ball had been
fired over from the war-vessels of the enemy during the morning hours, but they had been easily
dodged by the busy workmen.   Asa Pollard had
seen such missiles before, and made light of the
poorly directed shot.   But about midday this brave
son of Billerica, when seated on the embankment,
was struck by a cannon-ball, which severed his
head from his body.   The bloody scene was within
the presence of Colonel Prescott, who was passing
down the line at the very moment of the fatal
shot.   Then came the first confusion of the day.
Men left their places in spite of all orders.   They
were drawn to the spot by the dreadful fate of
their comrade.   Putnam came running up from
the rail fence, and with most positive words attempted to force them back into line.   Prescott
ordered the body buried immediately, saying,
'He's the first to fall, and the only one who will
be buried to-day.'   One of the officers is said to
have expressed surprise that the soldier should
be buried without a funeral service; but the gallant Prescott saw that the presence of death in
that form was not conducive to order, and considered that there was no other way to maintain discipline.   The enemy on the vessels had seen the
confusion resulting from that one successful shot,

BIRTHPLACE OF ASA POLLARD, BILLERICA

and redoubled their fire. The shot which struck Pollard came from the Somerset, the frigate which afterwards went ashore near Lieutenant's Island, off the Massachusetts coast ; and it is claimed that a portion of her hull is yet embedded in the sand of that place."

The body of Asa Pollard rests with the others in the soil which drank up their youthful blood. It was nearly a century before the people of his native town took any steps to perpetuate his memory; but on the centennial of his death, a tree was planted on the public Common, where it now flourishes to keep the young hero's memory green. Later, the Union School building was

DUDLEY FOSTER.

dedicated as the Asa Pollard School, and now the local society of the Children of the American Revolution is known as the Asa Pollard Society. The birthplace of the hero has also been suitably marked by the Billerica Historical Society and the Foster brothers, sons of Dudley Foster and Louise Pollard.

CHAPTER XXIII

A BOSTON FAMILY TAKES REFUGE IN CHELMSFORD.
THE TOWN OF BOSTON AFTER THE SIEGE

THE dew of only one night had moistened the little grave in Granary Burying-Ground where Robert and Mary Rand had laid their first-born to rest, when the sorrowful couple were aroused by the message, "The Regulars have marched out into the country to destroy the stores as it is supposed."

For nearly eleven months the people of Boston had suffered the hardships of the blockade. To be sure, the sympathetic patriots throughout the continent had ministered to them. South Carolina had sent two hundred barrels of rice, and promised eight hundred more. Wilmington, N.C., had sent two thousand pounds currency. Connecticut had sent over her flocks of sheep. All New England towns had shared their crops with their neighbors in Boston. Maryland and Virginia had contributed liberally. George Washington had headed a subscription paper with his personal gift of fifty pounds. The settlers beyond the Blue Ridge had contributed from their scant supply,

and sent it over the mountains to the distressed
and suffering in Boston. And with these repeated donations had come words of sympathy
and cheer. The ministers of Connecticut had
written, " The taking away of civil liberty will
involve the ruin of religious liberty also." The
people of Brooklyn, Conn., the home of General
Israel Putnam, had written, " Your zeal in favor
of liberty has gained a name that shall perish but
with the glorious constellation of· Heaven." Yet
notwithstanding all this aid, there was suffering
and untold anxiety in the blockaded town. It
was not confined to the poor by any means.
" The warehouses of the thrifty merchants were
at once made valueless ; the costly wharfs, which
extended far into the channel, and were so lately
covered with produce of the tropics and with English fabrics, were become solitary places ; the harbor, which had resounded incessantly with cheery
voices of prosperous commerce, was now disturbed
by no sounds but from British vessels of war."
No one could go in and out his own door without being scrutinized by the British guards that
patrolled the streets of the town. Even the sorrowful group that had made its way on the 17th
of April to the burying-ground had been under
the watch of the soldiers of the king. The grief
of the Rand family naturally led them to be more
sympathetic for the wounded and dying who were
brought in to Boston in the night of April 19 ;

but they were avowed patriots, and consequently not in harmony with the officials whose movements had occasioned the distress, and they could do but little for the sufferers.

The Rands were "well connected and well to do," but in this exigency were poor even in their wealth. Robert Rand, the head of the Boston family, was born in 1719. He was a descendant from Robert Rand of Lynn, who in 1692, by a vote in town meeting, was granted the right to sit with six other aged men in the pulpit. Mary, his wife, was daughter of William Simpkins, a jeweller and silversmith of considerable distinction. They were married on June 3, 1773, and had but just completed a year in a home of their own when the port of Boston was closed. Believing that an Englishman's home is his castle, the Rand family maintained their position until the infections that followed the army made it dangerous to health and life, when it was decided that Mrs. Rand should leave the town. A good many had gone to Chelmsford, and availed themselves of the hospitality bountifully extended to all ; and a home was found there for Mrs. Rand through the influence of her physician, Dr. Danforth. The change was made by his advice, and he naturally took steps to a   her in leaving the town. The restrictions in regard to the amount of goods taken away were very annoying to this family, for they had an abundance ; but Mrs. Rand in disguise presented herself for a permit. She had a suspicious trunk, which she refused to allow out of her sight, and this led the sentinel to oppose her going; but Dr. Danforth's son Tom, a family friend, yet a Tory, interfered with seeming roughness of manner, and said, " Let the old woman go ;" and she was allowed to leave the town. The contents of the trunk was chiefly gold coin, which was used by her for her own comfort, and in dispensing to 'the comfort of others who had fled from the blockaded town under less favoring circumstances. There was one memento, however, which the sorrowing mother could not leave behind in the deserted home. It was more precious to her than the coin which it accompanied; for it so vividly reminded her of the little one who had borne her name for a few short months and passed away, and whose silent resting-place was now at the mercy of the enemy. This memento was only a pincushion, on which the mother read, " Welcome, little stranger, to Boston, though the port is blocked up, 1774."

Chelmsford was truly a patriotic town, and her people were continually sending supplies, as were those of other towns, to the sufferers who were obliged to remain in Boston ; while those who made their temporary home in Chelmsford were as comfortable as kind, sympathetic patriots could make them. The slightest report of movements in Boston was eagerly scanned, and the news of the evacuation brought cheer to them all. The Rand family hoped to be soon re-established in their own home, but the army had left an entailment of disease which required the most vigilant

RAND PINCUSHION

attention and severe restrictions in order to eradicate it. In July, 1776, the selectmen passed an order that people going out of town must carry a certificate from the medical authorities proving that they had been "smoked and cleansed," and

were free from all possibility of infection. The repeated outbreak of the smallpox, and general dis-
arrangement of affairs, prevented individuals from
returning for many months. Among them was
Mrs. Rand. The year 1777 had come before this
lady again welcomed her friends around the family
hearth-stone in Boston. But the cradle left tenant-
less was again occupied; and there was recorded
in Chelmsford, "Born December 14, 1776, Mary,
daughter to Robert and Mary Rand of Boston."

Boston seemed to the returning family a very
different place from that which they had left.
Many of their neighbors who adhered to the king
had fled with the army and could not return,
while those who espoused the patriots' cause, and
remained in the country, found it the work of
months and years to restore their homes and public buildings to as good condition as they were
in when the army of the king took possession of
the town; and the old burying-grounds bear silent
testimony to the devastations of the army of the
king.

Four children grew up together in the home of
Robert Rand, but only three of them could claim
Boston as their birthplace. They were prominent
among the families of the enterprising merchants,
and popular in the best society of the town.

But a few months after the little stranger was
welcomed to the Rand family at Chelmsford, there
was a son born in the Fitch tavern at Bedford;

and he was called Jeremiah, after his father and grandfather. The war for independence was still being carried on, and. much of local military interest centred in this Jeremiah Fitch tavern. It was very natural that the namesake of the father should be early impressed with the story of the morning of April 19, 1775, and of his father's experience as sergeant of Bedford minute-men at Concord, and in the running fight of that day. These early impressions were never forgotten, but were often the subject of conversation by the old hearth-stone and in the busy world.

The family plan had been that Jeremiah should be trained to agricultural pursuits, and succeed his father on the farm, which was carried on in connection with the business of a country tavern. But the boy had no inclination in that direction, and at the age of fourteen years left home, and went to Charlestown with a capital of twenty cents, and unaided by any one set to work to procure employment. He soon secured a situation with Mr. Samuel Ruggles, and from that time relieved his parents from all pecuniary assistance. While in Charlestown the young man had constantly before his eyes the redoubt on Bunker Hill, and the hastily made graves of those who were companions in arms with his father when the Lexington alarm called them from their homes.

The success of the country boy, Jeremiah Fitch, while in Charlestown, made a way for him to cross

over to Boston, where he soon set up business for
himself, but by the failure of his patrons he was
involved in embarrassments; yet with the determination befitting a son of a hero of April 19, '75,
young Jeremiah struggled on until he had fully
extricated himself.

He was always esteemed for straightforward-
ness and integrity in his dealings; for nearly a
score of years he was a director of the Union
Bank and for the Mercantile Marine Insurance
Company. For many years he was a member of
the Board of Health, retiring in 1821 to become
a member of the last Board of Selectmen of the
town of Boston; in 1824 he was a member of the
Common Council, and in the following year an
Overseer of the Poor of the City of Boston.

It was his conduct in adversity that won for
him friends who offered capital and other assistance, with which he made his way to fortune.
But he never forgot his early associations. The
old tavern where his father served the minute-
men on the morning of April 19, 1775, was sacred
to him; and he cherished the hearthstone by
which he had been cradled during the war. His
delight was in ministering to the comforts of his
parents and friends of his youth.

As a successful, enterprising merchant of Corn-
hill, he met the beautiful young lady, Mary Rand;
and on May 10, 1804, they were married in Boston
by Rev. William Emerson, who, having left his

Harvard parish, had already made a decided impression as a dignified pastor of the First Church of Boston.

The united efforts of the young couple were rewarded with marked success ; public honors were justly conferred upon the merchant by his associates and fellow-townsmen. He occupied many positions of trust within the gift of the voters of Boston ; and as a mark of respect for the son of Old Bedford, the name of Pond Lane was changed to Bedford Street, which it now bears.

While in the midst of his flourishing business as an importer of dry goods, the second war with England came on. This brought vividly to mind the trying experiences of the Fitch and Rand families during the Revolution.

Having kept in family possession the old home at Bedford, Jeremiah Fitch had a safe retreat there ; and he recorded under date of September, 1814, " My family removed to Bedford in consequence of the war, moved my goods from the store the same day. Returned September 29, after about three weeks." Jeremiah Fitch repeatedly manifested his loyalty to his native town. His sentiments rebelled against the common use of the cannon-ball which, fired from the patriot camp of Cambridge, struck the Brattle-street Church during the siege of Boston. Mr. and Mrs. Fitch were attendants at this church ; and being a member of the standing committee, he succeeded in having the ball, that had done duty for many years as a weight at the front gate of a neighbor's residence, returned, and embedded in the front wall of the edifice, where it was kept so long as a reminder of the months when Gage's army was hemmed in by the Provincials.

The record of this worthy couple is with that of the truly successful of the world. The name

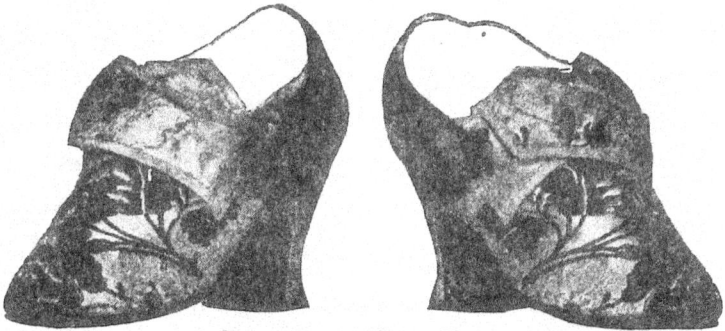

SLIPPERS OF MARY RAND

Mary Rand has been faithfully continued through successive generations ; and among the family treasures are a silver tankard made by William Simpkins the silversmith for his daughter Mary when she married Robert Rand ; the pincushion which marked the advent of the first Mary to the Rand family during the siege ; the slippers and a sample of the dress worn by Mary Rand when she married Jeremiah Fitch ; five generations of samplers, and other tangible reminders of two families worthy to be perpetuated in the annals of Boston and Bedford.

CHAPTER XXIV

FOUR EMERSONS. — PATRIOT PREACHERS OF THE
REVOLUTION. — ANCESTRY. — LETTER FROM REV-
EREND SAMUEL MOODY. — REVEREND DANIEL
EMERSON IN FRENCH WAR. — REVEREND JOSEPH
EMERSON IN THE ARMY. — COURTSHIP OF THE
MINISTER. — REVEREND WILLIAM EMERSON OF
CONCORD. — REVEREND JOHN EMERSON AND THE
TORIES

> 'Tis still observed those men most valiant are
> That are most modest ere they come to war.
>
> HERRICK.

THE act of incorporation by which early settle-
ments in New England were granted the legal
authority of towns was conditioned upon the settlement of an orthodox minister of good conversation, and a provision for his support. His was
the leading position in the town, and the influence
which he exerted was correspondingly great. His
judgment was seldom questioned, his authority
never doubted.

When the English and French were contending for possession in North America, the minister went forth, with his soldier parishioners, and

served as their chaplain. His voice was heard from the pulpit and from house to house in the interest of freedom during the years of the Revolution. In the siege of Boston he divided his time between his parish at home and his parish in camp. When the seat of war was removed from Massachusetts, the faithful minister did not hesitate to take up his cross and appear in the midst of the army, though far from his home. In many instances this trusted friend shouldered a musket and carried his Bible also.

As types of the patriotic ministers during the early and later wars may be cited the four Emersons. So large was their place in the affections of their people, and so broad was their influence, that they were styled "patriot preachers." They were Reverends Joseph, William, John, and Daniel Emerson, — settled ministers of the Congregational order in four prominent towns of New England when the Revolution burst upon the Colonies. Their respective parishes were Pepperell, Concord, and Conway in Massachusetts, and Hollis in New Hampshire. They had been laboring for the upbuilding of these towns for some years before the Revolution, and been faithful servants of the Crown. They had often read from their pulpits official proclamations for public fasts and thanksgivings, and sincerely offered up the prayer, "God save the king." But when Britain's sovereign proved unfaithful to his subjects, these Emersons espoused the cause of the oppressed. The alarm on that April morning, —

" Through every Middlesex village and farm,"

met with a ready response on the part of each of these ministers ; and before the evacuation of Boston one of them had passed from earth, and a second joined him before the close of the year 1776.

Hannah Emerson
Joseph Emerson

William Emerson
John Emerson

These men were not only closely allied in profession, but were united by the endearing ties of kinship. Reverends Joseph, William, and John were brothers, and their sister Hannah was the wife of Rev. Daniel Emerson. Thus four of the children of that noted minister of Malden, Rev. Joseph Emerson, were in full sympathy in their work at this trying period of the history of our country.

Among the ancestors of the Emersons in this country must be cited Rev. Peter Bulkley, a pio-

neer, and the first minister of Concord; Rev.
Joseph Emerson, a pioneer and minister of Mendon, who barely escaped with his life when the
village was destroyed by the Indians ; Rev. Samuel Moody, a pioneer and minister of York, Maine ;
and Deacon Cornelius Waldo, one of the Wenham
Colony, who emigrated in 1655, and became one
of the founders of the town of Chelmsford in the
Bay Colony.

Rev. Peter Bulkley was a man of considerable
property in Odell, Bedfordshire, England. He
was among those who, being silenced by Archbishop Laud for nonconformity, crossed the Atlantic in 1634 to New England, and became one
of the little company who pushed out through the
tangled wood, and founded the town of Concord,
and there spent most of his fortune as a pioneer
of civilization. "He was addressed as father,
prophet, and counsellor by his people, and by all
the ministers of the country." — SHATTUCK.

Rev. Joseph Emerson was settled in Mendon,
December, 1669. His salary was forty-five pounds
for the first two years, to be paid as follows : —

" Tenn pounds at Boston yearly at some shope there, or
in money at this town. The remayning to be made up, two
pounds of butter for every cow, the rest in pork, wheat,
barley, and soe to make the year's pay in work, Indian corn,
rye, pease, and beef. After the second year he was to be
paid fifty-five pounds yearly, and soe on as God shall enable
them. All differences between the minister and the town

were to be referred for adjudication, to the churches of Medfield, Dedham, and Roxbury." ·

This ministry was cut short by King Philip's war, in 1675, when Rev. Mr. Emerson fled to the home of his father-in-law, Rev. Edward Bulkley,[1] at Concord, and there died in 1680.

Rev. Samuel Moody, or Father Moody, of Agamenticus, was the valiant minister of York, Maine. He did not hesitate to exercise his full authority. "When the offended parishioners, wounded by his pointed preaching, would rise to go out of church, he cried out, 'Come back, you graceless sinners, come back!' And when they began to fall into ill customs, and ventured into the alehouses on a Saturday night, he would go in after them, collar the sinners, drag them out with rousing admonition. His charity was without stint. He gave away his wife's only pair of shoes from her bedside to a poor woman who came to the house one frosty morning barefoot. When his wife, trying to restrain his unreasonable generosity, made him a purse that was opened with difficulty, he gave away purse and all."

Deacon Cornelius Waldo of a family of London merchants was born in 1625. He came early to this country, and settled in Essex County, and later went with Rev. John Fisk and others to the

[1] Edward Bulkley left his parish at Marshfield to succeed his father at Concord, where he labored until his death in 1696.

town of Chelmsford, where he completed his useful life. A simple stone in the burying-ground
tells the following : —

HERE LYES YE BODY OF
DEACON CORNELIUS WALDO,
AGED 75 YEARS. DIED JAN. YE 3, 1700.
" The Memory of the Just is Blessed."

The line of connection is as follows : —

Rev. Joseph Emerson of Mendon married Elizabeth, daughter of Rev. Edward, and granddaughter
of Rev. Peter Bulkley of Concord. Edward, son
of Rev. Joseph Emerson and Elizabeth Bulkley,
married Rebecca, daughter of Cornelius Waldo.
Their son, Rev. Joseph Emerson of Malden, married Mary, daughter of Rev. Samuel Moody. Joseph, William, John, and Hannah were the children
of Rev. Joseph and Mary Moody Emerson.

While Edward Emerson of Chelmsford was not
a minister, he was early found to be a leader in
educational matters. He was the town's schoolmaster in 1698, and in 1703 was a member of a
board of school committee. On his grave-stone
he is thus recorded, —

MR. EDWARD EMERSON
SOME TIME DEACON OF THE FIRST CHURCH
IN MEDWAY.

He was noted for the virtue of patience, and it is a family
tradition that he never complained but once, when he said
mildly to his daughter, that her dumplings were somewhat
harder than needful, but not often. — O. W. HOLMES.

Our four patriot preachers were graduates of
Harvard College. They were young and unmar-
ried when they entered their pastoral work. Rev.
Daniel Emerson was from Reading. We shall

JOSEPH EMERSON'S CHAIR, PEPPERELL

consider him here for another reason than that
of marriage.

Elizabeth Bulkley, widow of Rev. Joseph Emerson who died at Concord in 1680, married, in
1682, John Brown, Esq., of Reading. This union
brought the Emerson and Brown children of

former marriages together, and resulted in the
marriage of Peter Emerson and Anna Brown,
who became the parents of Daniel Emerson. He
was born in 1716, and graduated at Harvard College in 1739. He was settled as the first minister of Hollis, N.H., in 1743, and in the autumn
of the following year brought his bride, Hannah
Emerson, from the Malden parsonage to his home
in the comparative wilderness.

The settlement of Rev. Daniel Emerson in a
home of his own with a guaranty of support ful-
filled the conditions of incorporation, and the
town of Hollis began a prosperous record.

While busy in clearing the land and erecting
homes, the settlers were obliged to turn their attention to war. The king's demand for service
was at the northward, and was met with a ready
response from the men of this new town, the minister among them.

It was my good fortune to meet in Hollis Mrs.
Levi Abbott, at her attractive home, within or
near the limits of the original grant to the minister, her great-grandfather. Mrs. Abbott said, —

" It was about twelve years after my great-
grandfather began his ministry among this people that he felt called upon to go into the army
contending against the French and Indians. Consequently he left his parish, his wife, and a half-
dozen little children, and went to the northward
as chaplain, in a regiment commanded by Colonel

Joseph Blanchard of Dunstable. He was absent about six months. During his absence he kept a journal, which is now treasured in our family. It is styled by the minister, ' A Journal of My Proceedings with the Army to Crown Point.' "

From the yellow leaves I have copied the following entries : —

July ye [8], 1755, *being Tuesday.*

Sat out from my own House after com''ng ourselves t' God by Solemn Pr. in wh. Br. Emerson was greatly inlarged. Went to Lichfield & Preached from ——, in wh. Exercise I enjoyed some inlargement. O that I might be used as an Instrument to Glorify God ! Went that night to Gen. Starks at Derryfield [Manchester] where I was kindly entertained with Rev. Dr. Cummings.

He preached on July 9, and then went on to Rumford (Concord, N. H.), where he was entertained by Mrs. Walker, the wife of the minister, and mother of Hon. Thomas Walker, a famous patriot in the Revolution. On Friday of the same week he went under guard to the army at Bakerstown, where he was kindly received " by ye Col's of ye Army," and began his service as chaplain. He records : —

" I lodged in ye Camp much better than I feared, slept some & rose refreshed early in ye morning."

On the following day he saw —

" Need of more wisdom, zeal & courage than in any station of life I have been placed in."

He preached twice on his first Sabbath in camp, but found the soldiers little disposed to attend. He notes that lodging on the ground was more bearable than at first.

On Monday, July 14, he writes : —

" I visited some of the inhabitants who came to Stevens-town while ye Regiment could protect them."

On the following day he was not able to go to prayer with the regiment, but two days later records : —

" Had a shock of ye fever & ague. Col. Blanchard prayed with ye Regiment ; at night was exceedingly kind, urged me to take his couch to lodge in. . . . This day wrote to my dear ch. & people."

On the 20th he made record of an order for the regiment to go to join the army at Albany, and on the following day, of his having leave to go home.

" To be with my dear family & people on the Day of Fasting & Prayer."

He preached at Suncook and Rumford on the way to Hollis, and recorded that it was harder to go from the ground to the bed than from the bed to the ground. He reached his home on the 22d, when his record is : —

" Almost overcome with the heat, but found my Dear Partner & children well. How pleasant it is & how great a Blessing to have such a wife as God has crowned me with."

The following day was observed as a Fast through the Province. The minister's parents came from Malden to visit their son.

On July 30, the Hollis minister set out for Albany, was joined by Colonel Blanchard, who accompanied him on the way to the Hudson River. They reached Albany on Tuesday, August 12, when Rev. Mr. Emerson made the following entry : —

"Found it a compact Place, but ye buildings not so gay as in our seaport town, tarried there all night & the next day, but I wanted to get to my Business at ye Flats 6 miles above Albany."

He speaks of being comfortable on his armful of straw.

August 24 was Sunday, and this chaplain preached to soldiers on both sides of the river. On the following day he dined with Colonel Schuyler[1]. Illness seems to have followed him, but he prayed four times each day. He divided his service between the troops lodged on either side of the river.

In the early days of September he records : —

"I saw some Indians who sang and danced in a very odd manner as did some before. Yy are pitiful looking creatures. I pitied Mr. Braynard and honored his memory more

[1] Colonel Schuyler was made a general by Washington in the Revolution, and in command of Provincial forces in New York for a time.

y^n ever w^n I saw ye poor People w^m he had spent his life among. Some told me y^t some of Mr. Bray^nard's Indians w^r among those I saw."

His journal continues with details of the journey, a skirmish with the French and Indians, and on September 19 he writes from Lake George to his wife. In this letter he says : —

" If you could by a window look into my heart I believe you would find that you possessed as much of me as ever woman did of any man's heart on earth."

This letter, penned one hundred and forty years ago by the patriot preacher of Hollis, is carefully treasured by his great-granddaughter. There is a family tradition that the letter was sent from Lake George to Hollis on the neck of a faithful dog that the minister had taken with him from his home for that purpose.

It is said that when Rev. Mr. Emerson was at Crown Point, and his regiment was ordered to present arms for inspection, he presented his Bible to the officer as his weapon.

At the opening of the Revolution the Hollis minister was about sixty years of age, and he did not enter the army; but his patriotic spirit had been duly impressed upon his people and family. His son Daniel was captain of the Hollis company, and went to Ticonderoga in July, 1776, and was also captain of a company enlisted in Hollis in

June of the following year. In 1778 he was in command of a mounted company which went to Rhode Island, and also of a company in Colonel Mooney's regiment, raised in 1779 for the defence of Rhode Island.

In the old burying-ground in Hollis may be seen a slab on which is chiselled the following : —

BENEATH THIS MONUMENT LIES THE MORTAL PART OF

REV. DANIEL EMERSON.

He was born at Reading, Mass., May 20, 1716. Graduated at Harvard University 1739, and was ordained April 20, 1743, to the Pastoral care of the church and congregation in Hollis which then consisted of only 30 Families. He was an honest man, given to Hospitality. An affectionate Husband, and tender Parent. A faithful friend and patriotic citizen. An Evangelical, zealous and unusually successful Preacher of the Gospel of Jesus Christ. Highly esteemed by his people, his praise was in all the churches. A.D. 1793 he voluntarily relinquished one-half his salary to promote the settlement of a colleague. From which time his pious walk and occasional labors evinced an unabating love for the cause of Christ, until nature failed and he fell asleep in Jesus SEPTEMBER 30, 1801, AGED 85 YEARS.

HERE ARE ALSO DEPOSITED THE REMAINS OF

HANNAH EMERSON,

WIFE OF THE ABOVE

AND DAUGHTER OF REV. JOSEPH EMERSON OF MALDEN.

She lived a pattern of filial obedience, respect and affection, and an example of conjugal love and duty ; a most tender indulgent and faithful Parent. The delight of her Friends and ornament of the Church. She lived the life of a true Disciple of Christ. In the constant exercise of active faith in His promise. And died in triumphant hope of everlasting life in those Regions where charity never faileth FEBRUARY 28, 1812, AGED 90.

Rev. Joseph Emerson was settled as the first minister of Pepperell, Mass., in 1746. He received, as did the Hollis minister, an allotment of forty acres of land, on which he built a house.

He was longer in becoming established in a home of his own than was his brother-in-law, Rev. Daniel Emerson. His journal, now in the possession of a descendant, shows the occasion of the delay with many interesting facts.

Tuesday, Sept. 6, 1748. Set out for Connecticut in company with Peter Powers of Hollis in order to go to New Haven commencement.

His journey and visits by the way occupied the time until the 14th, when he notes : —

Commencement, all things were carried on with the utmost decency. They come very little behind Cambridge itself.

Thursday, 15th. Breakfast at College & set out for home in company with Mr. Ellis of Middletown & arrived at his house in the evening about 34 miles.

He remained there and at Weathersfield until the 17th, when he resumed his journey in company with Rev. Jonathan Edwards of Northampton. They halted at Hartford, called at Windsor upon the father of Rev. Mr. Edwards, who was also a minister, and reached Northampton on Tuesday.

While here, Rev. Mr. Emerson met with Esther, the daughter of Rev. Jonathan Edwards. On the 21st he makes the following entry : —

Spent the day very pleasantly, the most agreeable family I was ever acquainted with, much of the presence of God here. We met with Mr. Spencer, a gentleman who was ordained last week at Boston, as a missionary to the Indians of the Six Nations. He purposes to set out to-morrow for Albany. The most wonderful instance of self denial I ever met with.

After taking leave of the minister who was on the way to Albany as a foreign missionary, the homeward journey was continued.

When back in his lodgings, the Pepperell minister records :—

Have not met with any difficulty in travelling about 300 miles. God's name be praised.

After four busy days in parish work and attention to his mother, who had come to visit her daughter at Hollis and son at Pepperell, he records :—

Sat., Oct. 1. I wrote two letters in the forenoon, one to Mr. Edwards of Northampton, and the other to his second daughter, a very desirable person to whom I purpose by divine leave to make my addresses. May the Lord direct me in so important affair.

Monday, 3. Set out with my mother for Malden. Dined at Col. Ting's & got as far as Reading. Lodged at Capt. Eaton's.

After four weeks spent in "journeyings often," like Saint Paul, and in close application to parochial work, together with some time spent in cutting corn-stalks, the parson records : —

Monday, Nov. 7. Set out some time before day on a journey to Northampton to visit Mrs. (Miss) Esther Edwards [1] to treat of marriage.

A subsequent record shows that the journey was performed in safety, but the hopeful parson adds,—

I could not obtain from the young lady the least encouragement to come again. The chief objection she makes is her youth, which I hope will be removed in time.

Months elapsed, and the young minister was compelled to abandon his fondest hope. He passed through the sentimental Gethsemane with true Christian fortitude, yet not without apparent mental and physical suffering, and at length married Abigail Hay of Reading. The minister with his bride opened the doors of their home to the people of his early choice.

I have shown in Chapter IV. that Rev. Joseph Emerson, the patriot preacher of Pepperell, was chaplain in the expedition to Louisburg, preached plainly of the duty of patriots during the French troubles, took a bold stand at the opening of the Revolution, and died a patriot's death, October 29, 1775, at the age of fifty-one years.

Rev. William Emerson married Phœbe Bliss, a daughter of his predecessor in the Concord min-

---

[1] Miss Esther Edwards became the wife of Aaron Burr, the president of Princeton College, and was the mother of Aaron Burr, the third vice-president of the United States, — a man of unpleasant memory.

istry. They established their home at the Manse,
and spent a few years in the enjoyment of the
entire confidence of their people, and in devotion
to each other and their children.

This Concord minister was a brave and determined "Son of Liberty." Bancroft has recorded
as testimony given him by veterans of that day's
experience that at the early morning alarm, rung
out by Amos Melvin, the sentinel at the Court
House, the minister turned out with the others
"his gun in hand." The school-boy's first lesson
in the history of Concord fight has contained the
old story that the minister of the town was one
of those who rashly advised that the early morning force should stand its ground on the Common
and abide the attack, but more experienced military men overruled in the excitement of the hour.
Additional testimony has come from a non-resi-
dent, who, working in Concord, was enrolled with
the minute-men. He said he felt he could not
stand when he saw the redcoats come in sight,
but was quieted and put in courage by Mr. Emerson's brave words, and hand laid on his shoulder.

The above should not be construed as conflict-
ing with the words of a famous author, quoted in
chapter ix. of "Beneath Old Roof Trees " — they
refer to different hours of the day. From the
family narrative we learn that when the Provincials retreated from the village to the opposite
side of the river, followed by the British, many

women and children took refuge in the yard of the Manse; and as the minister's wife and little children were in the house with no protector but an excited black man-servant (former slave), his duty was plain, and he stayed, as a faithful minister would, to protect his family, and comfort the crowd of helpless parishioners.

May not the expression, "Had not the friends around him prevented his quitting his doorstep," be a poet's account of the demands of a distressed people for the service and protection of their pastor? These duties caused the minister to be late at the river; but an official, who came a few days later to look over the ground, has recorded, "He saw all that went on, and at first was afraid his people would get excited and fire first, and after the British volley he feared they might not return it." After the enemy fell back from the bridge, Mr. Emerson went there, and was shocked at finding the soldier whom an over-zealous boy, seeing him striving to rise, had cut in the head with a hatchet.

We are indebted to the Rev. Mr. Emerson's journal for the account of the proceedings of April 19, 1775, as they impressed him. His record has been the foundation of the most reliable narrative of the battle on Concord soil. The same preacher has given us a vivid description of the camp at Cambridge during the siege. (See "Beneath Old Roof Trees," p. 73.)

Rev. William Emerson was of that class of which Bancroft wrote, " Eloquent and accomplished chaplains kept alive the habit of daily prayer, and preached the wonted sermons on the day of the Lord."

Writing from the camp to his wife at Concord, Mr. Emerson said, —

" There are many things amiss in this camp, yet upon the whole, God is in the midst of us."

On another occasion he wrote : —

" I despair seeing a battle fought this time coming down."

While in service in the northern campaign in 1776, Rev. Mr. Emerson's health failed, and he addressed the following letter to the commanding officer : —

TICONDEROGA, *Sept.* 10, 1776.

Sir, — My Ill State of Health is such that I am not able to perform the Duty of a Chaplain, and am advised by the Physicians to ask for a dismission from the Army, and shall be glad of your consent and assistance thereto.

WM. EMERSON.

To LT. COLL⁰. B. BROWN.

The Reverend Mr. William Emerson has my Discharge from the Northern Army of the United States of America. TYCONDEROGA, 10*th September*, 1776.

HORATIO GATES,
Major General.

The above letters are in the possession of the Emerson family at Concord.

Mr. Emerson started for home, reached Rutland, Vermont, and died there on October, 20, 1776. His body was interred with the honors of war by a detachment of Colonel Vandyke's Regiment, commanded by Major Shepard.

There is a table monument on Burying Ground Hill, Concord, on which the following is read : —

ERECTED BY THIS TOWN IN MEMORY OF THEIR PASTOR,

REV. WILLIAM EMERSON,

WHO DIED AT RUTLAND, VT., 1776, Æ. 33, ON HIS RETURN FROM THE AMERICAN ARMY OF WHICH HE WAS CHAPLAIN.

Enthusiastic, eloquent,
Affectionate and pious.
He loved his family, his people,
His God, and his country, and to this last
He yielded the cheerful sacrifice of his life.

Rev. John Emerson was two years younger than William, and did not make his advent to the Malden parsonage until Joseph had attained his majority. He was settled as the first minister of Conway, in Franklin County, in 1769. He had formed an attachment for a most estimable young lady in Boston before he had completed his studies; and when called to the new town in the wilderness, the brave Sabra Cobb went with him. The journey was made on horseback. They were married in Boston in 1770. It required moral heroism for a young lady to leave the society of the seaport town, and go to that distant settlement, where the people were doing the work of pioneers. Within a week after she reached Conway, she saw a bear looking into her bedroom window. The young preacher, in writing of himself, said it was literally John preaching in the wilderness.

The rustic people had prejudices to overcome, and it was a trying time for both parties. But the minister's wife soon endeared herself to the people, who admitted that she was a lady " if she came from Boston." One act shows her to have been a judicious, sacrificing woman. She was the possessor of a silk umbrella. Such a thing was not owned by the people of Conway ; and rather than give them occasion for jealousy, or have the appearance of being in any way above the women of the town, Mrs. Emerson never carried the umbrella, but long after made the silk into bonnets for her daughters.

We find that the Conway minister had an experience during the Revolution very different from that of his brothers in their parishes.

Rev. Daniel Emerson had some noted Loyalists in Hollis, and Rev. William Emerson had one in his own family, Daniel Bliss, Esq.; but Rev. John of Conway had a large number who adhered to the king, and were most reluctant to fall in with the patriots. In dealing with these Loyalists, or Tories, the young minister of Conway was severely tried. The following votes, passed during the Revolutionary times, serve to show the process used against those who were not in sympathy with the American cause : —

At a legal meeting held June 25, 1777, —
Voted, To try the minds of the town with regard to the enimical persons that the Selectmen have entered in a list and laid before the town as such separately.

After giving the list of Loyalists, they —

Voted, That Captain Alexander Oliver be the person to collect the evidence, and lay it before the court against the above enimical persons.

The meeting-house where Rev. John Emerson preached on the Sabbath was the place where the following peculiar action was taken : —

At a legal meeting held August 27th, 1777,—
Voted, That we proceed in some measure to secure the enimical persons called Tories among us. Then the question was put, whether we would draw a line between the Continent and Great Britain.
Voted in the affirmative.
Voted, That all those persons that stand on the side of the Continent, take up arms and go hand in hand with us in carrying on the war against our unnatural enemies, such we receive as friends, and all others treat as enemies.
Voted, That the broad alley be a line, and the south end of the meeting-house be the Continent side, and the north end be the British side ; then moved for trial, and found 6 persons to stand on the British side. . . .
Voted to set a guard over those enimical persons.
Voted, The town clerk immediately desire Judge Mather to issue out his warrants against those enimical persons returned to him in a list heretofore.

The Conway minister survived the war, and lived
to enjoy the blessings of liberty for many years.
He saw the settlement in the wilderness grow
from four hundred to two thousand inhabitants.

Rev. John Emerson kept a journal, as did the
other Emerson preachers, and the ministers of the
time generally. While these journals treat largely
of private matters, they also serve to show that
ministerial association was promoted by inter-
change of visits, and that the parsonages (ministers' homes) of New England were hostleries
where entertainment was freely dispensed. The
Conway minister's record of a journey to Boston in 1799 is of interest.

May 23. Set out on a journey to Boston . . . to consult
on the present critical and alarming state of our country and
to devise means for the suppression of infidelity. Rode this
day as far as Greenwich, dined at Mr. Parson's of Amherst,
and lodged at Capt. Rich's in Greenwich.

24th. Proceeded on my journey, dined at Mr. Avery's in
Holden (Rev. Joseph Avery the minister), and reached Harvard. Lodged at Dea. Whitney's.

25th. Rose early, breakfasted at my kinsman's, Mr. Emerson's [1] and went on as far as Concord by noon.

---

[1] Rev. William Emerson, pastor at Harvard from 1792 to 1799,
was son of Rev. William of Concord, and a nephew of Rev. John,
who made this visit just at the time when the First Church in
Boston was offering inducements to the Harvard pastor to exchange
his country parish for the more popular one at the seaport. He
did this in the autumn of 1799, and a Boston parsonage, instead of
that at Harvard, first echoed the voice of the boy Ralph Waldo
Emerson.

Rev. John Emerson continues his record : —

I was persuaded, contrary to my intention, to stay with Brother Ripley over the Sabbath.

26th, *Lord's Day.* Preached for Mr. Ripley. Had some freedom and satisfaction in the public service of the day. Preached to the acceptance of many, and I hope some benefit." [This visit at Concord was at the parsonage, "Old Manse," and upon his brother's widow Phœbe (Bliss) Emerson, who had become the wife of Rev. Ezra Ripley, the successor of his brother, the patriot preacher of Concord.]

27th. Set out early from Concord, and took breakfast at Dr. Osgood's in Medford (the minister's), and arrived at Malden in safety, after a pleasant and prosperous journey. Found my sisters well, and living together in harmony, which afforded me much satisfaction.

On June 13 he set out for home. Dined at Concord, drank coffee at Harvard, and proceeded to Bóylston. Lodged with Mr. Nash, the minister, and so on until he reached Conway.

In the old burying-ground of Conway may be seen a gravestone erected by loving hands, on which may be read : —

IN MEMORY OF
REV. JOHN EMERSON,
WHO WAS BORN AT MALDEN, NOV. 20, 1745,
WAS SETTLED TO THE WORK OF THE MINISTRY IN CONWAY
JULY 20, 1769.
& having preached the Gospel fifty-seven years,
He died June 26, 1826,
In the 81st year of his age.

" *Perfidem et Laborem ad Cœlum ascendit.*"

" He ascends to heaven through faithfulness and labor."

369

BRADDOCK, Gen 141
BRADSTREET, Simon 308
BRATTLE, 160
BRAYNARD, Mr 354 355
BRIDGE, Ebenezer 240 268 300
301 Mrs Ebenezer 300 Rev Mr
244 250 252 253 257 258 302
311 318 320 Sarah 301
BRITTON, Samuel 274
BROWN, Abel 133 Anna 351 B
362 Elizabeth 350 John 350
Joseph 87 Olive 328 Patty 326
Peter 322 326-329 Polly 326
Sally 326 Susan 327 328
William 178 327 328
BUCK, Richard 269
BULKLEY, Edward 348 349
Elizabeth 349 350 Peter 346
347 349
BULLARD, Rev Mr 48
BURGE, Cyrus F 107 135 David
273 Ephraim 135
BURGOYNE, Gen 37 49 50 140-
144 149 152 153 157 158 161-
163 166 171 173 174 259 289
John 165
BURR, Aaron 359 Esther 359
BUTLER, Benjamin F 51
BUTTERFIELD, Capt 251 Na-
thaniel 252
BYAM, Abraham 286 Amos 286
George 285 286 Isaac 286
Jacob 286 Sarah 286 Willard
259
BYHAM, Benjamin 252

- C -

CALLENDER, Gen 255
CAMBEL, William 274
CAMPBELL, John 133
CANADA JOHN, 59
CARLETON, Abigail 114 Gen 140
141 169
CARTER, Madam 155 Poley 320
Polly 321
CHAMBERLAIN, Aaron 246 John
62-67 Thomas 286
CHAMBERLIN, Aaron 250
Benjamin 39 Lydia 39 Phineas
39

CHAMBERS, John 274 William
274
CHAPLIN, Daniel 7 Sarah 7 8
Susanna 7
CHILD, Abram 9
CINCINNATUS, Lucius Quintius
25
CLARK, Jonas 96 243 300 303
Lucy 96 Miss 263 300 Mrs
Jonas 300 303 Mrs Thomas
300 Peter 201 Thomas 263 299
300 303
CLEAVES, Mr 222
CLOUGH, Mr 111
COBB, Sabra 363
COLBURN, 110 Enoch 128 129
Enoch Jewett 128 Hannah 135
James 133 139 144 John 102
(portrait) 103 106 107 139 144
156 Mother 104 Mr 166 172
Naomi 107 Nathan 133 Susan-
nah 139 Thomas 118 133
COLMAN, Dr 312
CONERY, Samuel 133
CONNER, James 269
COOK, Samuel 190
COOPER, Rev Mr 312
COREY, Aaron 4 Chambers 5
Giles 199 Nathan 4 Simeon
252
CORLISS, Helen 266 John 266
John L 266 Sally 266 Sarah
266
CUMINGS, Benjamin 133 John
115 133
CUMMINGS, Col 258 Ebenezer
108 Henry 301 Rev Dr 352
Sarah 301 William 108

- D -

DALAND, Benj 190
DALLIS, Lieut 262
DALTON, Charles H 248 John C
248 Julia Ann 248
DAMMON, Daniel 273
DANFORTH, David 274 Dr 336
337 Jacob 133 Tom 337
DAVERSON, Francis 274
DAVIS, Joshua 274 Mrs Sullivan
83 Sullivan 83

374

POLLARD, Asa 324 329-333
Edward 331 John 329 Louise
333 Mary 329 Solomon 330
POOR, Peter 118 120
POPE, Hannah 203 Joseph 203
Mehitable 203
PORTER, Benjamin 194 Eliza-
beth 200 Moses 194-196 Sarah
194 196
POWERS, Francis 119 Nahum
119 133 Peter 357 Sampson
133
POWNAL, Gov 310
POWNALL, Gov 15
PRATT, Thomas 119 133
PRESCOTT, 222 Abigail 22 24 39
Benjamin 5 6 21 22 Catherine
G 29 Col 23 24 26 27 35 37 49
55 68 69 77 91 115 118 323
326 332 Edith 26 Gen 255
James 6 7 John 6 7 Jonas 6
Mrs Col 25 Mrs William H 28
Oliver 6 24 Sarah 73 Susanna 7
William 5-8 11 16 19 22 24 25
28 29 34 38 39 41 73 102 119-
121 William G 26 William H
25 27 28
PRINCE, Asa 221
PROCTOR, Ezekiel 133 Lieut
252
PUTNAM, 229-231 279 332
Alfred P 194 209 210 Alfred
Porter 197 Amos 192 Arche-
laus 181 Daniel 200 217 218
David 200 204 Edmund 197
198 Elizabeth 200 Gen 255 256
Hannah 203 Israel 199-204 206
209 335 Jeremiah 222 John
199 200 221 Joseph 200 Mary
204 Mehitable 203 Miss 181
Molly 204 Nathan 198 199
Perley 186 190 198 Susan 200
Tarrant 197 Thomas 200

- R -

RAND, 335 338 342 Mary 334 336
339 341 343 Robert 334 336
339 343
REA, Caleb 194 Daniel 197 Sarah
194

READ, Esdras 293 Jacob 133
Mary 291
REED, Col 118 120 269
RICH, Capt 366
RICHARDSON, Ebenezer 288
Edward F 288 Francis 289
Hannah 291 John 288 Josiah
274 288 Oliver 273 288 289
Samuel 288
RIEDESEL, Baroness 153 (por-
trait) 154 156 165 167 169
171-174 Caroline 167 Frederi-
ca 167 Gen 156 165 167 169-
171 Gustava 167 Maj-Gen 149
164
RIPLEY, Ezra 367 Phoebe 367
ROBBINS, Sarah 278
ROBINSON, 220
ROBY, John 274
ROCHAMBEAU, Count 220
ROCKWOOD, Ebenezer 108 Sarah
7 William J 108
ROGERS, Major 45
ROYAL, Isaac 312
RUGGLES, Samuel 340
RUSS, Jonathan 133
RUSSELL, Jason 186 Richard 93

- S -

SANDERS, Benjamin 133
SANDERSON, Sally 91
SARTELL, Nathaniel 40
SAWTELL, Obadiah 77 86 99
Obadiah Jr 86
SCHUYLER, Col 354 Gen 142 153
Philip 173
SEAVER, Robert 133
SERVANT, Hagar 243
SEWALL, Joseph 227 Samuel
263
SEWARD, Thomas 48
SHATTUCK, Augustus L 60 61
Calvin 58 Experience 121
Jeremiah 36 60 119 121 John
59 Jonathan 60 Joseph 58 Mrs
59 Mrs Job 61 Mrs Joseph 58
Mrs Samuel P 62 63 (portrait)
Samuel P 62 (portrait) 68
Samuel Pepperell 59 William
57 58

375

WARNER (continued)
Richard 61 Seth 166 Walter 61
WARREN, 222 Benjamin 273 287
Edwin Henchman 287 Eliza A
295 Gen 34 35 Jacob 288
Jeduthan 287 Joseph 268 287
William 36
WASHINGTON, 9 47 53 91 128
129 148 156 189 219-222 354
Gen 121 217 George 92 318
334
WAYNE, Gen 9
WEBB, Jotham 190
WEBBER, Carrie Putnam 207
(portrait) Lewis Gleason 207
(portrait) Marcus Bernard 207
(portrait) Mary 204 205 (por-
trait) 206 Paul Baron 207
(portrait)
WENTWORTH, Benning 101 Gov
106 John 116
WHEAT, Lucy 136 Nathaniel 133
Thomas 120 133 136 Thomas
Jr 118
WHEELER, Ebenezer 133
Lebbens 133 Thaddeus 130
133
WHIPPLE, Gen 149
WHITCOMB, Col 77
WHITING, Leonard 62 Miss 300
Samuel 300
WHITNEY, Dea 366 Lydia 96
Mrs Phinehas 300 Pheneas 96
Phinehas 300

WILDS, Ivory 87
WILKINS, Bray 133 Israel 133
WILLARD, Samuel 2 Simon 306
WILLIAM, King of England 216
WILLIAMS, Luther H 55 Roger
327
WILLOE, Capt 171
WILSON, Isaac 193
WINTHROP, Dean 2 21 John 209
Robert C 49
WOLCOTT, Edith 26 Roger 26
WOLFE, 188
WOOD, Benjamin 5 37 William
119 133
WOODS, Henry 39
WORCESTER, 112 Abigail 114
Francis 113 114
WORCESTER (continued)
Jesse 122 124 (portrait)
Joseph E 125 Lucy E 114 122
Noah 114-117 121-123 133
Noah Jr 115 119 Sarah 124
(portrait) William 113
WRIGHT, Benjamin 133 Benja-
min Jr 133 Joshua 106 Mr 48
Mrs David 61 Uriah 133 Zach
259
WYMAN, Jesse 133

- Y -

YOUNGMAN, Ebenezer 129 133
Nicholas 129 Thomas 129

377

www.ingramcontent.com/pod-product-compliance
Lightning Source LLC
Chambersburg PA
CBHW071829270326
41929CB00013B/1936